The Balance of Terror

The Balance of Terror

*Nuclear Weapons and the
Illusion of Security, 1945–1985*

Revised and Updated

Edgar Bottome

Beacon Press   Boston

Beacon Press
25 Beacon Street
Boston, Massachusetts 02108

Beacon Press books are published under the auspices
of the Unitarian Universalist Association
of Congregations in North America.

92 91 90 89 88   8 7 6 5 4 3 2
Library of Congress Cataloging in Publication Data

Bottome, Edgar M.
    The balance of terror.

    Includes index.
    1. United States—Military policy.   2. Nuclear
weapons—United States.   3. World politics—1945–
I. Title.
UA23.B727   1986   355′.0335′73   85–47948
ISBN 0–8070–0520–7
ISBN 0–8070–0519–3 (pbk.)

To Howard and Roz Zinn

I appeal as a human being to human beings: remember your humanity, and forget the rest. If you can do so, the way lies open to a new paradise: if you cannot, nothing lies before you but universal death.

BERTRAND RUSSELL

Contents

Preface to the Revised Edition

This study represents a revised and updated version of *The Balance of Terror: A Guide to the Arms Race,* published in 1971. Minor changes have been made in the original text, represented in Chapters I-V. A new introduction and conclusion have been written and two new chapters have been added.

To those who gave of their time and energy in preparing the first edition, I again offer my thanks. I have received invaluable aid in writing this revised and updated study from Marge White, Rochelle Ruthchild, and Paula Bottome. To David Hildt and Susan Oleksiw go special words of thanks for their tireless editing of the manuscript. My thanks to Nancy Lattanzio and Caroline Birdsall of Beacon Press for their effort to maintain clarity in the manuscript. Howard Zinn and Philip Morrison contributed their own special knowledge, insights, and humanity to the study.

This book would not have been possible without the assistance, support, and understanding of my wife, Abigail, and the patience of our children, Lydia and Paul.

Edgar Bottome
Amesbury, Massachusetts
1985

Introduction

On August 6, 1945, the Japanese city of Hiroshima was destroyed by an atomic bomb. The decision by the United States to develop and use nuclear weapons had forever changed the "rules of the game" in international relations. By the mid-1950s, the world was entering an era when the balance of power could no longer be the organizing principle of international politics among nuclear-armed nations. A balance of terror had arrived. With over 50,000 nuclear weapons world-wide in the mid-1980s, nations can no longer claim to protect their people. The concept of national security has disappeared and has been replaced by varying degrees of national insecurity. Every nation in the world is subject to absolute destruction in less than one hour: There are no exceptions.

Since about 1955, the United States and the Soviet Union have had the capability of launching a nuclear attack on each other. No matter which side strikes first, both sides will be annihilated as functioning societies. The penalty for serious error in the conduct of foreign relations has become incalculably greater than at any other time in history. Yet the United States persists in efforts to integrate nuclear weapons into its over-all global strategy.

This book is about the military strategies and instruments used by the United States to pursue its foreign policy goals. It is also an effort to critically examine the development of the balance of terror and the concurrent arms race between the United States and the Soviet Union. In order to stop the arms race, much less reverse its course, we must try to answer three fundamental questions that have received too little attention over the past forty years. What purpose do nuclear weapons allegedly serve in the conduct of a nation's foreign policy?

Under what conditions will these weapons be used? And how did we arrive at the current impasse of massive nuclear overkill?

The international goals of the United States have been clear and remarkably consistent since the end of World War II. Since 1945 U.S. policy has never deviated from its support of the status quo in all noncommunist and nonsocialist countries. This policy is designed to maintain control over the allocation of world-wide resources and available labor and to ensure U.S. access to market and investment areas. No alternative forms of government could be allowed to replace existing friendly governments, since successful alternatives could demonstrate that there were different paths to national economic development from those approved by the United States.

Any failure to maintain the status quo in one nation, it was feared, would challenge the entire system. One nation's example would encourage other nations to follow. This is the domino theory, and its effect was not primarily geopolitical in nature. There was never any real danger of the Vietnamese Communists showing up in San Francisco, nor did Thailand or Burma automatically "fall" after the U.S. troops left Vietnam. The fear was less focused: Alternative systems shown to be successful in a Cuba or a Vietnam might infect other nations and thereby threaten the very roots of U.S. economic and political power. Viewed from this perspective the rationale for U.S. involvement in Vietnam, for example, is easier to comprehend. Thus, seeming contradictions between America's public statements and actual policies have a certain logic. Americans are told that their country champions democracy and freedom internationally, yet the United States supports Botha in the Union of South Africa, Pinochet in Chile, and Marcos in the Philippines. Although "freedom" is the banner waved for the American public, oppression is in fact supported if that is the price of keeping friendly governments in power.

Maintaining the status quo in a revolutionary world is no easy task. The United States failed to do this in China, Cuba, Vietnam, and Nicaragua. But instead of seeking the deeper causes of these failures, policy makers in the United States held the Soviet Union responsible for these successful revolutions. Instead of acknowledging that the Third World had entered a revolutionary era powered by the forces of nationalism and that the United States could not contain these powerful historical forces, the United States responded by further militarizing its foreign policy and becoming more dependent on nuclear weapons in the conduct of this policy.

To the casual observer, American policy may seem chaotic, lacking in purpose. Yet the philosophy and goals behind American policy since World War II have remained unchanged. The apparent chaos in American policy is a result of its failure and not its lack of consistency. In each case of major military failure, U.S. leaders redefined the role of the military and nuclear power in the conduct of policy. The Korean War was followed by John Foster Dulles' formal definition of "massive retaliation." Hard on the heels of the Bay of Pigs fiasco came Robert S. McNamara's "second-strike counterforce" and "flexible response." The war in Vietnam was followed by Richard Nixon's "controlled response," Jimmy Carter's "countervailing strategy," and Ronald Reagan's "winnable" nuclear war bolstered by his "Star Wars" concept. Each time a new course was chartered, the goal remained the same: to find a way to use nuclear weapons to prevent future failures.

For the purpose of analysis, the first forty years of the nuclear arms race can be divided into three distinct periods. The first period (1945–1961) originated with Harry Truman's "atomic diplomacy" and culminated with the Dulles Doctrine of "massive retaliation." During this period the United States had nuclear superiority and accumulated regional alliances world-wide.

The second period (1961–1979) began with McNamara's "second-strike counterforce" and "flexible response" doctrines and culminated with Nixon's "Vietnamization" and "surrogate gendarmes" (policies that would eventually fail in Iran and Nicaragua). During this period U.S. nuclear superiority was challenged by the Soviet buildup of intercontinental ballistic missiles (ICBMs). Many of the regional alliances foundered, and U.S. foreign policy failed to prove its efficacy in Cuba, Vietnam, Iran, and Nicaragua.

The third period (1979 to the present) began toward the end

of the Carter Administration. The past six years have seen further escalation of the arms race in an effort to achieve a first-strike counterforce posture that could "win" a prolonged nuclear war.

If the United States is given primary emphasis in my analysis, it is because the most striking fact to emerge from an overview of the arms race is that the United States has held a commanding lead in the development of nuclear weapons and the means of their delivery since the inception of the nuclear age. At every significant stage of the arms race, U.S. technology has been superior to that of the Soviet Union. This fact is often ignored and even more often distorted. But a look at the record will demonstrate that

—the United States first developed and used the atomic bomb (1945);
—the United States developed and put into operation the first intercontinental bomber force (the B-36 bomber, 1951–1952);
—the United States first introduced the concept of "forward basing" and placed medium-range nuclear bombers near Soviet territory (the B-47 bomber, 1952);
—the United States tested the first thermonuclear hydrogen bomb (1952);
—the United States had the first tactical nuclear weapons, weapons that could be used on the battlefield (1952);
—the United States put into operation the first medium-range ballistic missile force, around the Soviet Union (1958);
—the United States deployed the first significant intercontinental ballistic missile (ICBM) force (1958–1959);
—the United States deployed the first subsurface-launched ballistic missile (SLBM) force (1960);
—the United States first introduced operational multiple reentry vehicles (MRV) (1964) and multiple independent reentry vehicles (MIRV) on its ICBM (1970) and SLBM (1971) missile forces; and
—the United States developed the first operational radiation-enhanced nuclear weapon (the neutron bomb) (1981).[1]

By the mid-1980s, the United States had a clear technological and developmental lead in bomber technology, ICBM accuracy and development, submarine invulnerability and accuracy, cruise missile technology, and antiballistic missile technology and the use of space. Each of these technological developments and the consequent deployment of new weapons systems has meant an escalation of the arms race as the Soviet Union attempted to catch up with the United States.

In spite of the overriding reality of the balance of terror, the United States continued to behave as though it could somehow integrate nuclear weapons into a coherent and meaningful instrument in its foreign policy. Rather than accepting that the longer the arms race continues, the more insecure all nations become, the United States and the Soviet Union remained tied to the traditional belief that more weapons mean more security.

American policy makers have not been able to understand why the enormous destructive force represented by these weapons cannot be converted into political power guaranteeing the success of American global policies. Nor have American leaders yet recognized that nuclear weapons have no military use beyond their function as a minimum deterrent to an attack on the United States. American policy makers insist on envisioning a much broader purpose and potential use for these weapons and have broadened the concept of deterrence accordingly. Nuclear weapons are expected to:

(1) deter a direct attack on the United States by Soviet strategic weapons;

(2) deter a Soviet attack on Europe or the Middle East by a "first use" doctrine that "couples" the initial use of tactical nuclear weapons (small battlefield) to theater weapons (within Europe or the Middle East only), to, finally, strategic weapons (attacks on the Soviet Union);

(3) deter Soviet military action in the Third World by threatening the use of nuclear weapons; and

(4) deter any Soviet or Chinese response to American nonnuclear operations in the Third world.

American strategic doctrine makes nuclear and general purpose forces totally interdependent. Until this connection between nuclear and conventional forces is understood by the American people and particularly by the peace movement, there is no way to effectively challenge the dangerous and expensive policies of the American military establishment. For those who would change American policy, a fundamental understanding of the goals of that policy and the means used to implement them is essential.

Since the 1950s, the avowed doctrine of the United States has been to use nuclear weapons first in Europe (early 1950s) and the Middle East (1979) in the event of hostilities that the United States cannot win. This "first use" doctrine was based on a willingness of the United States to respond to nonnuclear warfare with small battlefield nuclear weapons and to escalate to strategic attacks on the Soviet Union if the military situation required it. By "coupling" the use of nuclear weapons in such a manner, the United States totally integrated nuclear weapons into its military strategy for the defense of Europe and the Middle East.

An essential corollary to the doctrines of "first use" and "coupling" is the U.S. acceptance of a first-strike counterforce doctrine. If the United States is willing to use nuclear weapons first and to escalate to attacks on the Soviet Union, it must be ready to attack Soviet nuclear delivery systems first or risk a Soviet attack that would surely annihilate American cities and possibly restrict the American ability to retaliate against the Soviet Union. The American doctrine of "first use" leads logically and inevitably to a first-strike doctrine.

By defining deterrence in its broadest sense and by "coupling" all levels of nuclear response, the United States attempted to create a nuclear "shield" behind which American conventional forces (the "sword") could operate in the Third World and Europe. This was clearly demonstrated by the threatened use of nuclear weapons in Korea (1950 and 1953), Vietnam (1954), Quemoy and Ma-tsu (1958), Berlin (1961), Cuba (1962), Vietnam (1968–1971), and the Middle East (1980–   ). These threats could only be made if the United States was prepared to launch a preventive first-strike attack against the Soviet Union.

Perhaps the single greatest barrier to understanding the arms race is the virtually impenetrable jargon that surrounds nuclear weapons. The United States has articulated and apparently discarded numerous doctrines and strategies for the integration of nuclear weapons into American military policy. The observer is confronted with an alien lexicon that is continually changing and undergoing redefinition: "massive retaliation," "first use," "second-strike counterforce," "controlled response," "surgical strike," "countervailing forces," "mutually assured destruction," and so forth.

It is one purpose of this book to go beyond the jargon—to analyze, not what is said, but what the United States is prepared to do. Strategic theory should not serve as a smoke screen for the reality of existing weapons and their designated targets. For example, Secretary of Defense McNamara's proclamation that mutually assured destruction (MAD) requires only the minimal nuclear forces needed to destroy the Soviet population centers needs to be examined in light of the buildup of a force of several thousand nuclear weapons—far in excess of the requirements of the MAD doctrine.

The very task of assessing U.S. nuclear capability is complicated by the fact that the U.S. government usually defines the arms race in terms of individual weapons systems rather than total delivery systems. For example, the correct claim will be made that the Soviet Union has more ICBM (intercontinental ballistic missile) warheads than the United States, but the fact that the United States has more total warheads than the Soviet Union will be ignored. Any analysis of U.S. strategy must include an assessment of all American nuclear systems that can attack the Soviet Union. All of the forces in the TRIAD of American strike forces must be taken into account, namely, (1) bombers and air-launched cruise missiles, (2) submarine-launched ballistic missiles, and (3) intercontinental ballistic missiles. In addition to the TRIAD, U.S. forward-based systems (FBS) that are capable of reaching Soviet territory need to be added: ground and sea launched cruise missiles, Pershing IIs, carrier aircraft, and fighter-bombers overseas. To omit any of these systems in comparing Soviet and American nuclear capability is to distort the truth.

Distortions of this nature have occurred regularly since the

1950s. American military planners have been extraordinarily successful in creating myths throughout the arms race. The "bomber gap," the "missile gap," the "security gap," the "window of vulnerability," and the "spending gap"—all allegations of Soviet superiority that turned out to be false—have been used to dramatically increase American military spending. When the various "gaps" have materialized, they have consistently favored the United States, not the Soviet Union. Yet the leaders who have perpetrated these myths do not seem to have ever suffered any loss of credibility, and in the mid-1980s the process continues.

The arrival of the balance of terror presented the Soviet Union with entirely different problems. Whereas the United States had emerged from World War II unscathed and in sole possession of the atomic bomb, the Soviet Union had suffered severe damage to its society and its economy. While U.S. leaders were trying to integrate nuclear power into their foreign policy, Soviet leaders in 1945 were trying to guarantee the internal and external security of the Soviet state. To achieve this goal, Soviet leaders pursued austerity and repression at home and established military dominance in Eastern Europe. Economic weakness, technological backwardness, and political uncertainty remained characteristic of Soviet society.

By 1949, the Soviet Union had developed the atomic bomb and by the mid-1950s it had the intercontinental bomber force to deliver it. To a limited degree, it also integrated nuclear power into the conduct of its foreign policy. The Soviet development of a nuclear capability represented a number of short-range advantages, among them status as a great power and temporary equality with the United States in a bipolar world. In addition, nuclear weapons allowed the Soviet Union to resist Western pressure. Both the United States and the Soviet Union eventually adopted a nuclear policy aimed at maintaining their respective control over Europe and both threatened the destruction of Europe should this hegemony be challenged.

Faced with American nuclear superiority, the Soviet Union did not fully integrate nuclear and conventional forces and policies. The Soviet Union increased its nonnuclear forces and was more hesitant than the United States to threaten the use of nuclear weapons. Only in the Cuban missile crisis did the Soviet Union place its nuclear weapons on alert, and it was forced to back down under extreme U.S. pressure.

In their effort to maintain the status quo on the Soviet frontier, the leaders of the Soviet Union demonstrated the same lack of understanding of nationalism that characterized American leadership. Soviet military forces were used in the German Democratic Republic, Hungary, Czechoslovakia, and Afghanistan in an effort to prevent the independence of Soviet client states. The Soviet Union demonstrated in a clear and brutal fashion that it would not tolerate any challenge to its hegemony in Eastern Europe or along its southern border.

The United States and the Soviet Union emerged as social and political rivals in an essentially bipolar world. Yet both were imperial systems in decline, neither in control of its client states and junior partners. Although both nations preferred to maintain a world divided between two superpowers, in the latter part of the twentieth century the world was slowly dissolving into a multipolar world with at least four major centers. China, Europe, and possibly Japan would not remain second-rate powers indefinitely and no amount of Soviet or American effort could prevent the emergence of these areas as equal powers. Change would not happen overnight, but by the 1980s the bipolar world was disappearing.

Perhaps the ultimate irony of the Cold War is not the great differences between the United States and the Soviet Union, but the similarities of these two nations. Both nations are conservative in protecting the status quo in areas considered to be vital to their national interests. Both nations are faced with a revolutionary world that neither can control. Both nations are facing a relative decline in national power. Both nations are forced to use military power as a demonstration of weakness rather than as a mark of national strength. Both periodically face foreign policy difficulties that threaten the stature of their political leaders. And, finally, both are confronted with the disintegration of a bipolar world that both are trying to maintain.[2]

Yet the Cold War continues. The American system promises liberty and freedom, and the Soviet Union claims that it can deliver equality and meet social needs. Neither system has fulfilled its ideological promises and each perceives the other as diametrically opposed to its own ideology. The "socialism" of the Soviet Union represents the ultimate alternative system to the "free enterprise" of the United States. As the Soviets see it, the military power of the United States and its allies threatens continued Soviet survival in a hostile world.

Antagonism is increasing and it is fortunate for the world that Europe is the only place on the globe where the armies of the two nations stand face to face. While each side hopes for the internal collapse of the other, the bipolar world is disintegrating around both. If nuclear war can be prevented, the twenty-first century will bring significant changes in the political and economic configuration of the globe.

Surviving to the year 2000 represents a unique challenge in the nuclear age. According to Alan Wolfe, "the campaign to control nuclear weapons and the effort to teach about them are indistinguishable."[3] It is hoped that by analyzing the origins, causes, and misperceptions of the arms race, we can find ways to reverse it. The secrecy, complex technology, ideologies, and jargon that surround the arms race make understanding difficult. Yet until we understand the arms race, we cannot stop it.

NOTES

1. See the excellent book by Thomas B. Cochran, William M. Arkin, and Milton M. Hoenig, *Nuclear Weapons Databook,* Vol. I, *U.S. Nuclear Forces and Capabilities* (Cambridge: Ballinger, 1984).

2. The author would like to acknowledge his appreciation to Michael Cox for his unpublished study "Rethinking the Cold War." Professor Cox teaches in the Political Science Department, Queens University, Belfast, Ireland.

3. Alan Wolfe, "American Democracy and Nuclear Weapons," *World Policy Journal* (Fall 1984), p. 108.

The Balance of Terror

I

Early Years of the Arms Race

(1945–1952)

The balance of terror between the United States and the Soviet Union did not become a reality until 1955–1956 when the Soviet Union developed its first operational intercontinental bomber capable of reaching the United States. Once the Soviet Union could deliver hydrogen weapons on the United States, the balance of terror between the two superpowers became the dominant, underlying military-political factor in the conduct of great power diplomacy. However, from 1945 to 1949 the United States possessed a monopoly on nuclear weapons and then from 1949 to 1955 a monopoly on the means to deliver these weapons. During this decade of American absolute superiority, the events surrounding the arms race made the reality of the balance of terror in the mid-1950's inevitable. Therefore, in order to understand the balance of terror and its origins, it is essential to sketch briefly these early years of the arms race between the United States and the Soviet Union.[1] This discussion will center around three basic questions: 1) the nature of American and Soviet disarmament following World War II; 2) the B-36 debate and the decision to build the hydrogen bomb; and 3) National Security Council Paper #68 and the Korean War.

POSTWAR DISARMAMENT?

There have been numerous estimates on the extent of Soviet and American reductions of manpower immediately following World

1

War II; the fact that both drastically reduced their military manpower is not challenged, although many Americans still believe that the United States disarmed after World War II, while the Soviet Union maintained large numbers of men under arms in preparation for future aggression. In the atomic age the number of men under arms is only one indication of a nation's military strength, but it is an important one. Both P. M. S. Blackett and Raymond Garthoff have accepted the following figures: from 1945 to 1948 the Soviet Union reduced its military manpower 75 percent from 11,365,000 to 2,874,000; while the United States reduced its military manpower 87 percent from almost 12,000,000 to 1,500,000.[2]

But manpower figures do not tell the entire story. At the end of the war, the Soviet Union had secured its borders from the threat of foreign invasion. In any calculation of national security, however, the Soviet Union still remained extremely vulnerable to attack due to the new developments in heavy long-range bombers and the existence of atomic weapons. In 1945 only the B-29 heavy bomber could carry the cumbersome early A-bombs, weighing about five tons, and only the United States had the B-29 bomber* *and* the air bases near enough to Soviet territory to deliver these weapons.[3]

In the late 1940s the United States not only had well over 1,000 B-29 bombers, but also had foreign airfields well within range of *all* of the major cities of the Soviet Union. The United States had major airfields in Greenland, Iceland, Okinawa, Japan, and Alaska. In addition to these bases, the United States began to acquire additional airfields on the perimeter of the Soviet Union. Listed below are the countries that the United States approached for airbase leases and the dates of the initial discussions:

> Spain—1945
> Saudi Arabia—1945
> Tunisia—1946

* The B-29 had a range of approximately 2,000 miles. That is, it had the capability to strike a target 1,000 miles from its base and return, or make a 2,000 mile one-way trip.

French Morocco—1951
Turkey—1946

The United States eventually built strategic military bases in all of these countries.[4]

But the existence of a large number of bombers and foreign bases near the Soviet Union obviously had to be accompanied by the atomic weapons to be delivered by this bomber force. Although the exact rate of American production of atomic bombs following the war is a well-guarded secret, it would appear that by 1948 the United States had produced approximately 50 atomic bombs and had the means to deliver these weapons. At the end of the war Secretary of State Byrnes declared, ". . . we should continue the Manhattan Project [the secret project to build the atomic bomb] with full force."[5] The fact that this work continued at a rapid rate after the war was later confirmed at the Oppenheimer Hearings.[6] By 1949 the United States had between 500 and 800 B-29s stationed at overseas bases within range of the Soviet Union,[7] and estimates at that time placed the atomic bomb arsenal in the hundreds.[8]

On the other hand, the United States did not develop a large, effective ground force capable of what was to become known as a limited conventional war. The decision had been made by the United States government to rely on atomic weapons as the major military instrument of diplomacy. It was felt that this form of "atomic diplomacy" was the most effective way to protect American interests and contain what U.S. leaders perceived as an aggressive, hostile Soviet Union.

The existence of the growing American nuclear strength placed the Soviet Union in an extremely vulnerable position. Although the Soviet Union exploded its first atomic bomb in 1949, this still did not resolve the fundamental problems surrounding the security of Soviet territory. By 1947, the Soviet Union was beginning production of the Tupylov-4 (the TU-4, nicknamed "BULL" by the United States). This aircraft was a copy of the American B-29 and could not deliver atomic weapons on the United States without either foreign bases close to the United States or in-flight refueling. The Soviet Union had no such bases and did not develop in-flight refueling until 1957, or possibly not until as late as 1959.*

In its simplest terms, this means that the Soviet Union had no direct means of deterring an American atomic attack on its territory from 1945 to 1955. The only means available to the Soviet Union to prevent such an attack was to raise the strength of the Red Army to a level where it could not possibly be challenged on the Eurasian land mass. This is exactly what the leaders of the Soviet Union proceeded to do. The number of men under arms in the Soviet Union increased from approximately 2.8 million in 1948 to over 5.7 million by 1955 (See Appendix B.)† With this large number of fighting men under arms, the leaders of the Soviet Union could seriously threaten the security of Western Europe, even if attacked first by the United States.

By 1949 the first major stage of the arms race was completed. The United States increasingly relied on its growing monopoly in the means of delivering atomic weapons. On the other hand, the vulnerability of the Soviet Union to American air power led the Soviet Union to increase the size of the Red Army to a point where it could march across Europe in the event of an American attack on Soviet territory. In a very real sense, Western Europe had become a Soviet hostage in order to deter an American

---

* In-flight refueling is a method whereby an aircraft in the air can be refueled by a tanker aircraft and thus substantially increase its range. Evidence of the Soviet capacity for in-flight refueling is difficult to find. This information is extremely important in any determination of Soviet strategy and intentions during the period prior to the development of an intercontinental bomber force in 1955. After 1955, the importance of a Soviet in-flight refueling capability decreased due to the introduction of the intercontinental bomber, the Bison. The fact remains that from 1945 to somewhere around 1954–1955 the Soviet Union was incapable of delivering atomic weapons on the territory of the continental United States (see: H. S. Dinerstein, *War and the Soviet Union*, rev. ed., New York: Frederick Praeger, 1962, p. 230; and *The New York Times*, news article by Hanson Baldwin, March 25, 1959.

† It is interesting to note that once the Russians had an operational intercontinental bomber in 1955, Soviet force levels began to go down and were down to 3.6 million men under arms by 1960.

attack on Soviet territory until the Soviet Union could develop its own atomic arsenal and delivery system.

The United States did not disarm following World War II, but simply shifted its emphasis from a large army and navy to belief in the efficacy of the air force and the atomic bomb as the major military instruments of American foreign policy. In the case of the Soviet Union, this nation responded in the only manner possible in face of the American atomic monopoly; it increased the size of the Red Army.

In view of this American strategic superiority over the Soviet Union, what is most surprising about the development of American postwar attitudes and military policy was the lack of sustained, energetic debate on the assumptions made by American leadership and the policies these assumptions were producing. Some Americans raised their voices in protest, but in reality there was never a sustained public debate. The major voice of dissent during this early period of the cold war was Secretary of Commerce Henry Wallace: he lost his job for his efforts. Although the Wallace movement of later years was disowned by Wallace himself, the fundamental questions raised as early as 1946 by Mr. Wallace deserve careful consideration. If more Americans had sincerely asked these questions, there is a chance that the Cold War and the arms race might have both taken a very different course. Mr. Wallace asked:

> How do American actions since V-J day appear to other nations? I mean by action concrete things like $13,000,000,000 for the War and Navy Departments, the Bikini tests of the atomic bomb and continued production of bombs, the plan to arm Latin America with our weapons, production of B-29s and planned production of B-36s, and the effort to secure air bases spread over half the globe from which the other half of the globe can be bombed. I cannot but feel that these actions must make us look to the rest of the world as if we were only paying lip service to peace at the conference table.
>
> These facts make it appear either 1) that we are preparing ourselves to win the war which we regard as inevitable or 2) that we are trying to build up a predominance of force to intimidate the rest of mankind. How would it look to us if Russia had the atomic bomb

and we did not, if Russia had 10,000 mile bombers and air bases within 1,000 miles of our coastline and we did not.[9]

However, these questions were evidently not considered debatable, for on September 20, 1946, Secretary Wallace was dismissed from the Truman Cabinet.

THE B-36 AND THE H-BOMB

When the debate over American military policy finally emerged publicly in the United States, it did not pertain to the nature of the challenge (this was accepted) as being an aggressive, hostile Soviet Union, but to the type of weapons systems that America needed to meet the challenge. That is, whether to build bombers or aircraft carriers, whether to develop the H-bomb or stay with the less powerful fission A-bomb, and whether to use Universal Military Training (UMT) or rely on a more limited draft system to meet the military manpower needs of the future. All three of the questions had been discussed as early as 1945, but it was in 1949—marked by the testing of the first Soviet atomic bomb, the Berlin blockade, and the victory of Mao's forces in China—that the debate emerged into a full-scale public discussion.

The major manifestations of this debate surrounded the question of whether or not to build the B-36 intercontinental bomber. The importance of this controversy was not the actual decision to build the B-36 because it became obsolete shortly after it went into production, but that it laid the foundation and established the methods and procedures that were to be followed in future debates on any given weapons system. Therefore, a rather detailed analysis of the B-36 controversy is an essential first step in order to understand the domestic forces that produced the arms race.

The debate offered an almost classical split of the military forces involved in American defense policy formulation. It is an excellent case study of the early stages of interservice rivalry and the conflict over strategic doctrines of American military policy that have characterized the entire postwar period. The

B-36 controversy centered on two questions: the nature and length of a future war; and the weapons systems needed to fight this war. The Army, Navy, and the Air Force along with their industrial, journalistic, and congressional friends lined up on opposite sides and the debate was on.

During this early controversy, a standard procedure was established for future conflicts among the military services for budgetary allocations. Under this procedure, each branch, along with its various industrial and political allies, would devise a military strategy to increase its appropriations. Then, each group would come before Congress and the nation and claim that its particular strategy and given weapons system had to be implemented or dire consequences for American national security would result. This recurrent effort literally to terrorize Congress and the American people continues to this day as each of the services raises the specter of an enemy prepared or preparing to fight its kind of war.*

The B-36 was strictly an Air Force weapon and, of course, the Air Force wanted it produced and deployed immediately in large numbers. At this time (1949) and to the present, the United States Air Force has claimed that any major war with the Soviet Union would be a relatively short one and that air power would be the decisive weapons system in this type of conflict.† The Air Force in 1949 was still enthralled with Douhet's theory of air power and its efficacy in winning wars by mass bombing.[10] This early strategy was based on an exag-

---

* Perhaps the best early example of this approach occurred in the immediate postwar period. In 1946, a specially equipped American B-29 had proven that trans-Arctic flights were, in fact, possible. At this time the UMT debate was taking place and advocates of this program and a large ground army immediately invoked the specter of an enemy using this route to drop "hordes of airborne troops" on the United States. The advocates of a large army further claimed that these airborne troops could not be overcome by a small army and therefore the size of the existing army should be increased. (*The New York Times,* October 7, 1946.) Needless to say, the fear of "hordes of airborne troops" descending on the United States was not the most realistic assessment of the situation in 1946.

† In 1949, the Air Force was probably wrong in its assessment. Today there is not much question that after a massive thermonuclear exchange the war

gerated belief in the destructive power of these early atomic weapons which it was thought would lead to a rapid Soviet surrender. Likewise, in the late 1940s, the Air Force believed atomic weapons were too scarce to be used on Soviet military forces and therefore they would have to be used on Russian cities. The result was that the Air Force saw the B-36 as a means of delivering atomic weapons on Soviet cities and not as a means of attacking Soviet military targets.

But if the Air Force was to get its B-36, the United States Navy was afraid that not only would it be denied its new "super carrier" but also that its actual aircraft carrier force would be reduced from fourteen to six.[11] The major spokesman for the Navy position was Admiral Arthur W. Radford; he argued against the Air Force "counter-city doctrine" on the following grounds:

(1) The next war would not be won quickly by atomic weapons.

(2) The morality of attacking Soviet cities was highly dubious.

(3) It was contended that all nations would lose the peace.

(4) And, finally, that the military need facing the United States was not for a means to attack Soviet cities, but for the capability to attack the enemy's atomic installations and the airfields of the Soviet's long-range bombers.[12] (They had none in 1949.)

It was further agreed that there was a definite need to meet limited aggression with ground forces, and the Army continued to push for UMT.[13]

The major spokesman for the Air Force point of view was the Secretary of the Air Force, Stuart Symington. Secretary Symington accused the Navy of grossly underestimating the potential air power. He continued by stating that it was not

---

would be over, and so probably would human life on this planet. This Air Force belief in the efficacy of the use of air power continued to reappear throughout the arms race. The fallacious belief that air power could win a war was amply demonstrated in Vietnam.

true that the Air Force favors "mass atomic bombing of civilians." Yet Secretary Symington proceeded to advocate just that when he stated that if the country's safety was at stake:

> I can't see the difference between trying to stop a man at a lathe building a bomber to attack us and trying to stop a soldier.[14]

No matter what the major spokesmen at the top were saying, the fact remains that the B-36 was designed primarily to attack cities. First, the B-36 was not designed to attack specific objects, but "was primarily for area attacks on cities" due to its limited accuracy at an altitude of 40,000 feet, from which it would be forced to bomb due to Soviet air defense.[15] Second, in 1949 there was no Soviet delivery system for the B-36 to strike. The Soviet Union did not have a delivery system capable of reaching the United States and was not to have one until 1955. By that time the increasing obsolescence of the B-36 led to its replacement by the B-47 medium-range bomber and eventually by the B-52.*

In 1949, the Navy argued in humanitarian terms that were rare in later years. One Navy admiral characterized strategic bombing of the type advocated by the Air Force as "ruthless and barbaric" and went on to say that the Air Force strategy would mean the "random slaughter of men, women and children in the enemy country."†

* The B-47 was built in large quantities by the United States (over 1,200 bombers). It had a range of 3,600 miles and could carry a nine-ton bomb load. (Dinerstein, *War and the Soviet Union,* p. 23.) It was stationed primarily at American overseas bases in Greenland, Iceland, Britain, North Africa, Saudi Arabia, the Philippines, Formosa, Okinawa, and Japan. (Blackett, *Atomic Weapons,* pp. 51–56.) The B-47 had an in-flight refueling capacity. The B-52 was built in smaller quantities (around 500 were operational at any given time) and could reach the Soviet Union from United States SAC bases. The reader should keep in mind that the Soviet Union has never had more than 300 operational bombers capable of reaching the United States. (See Appendix A.)

† *The New York Times,* quoting Admiral Ralph Ofstie, October 12, 1949. It is interesting to note that this Navy argument against city strike weapons never came from advocates of the Regulus and later the Polaris systems in the late 1950s and early 1960s. These earlier submarine missile systems

Obviously the B-36 debate went far beyond humanitarian concerns. It was not only a debate over American strategic doctrine and the budget, for even at this early stage the Navy felt that it could conceivably be fighting for its very existence. After the Air Force was separated from the United States Army, a number of Navy men began to fear that the role of the Navy would be drastically reduced and permanently relegated to an inferior position behind the Army and the Air Force. Added to the Navy's suspicions was the fact that at this time a successful attempt was being made to reduce the air arm of the Navy, and plans for a large aircraft carrier had recently been scuttled.[16] Along with attacking the B-36 the Navy constantly called for increased appropriations for naval requirements throughout the world in order to avoid a long "siege war."[17]

The final results of the B-36 debate had a lasting impact on American military strategy. First, the B-36 was approved, put into mass production, and became the major SAC bomber until the B-47 and the B-52 came along. American willingness to mass produce this weapon and keep its navy and army at reduced levels indicated that the United States would continue to rely on atomic and then thermonuclear weapons to deter war and to gain its diplomatic objectives (the decision to build the H-bomb had been made at the same time as the B-36 decision had been made—see below). Second, the American decision to build the B-36 was a commitment on the part of the United States to a doctrine of massive retaliation or, more

---

were fairly inaccurate when compared to bombers or fixed-position ICBMs. Later, Polaris generations (A-2 and A-3) did achieve a degree of accuracy but still did not qualify as a counterforce system. Also, the Navy's humane concern of 1949 did not seem to have been present in 1947 when the Navy Department ruled out long-range bombers as "insufficiently reliable," and in turn called for the delivery of atomic weapons from floating bases 500 miles off of the enemy's shore (presumably an aircraft carrier) or by short range missiles of the V-2 types. (*The New York Times,* April 10, 1947.) This Navy reaction was triggered by an earlier War Department study which concluded that the strategic bomber was the "single most important element of our military capabilities." (*The New York Times,* April 19, 1947.)

aptly, of threatening the Soviet Union with a massive city strike if war came. The United States was not capable of any other type of immediate response to a major Soviet challenge. American air power was to counterbalance the Red Army. Third, the initial fight over American strategic doctrine was won by the Air Force, and this pattern of Air Force preponderance continued until the Kennedy years. And, finally, the B-36 debate was the last major debate in which any of the military services would feel that its very existence or over-all importance was challenged. From this point on, debates would center increasingly, not on whether a weapons system should be built, but which of the military services should build any given system. Each of the military services felt confident that a certain percentage of the defense appropriation "belonged" to a given branch even if it did not get prime responsibility for a system.

The decision to produce the B-36 was not the only major American strategic decision in 1949. Under the stimulus of the rather surprising Soviet test of an A-bomb in August of that year, the United States had evidently decided by November 1949 to proceed with the development of the hydrogen bomb.[18]

It should be emphasized that the decision to build the H-bomb was an important one for all mankind as well as a revolutionary development for the future of delivery vehicle systems. The atomic bomb had proved its destructiveness; however, weapons in the kiloton range were relatively low in explosive and radiation yield when compared to the megaton range of thermonuclear weapons.* Atomic fission weapons did not appear to threaten the existence of mankind; thermonuclear fusion weapons did.

A single megaton warhead (the one used on the American Minuteman II) can cause severe blast damage to an area of 60 square miles and do moderate damage up to 110 square miles. Or, put another way, moderate damage would be suffered over an area with a radius of approximately 6 miles.[19] A ten

---

* One kiloton is the explosive equivalent of 1,000 tons of TNT, whereas one megaton is the equivalent of 1,000,000 tons of TNT.

megaton explosion (an American B-52 carries four of these) can destroy an area of roughly 400 square miles and cause serious damage within a radius of about 12 miles.[20] In other words, a ten megaton bomb exploded over London (the largest land area of the world's cities) would destroy most of London, or 3 one megaton explosions spread over the city of Boston would effectively destroy that city.

The exact effects of fall-out in the event of an all-out thermonuclear exchange of the over 10,000 megatons possessed by the United States and the Soviet Union are not fully known. But there is a real possibility that the fall-out from these explosions would destroy human life; if it did not completely destroy it, it could very drastically alter the entire genetic make-up of what we now call human beings. Any attempted explanation of the possible effects of thermonuclear war is truly impossible. The destruction and horror not only stagger the imagination but go completely beyond it.[21]

Aside from the unbelievable power unleashed by the introduction of hydrogen weapons and the fact that they laid the foundation for a balance of terror which had not existed before, thermonuclear weapons also had a major impact on the strategic thinking of American policy makers. The future strategies to be adopted by the United States relied directly upon the existence of these terror weapons and their threatened use (e.g., massive retaliation or second-strike counterforce).

Before long, each of the military services (and their allies) had developed strategies and weapons systems designed to maximize their role in the thermonuclear age. For the Air Force, hydrogen weapons strengthened their belief in the efficacy of the bomber that could now carry the equivalent of 40,000,000 tons of TNT. Likewise, thermonuclear weapons eventually made the intercontinental ballistic missile system (ICBM) a "viable, economic" possibility for future Air Force systems. For the Navy, the argument was strengthened for the heavy aircraft carriers and, more important, the Navy began development of what was to be a number of generations of submarine-launched thermonuclear missiles—Regulus, Polaris, Poseidon. The Army also got a number of intermediate-range ballistic missiles—Redstone, Jupiter, "the atomic cannon," and, more important, it was assigned the air defense role which led to the antiballistic missile systems—Nike X, Sentinel, Safeguard. The military services believed they could not fail in devising a strategic doctrine to apply thermonuclear power in the conduct of the missions assigned to them. They did not fail.

The fact remains that the introduction of thermonuclear weapons assured the reality of a balance of terror between two powers if they would admit that it existed. The problem has been that the United States government has continually tried to convince the American people that some additional weapons system would add to a security that the government has not been able to guarantee since 1955 nor will be able to guarantee in the future (MX, "Star Wars," and the B-1 notwithstanding).

By the end of 1949 and on the eve of the Korean War, not only had the United States decided to build the B-36 bomber and the hydrogen bomb, but this country was also in the final stages of "enormous growth" of the Strategic Air Command (SAC), which had engaged in a crash program to reach maximum strength by January 1949. A peak in American atomic weapons production had also been announced by the Atomic Energy Commission on January 21, 1949. And in February of that year, the United States announced that an American B-50A bomber had flown around the world nonstop, demonstrating not only American advances in prop-jet aircraft, but also a substantial in-flight refueling capability.[22]

It should be noted that the decision on the B-36 and the H-bomb can claim to have been a direct result of the Soviet A-bomb test in August 1949, but under no circumstances can this reason be used for the strengthening of SAC or the increased production of atomic weapons earlier in the year.

By 1949 and early 1950, the United States represented a formidably armed nation for strategic, atomic warfare with the Soviet Union. There appears to be no question that the United States could have inflicted an extremely severe blow on the Soviet Union. If the United States had attacked with over 50 atomic weapons, it could have done more damage in twelve hours than that done by the Nazis in four years of war. It

also appears that by this time the American people approved
of this massive armaments effort, and specifically approved of
the preponderant effort being given to the Air Force over the
other two services.[23]

KOREA AND NATIONAL SECURITY PAPER #68

The commonly accepted belief that the United States disarmed
following World War II was one more in a rather long list of
postwar myths that surrounded American military policy. Another of these myths is the continued belief that the United
States decided to increase its arms expenditures drastically in
response to the war in Korea and that it was this conflict which
led to the tremendous increase in the military budget for 1951.
Yet, a close scrutiny of the facts surrounding this budget increase indicates that the *decision* to increase the military budget
threefold was made almost four months *before* the Korean
War started.

Prior to the fiscal 1951 military budget, American military
spending had ranged from $11 to $14 billion a year (5 to 7
percent of the Gross National Product, a figure that has not
fluctuated greatly over the years). A combination of conservative economic forces in the United States and a degree of
confidence in American military security had led to the belief
that this amount of spending was the minimum necessary for
the security of the United States.

The decision to build the H-bomb and the B-36 were, in part,
responses to perceived challenges, but even with the decision
to build these two weapons systems, the United States still had
not defined its over-all military doctrine. The attempt to do so
was National Security Council Paper #68 (NSC #68).

This document was drawn up in February 1950 and was re-
viewed by President Truman in April 1950. It was considered
"the first comprehensive statement of national strategy."[24] NSC
#68 represented a major assessment of American defense pol-
icy. It is interesting that the original authors of the ideas of
NSC #68 were civilians from the State Department and not
military from the Pentagon. And, although NSC #68 was later

accepted by the military, it was the civilian sector that came to the conclusion that the American military response to the Soviet challenge was not adequate. It was believed that the Western powers lacked a conventional capability in Europe and were critically weak in this area. Furthermore, it was estimated that by 1954 "the Soviet Union would have the nuclear *capability* [emphasis added] to launch a devastating attack on the United States."[25] The paper rejected the choices of doing nothing, launching a preventive war, or withdrawing to "fortress America"; instead, the paper advocated

> . . . an immediate and large-scale build-up in our military and general strength and that of our allies with the intention of *righting the power balance* [emphasis added] and in the hope that through means other than all-out war we could induce a change in the nature of the Soviet system.[26]

It was estimated that the implementation of the policies and programs recommended by NSC #68 would cost approximately $35 billion. This represented a threefold increase in American defense spending over that originally planned for Fiscal Year 1951.[27]

An analysis of NSC #68 reveals not only some of the basic thinking on national security problems in early 1950, but also some of the basic assumptions that have dominated postwar national security policy. Three recurrent fallacies appear in the assumptions behind NSC #68:

(1) The tendency to base policy exclusively on the maximum Soviet capability rather than on a mixture of Soviet potential and a realistic assessment of Soviet intent.

(2) The American belief that as they approached the thermonuclear balance of terror they were still working within the framework of the balance of power.

(3) The assumption that ". . . we could induce change in the nature of the Soviet system" by American military programs.

These three assumptions (along with others) furnished recurrent themes in the military policies of the Cold War. When

NSC #68 defined the period of maximum danger of Soviet attack as 1954, it established a precedent that is still followed, that is, an estimate based on Soviet capability and possible future threats to American security. For example, the belief in 1950 that the Soviet Union would have the capability to launch a devastating attack in 1954 proved to be false. Yet this did not prevent advocates of the "bomber gap" from making the same threat in 1955 about a Soviet attack in 1957, nor proponents of the missile gap from predicting in 1958 the same fate for the United States in 1961. And in 1970, the same predictions were made with regard to the devastating surprise attack that the Soviet Union could launch in 1975 with the SS-9 missile. At some point in the propagation of these dire but unfulfilled predictions one would think that the credibility of those making such predictions would be challenged. These exaggerated estimates of Soviet military capability had begun early in the arms race and they continued right through the Reagan Administration.

Before NSC #68 could be implemented, the Korean War started in June 1950. From the outset, one fact of American military planning became obvious. The United States had prepared for the wrong war, in the wrong place, and at the wrong time, and was involved in a type of war that it was least prepared to fight. Post-World War II military planning had been based on the belief that the United States could use its monopoly on the atomic bomb and the means to deliver it as a deterrent to any type of war initiated by the Soviet Union. This policy may have been correct if aggressive intent on the part of the Soviet Union is accepted, but the United States had not foreseen or planned for participation in a war such as Korea—a war in which the Soviet Union was not directly involved and which may have started without Soviet control and direction.

Thus, in June 1950, the United States found itself with an extremely limited conventional capability—only ten understrength divisions, eleven regimental combat teams, and two understrength Marine divisions.* At the same time, the United States had 48 aircraft wings including 18 SAC wings (at 45 planes

* An A.aerican division has approximately 15,000 men.

each for a total of 810 bombers).[28] As General James Gavin later pointed out, the United States had placed its complete reliance on air power, and therefore:

> . . . the greatest industrial nation of the world could do no better than to airlift two rifle companies and a battery of artillery to meet six aggressor divisions in the initial stages of the [Korean] war.[29]

In order to correct this critical manpower shortage in conventional forces, the United States mobilized over 650,000 reservists and National Guard troops and inducted another 585,000 men into the armed forces during the first year of the Korean War.[30]* The United States eventually placed 253,250 American troops in Korea by June 30, 1951; by June 30, 1952, there were 265,864; and by July 31, 1953, the total United States manpower in Korea was 302,483 men.[31] At the end of the Korean War, 33,629 Americans had died in combat; 20,617 were listed as dead from other causes; and 103,284 men had been wounded.[32] As the casualties increased and the war continued, the frustration and anger of the American people also increased to the point where Truman's heir-apparent, Adlai Stevenson, was easily defeated by Dwight Eisenhower in the 1952 election.

---

* Total American military strength went from 1.7 million men in 1948 to a total of 2.8 million men in 1951. Huntington, *The Common Defense,* p. 54.

II

The Eisenhower Years: Massive Retaliation
and Collective Security

(1953–1957)

MASSIVE RETALIATION

The Korean War and the election of Dwight Eisenhower signaled the end of an era in American defense policy. From 1945
to 1953 American military policy had not been clearly articulated. Despite the discussions within the Truman administration of NSC #68, the public had been content to drift along,
secure in the belief that the American atomic monopoly and
means of delivery guaranteed American and Western European
security. The first stirrings of an attempted policy definition had
occurred periodically in the past, but these discussions did not
lead to an explicit statement of American strategy. The Korean
War cut these discussions short as the United States mobilized
to fight this confusing and frustrating conflict. Therefore, when
Eisenhower came to the White House in 1953, there was no
clearly defined policy toward the use of atomic weapons, nor
had American policy been declared toward those areas of the
third world not immediately involved in the politics of superpower diplomacy.

The main architect of American foreign and military policy
from 1953 to 1959 was Secretary of State John Foster Dulles.
And, in his view, the many problems facing the United States

in 1953 were epitomized by the threat from the world Communist movement and the aggressive intentions of the Soviet
Union. Yet it appears that Dulles not only misunderstood Soviet
policies during this period (they were conservative and counter-
revolutionary), but he also failed to grasp the rapidity with
which technological developments were making obsolete the
balance of power concept and, therefore, the strategy of thermonuclear bluff that he implemented. Thus, the failure of the
rather elaborate alliance systems created by Secretary Dulles
was matched by the equally futile effort on his part to implement a policy based on an unrealistic and highly dangerous
bluff—massive retaliation.

Although the doctrine of massive retaliation and the establishment of a number of complicated alliance systems are closely
related, it is desirable temporarily to separate them for analytical
purposes. However, the reader should keep in mind that the
strategy of massive retaliation and the surrounding of the Soviet
Union (and China) with alliance systems were both part of the
over-all American policy of containment, and on occasion were
used in an attempt to strengthen the unstated but implied policy
of "liberation."

This policy called for an American attempt to "roll back" the
Iron Curtain to "free" those countries with Communist governments. Although at times the rhetoric of such a policy was present in official government statements, the fact remains that
during the Eisenhower Administration the United States had no
military alternatives outside the use of atomic weapons; and
nuclear weapons could not "roll back" the Iron Curtain without
serious risks to the United States. The best example of this was
the inability of the United States to react in any military manner
to the Soviet suppression of the Hungarian revolution in 1956.
Five American divisions, or twenty NATO divisions in Central
Europe simply could not challenge the Red Army in Hungary
with any prospect of success.

Following the Korean conflict, there was a great deal of
revulsion and frustration in the United States concerning the
limited application of American power in this "police action."

Many Americans were aware of this nation's great nuclear strength and believed in the invincibility of the armed forces of the United States once this country mobilized. These Americans could not comprehend the subtle reasoning (or did not agree with it) behind fighting a war other than one aimed at total victory, particularly if the United States could win the war without the use of nuclear weapons.[1] One of the major forms in which this frustration manifested itself was the increasing demand on the new Eisenhower Administration for a clearly stated, applicable means of using the nuclear power of the United States to implement American policies.

The problem of defining American strategy was further complicated by the existing rivalry between the military services. The Army and the Navy emerged from Korea with their belief intact in the need for strong conventional forces and the ability to transport them to any point necessary. For them, Korea confirmed the lessons of World War II. On the other hand, the Air Force contended that no nation would risk aggression in the face of an overwhelming American Air Force that could deliver large numbers of nuclear weapons anywhere in the world. They maintained that American air power should be able to destroy the atomic capability of any nation and that if this capability existed, there would be no need for the specialized forces required to fight limited wars. The power of the Air Force would be sufficient to deter any type of Soviet aggression. As will be seen, with the introduction of the doctrine of massive retaliation, the Air Force emerged as the most powerful of the military services with by far the largest percentage of the defense budget allocated to it.

Although the doctrine of massive retaliation was not officially stated until January 1954, its foundation and underlying philosophy became apparent during the first year of the Eisenhower Administration. In President Eisenhower's State of the Union message in February 1953, he stated that the free world could not leave to the aggressor "the choice of the time and place and means to cause the greatest hurt to us at the least cost to himself."[2] He then set forth his Administration's policy for obtaining national security without excessive defense spending:

To amass military power without regard to our own economic capacity would be to defend ourselves against one kind of disaster by inviting another. . . . The biggest force is not necessarily the best.[3]

The President's goal of balancing military requirements and economic capacity of the United States proved to be difficult to achieve. The Eisenhower Administration became ensnarled in the same dilemma that frustrated the Truman Administration. In more precise terms, the dilemma was how to maintain United States security and the military posture believed necessary to conduct foreign affairs while at the same time following a domestic policy of solvency and expansion of essential domestic programs.[4]

The traditional American approach of preparing for war by planned mobilization of manpower and industrial resources over an extended period of time appeared to be outmoded in the nuclear age, and the new strategy of deterrence through readiness accentuated military versus nonmilitary claims on scarce resources.[5]

President Eisenhower continued to state many of the more significant aspects of the doctrine of massive retaliation before its formal announcement. In his second State of the Union message, he announced: "We shall not be the aggressor, but we and our allies have and will maintain a massive capacity to strike back."[6]

The formal announcement of the doctrine of massive retaliation was made by Secretary of State Dulles on January 12, 1954. The original doctrine had two basic precepts—one dealing with the cost of deterrence and the other with the response of the United States to aggression. The Secretary of State declared: "We want for ourselves and for others a maximum deterrent at bearable costs."[7] In order to secure the two goals of security and solvency, the Eisenhower Administration initially adopted a dual posture to prevent Soviet aggression. Strategically, the policy of threatened massive retaliation emerged to deter Soviet aggression. On the tactical level, especially in Western Europe, it was felt that should deterrence fail, the United States would have the option of using nuclear weapons first rather than being forced to choose between capitulation or all-out war in the event of Soviet aggression. This dual strategic and tactical task was to be accomplished by getting "more bang for the buck" than would have been possible under more conventional forms of defense planning.

By publicly articulating the official doctrine of massive retaliation, Secretary Dulles exposed it to open scrutiny and debate. The debate was not long in coming, and it revealed that a degree of ambiguity and confusion arose from the original statements. The combination of continued debate and the subsequent Administration attempts to clarify the new doctrine continued until the concept changed and was eventually discarded.

The first express criticism raised the question of the President's constitutional authority to initiate massive retaliation,[8] and other critics questioned its credibility in the mind of a potential aggressor.[9] The problem of constitutionality was never seriously discussed, but the question of credibility was a constant factor throughout the debate.[10]

Due to the criticism and confusion arising from the original statement in January, Secretary Dulles attempted to clarify the doctrine and to answer his critics in the April 1954 issue of *Foreign Affairs*. He began by restating what he believed to be the basic question concerning the maintenance of free world security, that is: "How should collective defense be organized by the free world for maximum protection at minimum cost?"[11] Mr. Dulles believed that to allow the aggressor to dictate the battle conditions and thereby to engage the "free world" in a struggle involving manpower was to encourage aggression. He thought that the aggressor would be tempted to attack in places and by means where, at a minimum cost to himself, he could impose the greatest burden on the United States. If the "free world" responded to this strategy, it could bankrupt itself and not achieve the security required.[12] Secretary Dulles attempted to forestall any act of aggression when he stated:

> The potential of massive attack will always be kept in a state of readiness, but our program will retain a wide variety of means and scope for responding to aggression.[13]

Despite the reference to a "wide variety of means," this policy was based on the belief that it was impossible for the "free world" to build up adequate conventional defense forces around the Communist perimeter. By claiming that the United States could choose the time, place, and means of warfare, there was a strong implication that local conflicts might be escalated as to the place and methods of retaliation. The doctrine of massive retaliation implied the threat of and preparation for total war in an effort to prevent not only all-out war but also limited warfare.

Despite this clarification, the exact response of the United States to any given act of perceived Soviet aggression remained vague, probably on purpose. By not stating exactly what aggressive act would initiate instant retaliation, or the exact nature of the retaliatory act, Secretary of State Dulles hoped to prevent all types of aggression or any challenge to the status quo.

However, the doctrine and its clarification had hardly been announced, when just the type of "aggression" that it was allegedly intended to prevent was succeeding. In Indochina, a supposedly Russian-directed war was rapidly approaching its decisive stage, and it was becoming apparent that the French would be forced to abandon the area unless substantial American military forces were forthcoming. Although some consideration was given to the use of American forces, both conventional and atomic, the decision was made in Washington not to do so. Thus, the first test of massive retaliation as a doctrine resulted in American inaction.

For complete credibility, such a doctrine should have been based on a United States counterforce posture—United States ability to strike first at the enemy's nuclear capability, destroying enough of its delivery system to prevent an unacceptable second strike by the enemy. Unless the United States possessed this capability, it made no sense to retaliate massively against limited aggression if the United States would suffer unacceptable damages in return. Ironically, Secretary Dulles announced the new doctrine almost at the time that the United States was losing its ability to attack the Soviet Union without the certainty of an unacceptable Soviet counterattack. Prior to 1954–1955, the United States could have launched an atomic attack on

Soviet territory and not received a single atomic bomb on its soil in retaliation. But by the time of Dulles' announcement, the Soviet Union had 300–400 nuclear and thermonuclear weapons and was beginning to produce operational long-range bombers to deliver them.[14] After 1955 there could be no certainty that the United States would not receive a devastating nuclear attack on its major cities in the event of war with the Soviet Union.

Massive retaliation could deter local aggression only so long as there existed a reasonable prospect of an immediate victory in all-out war and so long as the potential aggressor understood this. However, the possibility did exist that the doctrine of massive retaliation, even though not supported by a guaranteed American counterforce posture, would still be an effective deterrent to limited war if a potential aggressor was convinced that American prestige and honor were so involved in a dispute that the United States would respond massively to limited aggression. Nonetheless, as Soviet nuclear strength increased, the credibility of massive retaliation weakened.

Except for an atomic attack on the United States, the doctrine of massive retaliation was—in its simplest terms—a bluff. From 1956 on there was no way that the leaders of the United States could be *certain* that this country would not be seriously damaged in the event of a thermonuclear exchange with the Soviet Union. It made no sense to base American military policy on a threatened reaction that could lead to the destruction of American society. Yet, many contend that even if the policy was a bluff, it worked in that there were no examples of overt Soviet aggression during the period 1954–1960. This assumption, of course, was based on the belief that the Soviet Union was an aggressive nation during the 1950s just waiting for the chance to attack. Outside Eastern Europe there is really no evidence to support this contention. The best example of Soviet aggression during the Eisenhower Administration was the suppression of the Hungarian revolution; American inaction during this conflict is well known. On a more hypothetical level, let us assume the worst and speculate for a moment on the American reaction to a Soviet invasion of Turkey. Here would be a classic case of clear aggression and the application of Dulles' doctrine of massive retaliation. For the United States to respond to this aggression by entering into a race of mutual annihilation with the Soviet Union hardly seems to be a rational reaction. It can certainly be argued that the destruction of fifty of America's largest cities is an incredibly high price to pay, especially when existing Soviet ground forces would have probably overrun Turkey anyhow. The doctrine of massive retaliation and its accompanying weapons systems meant that the United States was left with only a nuclear response to any military action it perceived as hostile or a threat to a friendly government.

TACTICAL NUCLEAR WEAPONS AND NATO

As it became increasingly evident that American military power could deter an all-out attack on the United States, but not necessarily stop more limited aggression, the question arose as to the means by which limited aggression could be prevented. In keeping with the desire of the Administration to provide security and solvency, the decision was made in 1954 to equip ground, air, and naval forces with tactical nuclear weapons.*

As early as 1951 the United States had successfully tested tactical nuclear weapons, and American leaders began to discuss the possibility of using them in the initial stages of limited hostilities rather than resorting to the use of strategic weapons.[15] The Navy rapidly developed the capability to launch carrier aircraft with atomic bombs, and the Army began development of the "atomic cannon." By 1953, the United States had over $10 billion invested in its atomic program, with over 90 percent of it for military purposes. By this same year, the United States was approaching a stockpile of 1,000 atomic weapons, and production costs for each additional weapon were down to about $1 million each. Finally, the appropriation of $3 billion in

---

* The distinction between tactical and strategic nuclear weapons is difficult to make. But, for the purposes of this study, it would mean that the United States and the Soviet Union might use "low yield" tactical atomic weapons (1–20 kilotons) against hostile forces engaged in Europe, but would not resort to "high yield" strategic weapons against each other's homelands.

1953 for atomic facilities guaranteed the existence of an extremely large American nuclear stockpile.[16]

In 1951, in recognition of the impact of tactical nuclear weapons, Senator Brian McMahon had called for a sixfold increase in American atomic production,[17] and by 1953 he summed up the results of this program:

> Five years ago neither the professional soldiers nor the atomic scientists foresaw what will turn out to be the great military revolution —the use of atomic energy as firepower in the hands of troops, sailors, and airmen. It was this revolution that brought about the requirements for great numbers of atomic bombs.[18]

But Senator McMahon had only stated the most obvious result of the decision to arm American conventional forces with nuclear weapons. What he did not state was the fact that the American decision to deploy nuclear weapons in Europe was a direct result of the fact that the North Atlantic Treaty Organization (NATO) nations had failed to meet troop quotas established at an earlier date.

By the end of 1949 or early 1950, the United States had made the dual decision of *attempting* to confront Soviet military power in Europe with a conventional response and of completely reassessing its policy toward rebuilding and eventually rearming Germany. Obviously these two decisions were closely interdependent. It did not make much sense to rearm Western Europe without rearming Germany. As later events demonstrated, even with Germany rebuilt and rearmed, the NATO allies have never had much certainty that the conventional defense of Europe was possible in the face of a determined Soviet attack.

Officially, NATO was formed in 1949, and its initial military goals were the establishment of 20–22 divisions. By the 1980s, no *feasible* defensive forces had been raised to protect Western Europe should the Soviet Union launch a conventional attack. The decision to rearm this area placed a heavy burden on the already strained economies of these nations. The reality of the conventional rearmament program in conjunction with the growing American atomic capacity is certain to have appeared as a threat to the Soviet Union, if for no other reason than as an apparent attempt on the part of the West to remove Western Europe as a hostage in the event of an American atomic attack of Russia.

By 1949, the Soviet Union had 50–60 well-equipped and combat-ready divisions in Eastern Europe and the western part of the Soviet Union. Against this force, the five European nations could boast a maximum of six divisions—three French, one British, one Belgian, and one Dutch.* The United States could have possibly added one or two divisions to this force, while the Soviets could have brought their total strength up to 150 divisions within a month.[19] This discrepancy among conventional forces was recognized by Western leaders. In 1952 at the Lisbon Conference the NATO allies approved a plan that called for 50 NATO divisions (half active, half reserve) by the end of 1952, 70 by the end of 1953, and 97 by the end of 1954.[20] These goals were never met. The fact is that at no time since World War II has the NATO Alliance had more than 30 combat-ready divisions in northern Europe (and most of the time less than this).

When it is also recognized that many of these Western divisions were stationed in areas other than the crucial North German Plain invasion route, including at a later date the entire United States Seventh Army, the inadequacy of the NATO conventional forces in Europe becomes even more apparent. As will be shown in Chapter III, contrary to the Pentagon's public relations effort, at no time since World War II have the NATO forces had a credible nonnuclear response to a Soviet attack on the North German Plain (roughly a line running from the German cities of Kiel, Hamburg, Hannover, and Giessen). Without adequate conventional defensive forces in this area, and in the absence of the use of atomic weapons, it would probably have taken the Soviet Union about eight days to take the critical ports of Antwerp and Amsterdam.

---

* The number of men in a division varies greatly, but roughly Soviet divisions were approximately 10,000–12,000 men, with Western divisions running approximately 15,000 men (sometimes reinforced from 18,000 to 20,000 men).

By 1953, the NATO powers were nowhere near the 70 divisions envisioned at Lisbon; as a matter of fact, NATO combat-ready strength in Central Europe at this time was under twenty divisions and showed no signs of significantly increasing. It was in this context that the decision was made to deploy tactical nuclear weapons instead of the manpower that the European nations were either unwilling or unable to contribute. This represented a major shift in NATO strategy. And, although it was not realized at the time, the decision to attempt the defense of Europe with atomic weapons in 1954 was the final admission that the NATO powers could not or did not feel it necessary to defend Europe with conventional forces, and never again were the high goals of the Lisbon Conference set by the NATO nations.

The controversy over the efficacy of the substitution of firepower for manpower began almost immediately and still has not been resolved. The United States initially placed a great deal of faith in the concept of the use of tactical nuclear weapons to *defend* against an attack on Western Europe. But as the weapons systems evolved and the age of nuclear plenty became a reality, the validity of this belief became open to doubt, and some serious observers began to regard the existence of thousands of tactical nuclear weapons in Europe as more of a deterrent force than as a viable defense against Soviet attack.

As the number of tactical nuclear weapons in Europe continued to grow during the 1950s, two fundamental questions arose concerning the value and possible use of these weapons should the need arise to fight with them. The first question concerned tactical military function; the second question was fundamentally a humanitarian and moral one.

The debate over whether tactical nuclear weapons would militarily favor the offense or the defense in the event of hostilities has not been resolved. Since they have never been used in a tactical situation, the exact effect is not known.[21] However, it does appear that their use would place a large premium on well-trained manpower reserves, mobility and dispersion of forces, and maneuvering territory available to the opposing forces. If this is the case, and tactical nuclear weapons are considered as a defense force in Western Europe, the advantage would appear to rest decisively with the Soviet Union. For, throughout the arms race in Europe, Soviet superiority in these critical areas seems to be fairly clear.

But the humanitarian question overshadows this military problem and reduces it to meaninglessness.* As the number of tactical nuclear weapons increased in Western Europe, the real possibility began to emerge that the use of these weapons would result not in the defense of this area, but in its destruction. During the 1950s American leaders and some scholars† advocated and planned for the use of these weapons to defend Western Europe; but it would seem that the morality and efficacy of this plan could be seriously challenged by concerned Europeans and, of course, that is exactly what happened. First DeGaulle and then progressively more European leaders began to wonder about the wisdom of defending Western Europe by destroying it. It is one thing for the leaders of the United States and the Soviet Union to speak of a land war in Europe which would almost inevitably result in the use of tactical nuclear weapons; but it is quite another matter for Europeans, both east and west, to contemplate this approach with equanimity.

In spite of the growing awareness of the destructiveness of tactical nuclear war and the fact that the use of these weapons would probably favor the Soviet Union if they favored either side, NATO did not develop an adequate conventional defense against any major attack on the main front of Central Europe. The early acceptance of the idea that tactical nuclear weapons diminished the need for troops naturally tended to counteract efforts to build a conventional military force in Europe. As a consequence, in Europe there was almost no capacity for defense by conventional means. If deterrence failed, there would be no choice but to surrender Europe or run the risk of destroying it.

---

* The reader should be reminded that the average tactical nuclear weapon had an explosive power of 1–20 kilotons. The Hiroshima bomb was approximately 15 kilotons.

† See Henry Kissinger, *Nuclear Weapons and Foreign Policy*. Kissinger later changed his mind about the use of tactical nuclear weapons in the defense of Western Europe.

The American decision to emphasize firepower over manpower and the attempt to implement the doctrine of massive retaliation and its lesser corollary—deploying tactical nuclear weapons—meant that during the Eisenhower years the Air Force had won the interservice rivalry for budgetary funds. From 1955 to 1959 military appropriations were divided among the services in the following manner: Air Force, 45 percent; Navy-Marines, 28 percent; and the Army, 23 percent.[22] During this period, the number of men in the Army and Navy declined, as did the number of combat-ready Army divisions and active naval ships. At the same time, the number of men in the Air Force and the number of Air Force wings increased substantially.[23] However, almost inadvertently, an important long-range consolation prize was given to the Army in the form of its new atomic missions—atomic artillery and eventually air defense. In the long run this meant additional appropriations for the Army which placed it in the technological position to challenge, temporarily, the Air Force missile programs (see next chapter). More important, the Army combined this early technological progress and its assigned air defense mission to the early Nike antiaircraft systems and eventually to the much more lucrative ABM (antiballistic missiles) systems that were developed (Nike-Zeus, Nike-X, Sentinel, Safeguard, and "Star Wars").

Samuel Huntington has contended that the original Dulles announcement of massive retaliation represented the "New Look" of the Eisenhower Administration and that this doctrine aimed at superiority in strategic weapons while accepting inferiority in conventional forces. Mr. Huntington further contends that this policy was changed about 1956 by the introduction of the "New, New Look" which assumed superiority in neither, but adequacy in both.[24] Yet throughout the Eisenhower Administration the United States remained vastly superior in strategic weapons and maintained a very limited conventional capability. This situation was probably best reflected by the fact that at no time during this period did the NATO allies have a conventional option in Europe in the event of a strictly conventional attack. The reality of this policy was demonstrated at a later date when the United States was strapped for a conventional force of approximately six divisions for an invasion of Cuba after the Bay of Pigs operation had failed.[25]

COLLECTIVE SECURITY

In an effort to make the doctrine of massive retaliation more credible, Secretary of State Dulles not only continued the alliance-building of his predecessors, he expanded the American attempt to guarantee the protection of its national interests and contain communism through collective security arrangements. The promise to respond "at places and with means of our own choosing," so the thinking went, would certainly be more believable if the United States had a tighter set of alliance systems surrounding the periphery of the Soviet Union and China.

Thus, by 1955 the United States had literally allied itself with every nation near the Soviet Union or China that would enter into a collective security pact or associate itself with the United States or its allies. These alliances, both multilateral and bilateral, were set up without regard to the political system of the nation involved, so long as the governments did not call themselves Communist. The keystone of this system of collective security was NATO.

The American decision to establish a European alliance system effectively reduced the future options of American foreign policy and proved to be one of the critical decisions in solidifying and guaranteeing the continued development of the Cold War. At this point, a few examples will illustrate some of the costs of establishing this alliance. In terms of Soviet-American relations, the most costly of these sacrifices can be traced to the decision to rebuild and then rearm Germany. This decision produced predictable Soviet hostility and eventually the Warsaw Pact. Likewise, part of the price for French support of German rearmament was increased American support for French attempts to maintain its colonial empire in Indochina and then Algeria.

The efforts of John Foster Dulles finalized American policy toward Europe for many years. Although his threats of an

"agonizing reappraisal" initially failed to gain French support for the European Defense Command, the French finally
approved of West German rearmament and the acceptance of
West Germany into NATO. In addition, Dulles' efforts to apply
the doctrine of massive retaliation to Europe meant that it was
then possible for a world-wide thermonuclear war to be fought
without European consultation, much less approval.* The introduction of American-controlled tactical nuclear weapons
meant that an atomic war might take place on European soil
before the governments of Europe had a chance to prevent it.
Neither of these latter possibilities proved to be particularly
appealing to the thinking European.

However, there appears to have been a deeper, more fundamental difference between the American and European approach
to European Security—a difference that has constantly weakened the NATO Alliance and will probably destroy it in the
long run. As early as 1953, this difference was noted by Hanson
Baldwin when he stated: "Europe simply does not take the
threat of imminent war as seriously as the United States
does. . . ."[26] While American strategists and politicians planned
for the invasion of Western Europe by the Soviet Union, Western Europe gave some lip service to this threat, offered token
defense forces, and then proceeded to allocate their resources,
first toward the rebuilding of Europe and then toward the ex-
tension of European prosperity. (Germany is the possible
exception to this statement.) European support was greatest
during the early years of the Alliance when these nations were
dependent upon the good will of United States capital and foreign aid; but once currency convertibility and relative prosperity had been achieved, European ardor for rearmament and
NATO cooled noticeably. This tendency was apparent by 1953,
when it became obvious that the NATO nations were not going

---

* In March 1954, Secretary Dulles announced that he interpreted the doc-
trine of massive retaliation and the NATO commitment to mean that the
United States President could retaliate "instantly" without consulting
Congress in the event of an attack on American allies in Europe. *The New
York Times,* March 17, 1954.

to fulfill even the minimum force levels agreed upon at the Lisbon Conference.

The argument that the introduction of tactical nuclear weapons obviated the need for conventional forces is a classic evasion of the issue. The American decision to introduce these weapons into Europe was based on the clear recognition that the European nations were not going to rearm sufficiently and therefore the introduction of tactical nuclear weapons was the only alternative open to the United States unless this country wanted to undertake the conventional defense of Europe by itself.

By 1955, American diplomacy had succeeded in placing tactical nuclear weapons in Europe. It had also succeeded in gaining approval for the rearmament of Germany and the admission of West Germany into the NATO Alliance. But two months following the admission of West Germany, the Soviet Union responded by forming its own alliance system in Eastern Europe—the Warsaw Pact.

Yet even the formation of the Warsaw Pact did not seem to disturb unduly the defense plans of Western Europe. If the nations of Western Europe had truly feared a Soviet invasion, they would have spared no effort to arm themselves with adequate forces for the conventional defense of Europe. Western Europe had the manpower and the industrial capacity by the mid 1950s; the failure to use it was based on their assessment that a Soviet attack was not imminent.

However, the finalization of NATO was not Dulles' major contribution to the American policy of collective security. Dulles formulated and implemented two other major alliance systems to contain what he viewed as the aggressiveness of communism. At the primary initiative of the United States the Baghdad Pact (later, Central Treaty Organization—CENTO) and the Southeast Asia Treaty Organization (SEATO) were formed. Even at the time, the efficacy of both of these systems as meaningful collective security arrangements was open to serious doubt. By the end of the Eisenhower Administration, Iraq had pulled out of CENTO, and this alliance was in a state of steady decline and irrelevance.[27] On the other hand, by 1960 the SEATO agreement was just beginning to be used as one of the major justifications for American involvement in Southeast Asia. By 1970, the damage done to American and world interests because of the manner in which this alliance was interpreted was staggering. Following Vietnam, SEATO became ineffective.

Although Dulles constructed the underlying diplomatic-military system that was to continue throughout the Eisenhower Administration, the President seemed to demonstrate an awareness of the meaning of the thermonuclear age that his Secretary of State lacked. This tendency on the part of the President to be doing or saying one thing while members of his Administration were reacting in a different or opposite fashion reappeared throughout this Administration. (See below on the missile gap period.)

President Eisenhower stated as early as 1954:

> We have arrived at that point, my friends, where war does not present the possibility of victory or defeat. War would present to us only the alternative of degrees of destruction. There can be no truly successful outcome.[28]

This solid analysis by the President was confirmed several months later by a report of the Atomic Energy Commission on the hydrogen bomb tests of March 1954 which had polluted an area of 7,000 square miles with deadly radioactive fall-out. Several years later, Secretary of Defense Charles Wilson warned Congress that the atomic stockpiles of both the United States and the USSR were approaching the point where they could "practically wipe out the world."[29]

This growing awareness of the power of thermonuclear weapons did not serve as a brake on the arms race; rather, it seems to have escalated it. As seen above, as early as 1951 United States Air Force spokesmen had begun to cast doubts on the ability of United States strategic forces to deter an attack by the Soviet Union.[30] With the arrival of the thermonuclear era in 1953, this fear evidently persisted as Pentagon strategists began to calculate that the strategic balance was turning against the United States.

THE BOMBER GAP

In view of the fact that the Soviet Union did not possess a bomber that could reach the United States, it seems reasonable to speculate that the threat perceived by the Air Force was not the Soviet Union, but a budget-conscious Republican administration. An administration committed to stabilizing, if not reducing, the military budget was a threat to all the military services, but particularly to the Air Force with its large share of the existing budget. The bulk of the Eisenhower Administration's reductions in the Truman budget had occurred in the Air Force allocations. President Eisenhower had also abandoned the Truman target of 143 Air Force wings by 1956, with the new goal being 114 in Fiscal Year 1954 and 120 for 1955.[31]

Thus, by 1955, the foundation for the "bomber gap" had been laid. In the next chapter we will go into considerable detail as to where the later "missile gap" came from, the forces that produced it, the weaknesses in American decision-making it illustrated, and the degree of interservice rivalry involved. Therefore, in dealing with the bomber gap the discussion will be limited to the basic facts surrounding this example of myth creation in American defense policy, rather than examining the bomber gap in great detail.

The bomber gap, in its most basic form, was the belief by many American leaders that the Soviet Union had the capability and desire to mass produce a large number of Bison bombers in preparation for an attack on the United States that would destroy the American ability to retaliate. Although a number of civilian and military leaders had believed all along that the Soviet Union was preparing to attack the United States, the Soviet Air Show in July 1955 seemed to offer them proof of this contention. At this air show, for the first time the Soviet Union displayed their *first* intercontinental bomber, the Bison (officially the M-4, a rough equivalent of the already operational

American B-52). The Soviets not only displayed this bomber flying in squadron formation (ten planes), but also appeared to have large numbers of Bisons in the air that day. It was from this allegedly impressive display of air power that many Americans, especially the Air Force, contended that the United States was in danger of losing its strategic advantage and would be imperiled by a Soviet Bison attack in about two years. (It should be noted that the period of "maximum danger" had shifted from 1954 to 1957.) American estimates indicated that the Soviets *could* quickly build over 600 of these aircraft.[32] The belief that the Soviet Union would maximize this capability led U.S. Air Force General Curtis LeMay, to comment that this huge Soviet bomber build-up could lead to a 2–1 Soviet advantage over the United States.[33]

Later evidence indicated that the Soviet Union had attempted to create the illusion of strength to conceal their weakness in long-range delivery systems. To create this impression, they had their one existing squadron of ten Bisons flown repeatedly around the review stand in a wide circle.[34] Evidently the Soviet Union had the *capability* to produce large numbers of Bisons, but they simply chose not to allocate their resources in this manner. As a matter of fact, the Soviet Union has *never* possessed at any one time more than 300 bombers capable of reaching the United States, while under the impetus of the "bomber gap" the American strategic bomber force soon reached about 500 long-range B-52 bombers and over 1,500 medium-range bombers capable of reaching the Soviet Union from either foreign bases or with the aid of in-flight refueling.[35]

The Soviet attempt to create an illusion of strength succeeded only too well. Many Americans believed that the Soviet Union had achieved strategic superiority over the United States, and this country began a massive build-up of its strategic forces. Thus, when the "bomber gap" did appear, it appeared in favor of the United States by about a 5–1 ratio. Common sense would indicate that the Soviets might have learned a lesson about the American reaction to a possible strategic inferiority, but they repeated exactly the same error at a later date during the "missile gap" period and with exactly the same results—an overwhelming increase in American missile superiority. In the long run, this Soviet error cost the Soviet Union a great deal of money and led to an escalation of the arms race that they neither wanted nor could afford. In trying to create an illusion of strength in the face of American superiority, Soviet leaders played right into the hands of the American military and their numerous allies.

Thus, the Soviet Union seems to have learned the wrong lessons from the "bomber gap." Instead of realizing the extreme dangers of arms escalation because of American sensitivity to possible threats to its strategic superiority, they learned only that some forces in the United States could be falsely led to believe (or claim to believe) that America's strategic power was inferior. Obviously, the American willingness to propagate its own strategic weakness in the face of projected Soviet forces is at least partially traceable to the military-industrial drive for more funds for future weapons systems. The forces supporting higher military budgets had learned early in the arms race that there is no better method of increasing the military budget than that of convincing Congress of some *future* threat to American security by the Soviet *capability* to produce a weapons system. The fact that the Soviets have never developed these systems in the form predicted has not in the least reduced the effectiveness of this tactic.

At a later date, some observers claimed that the Soviet Union had tricked the United States into believing that they were mass producing bombers when actually they were engaged in a "crash" missile-production program.[36] There does not appear to be much doubt that the United States was tricked by the Soviet Union, but this was not because the Soviets were engaged in a "crash" missile-building program. It seems more likely that the Soviet Union was diverting some resources to missile development (but not necessarily to programmed missile production), and that they were using the remainder of their available military resources for the modernization of the Red Army.

It would appear that during the postwar period the Soviet Union explicitly rejected the idea of surprise attack both in theory and in the weapons systems built. The fact that the Soviet

Union had the *capability* to build large numbers of Bisons but chose not to do so, even in the face of overwhelming American superiority, is another indication of the soundness of this analysis.

Theoretically, the Soviet Union explicitly rejected the decisiveness of a surprise thermonuclear attack in 1955. Raymond Garthoff, quoting Soviet Marshal Rotmistrov, in an article in *Military Thought* (February 1955): "Surprise attack by itself still does not and cannot provide complete victory in war or in an operation."[37] Under both Stalin and his successors, the leaders of the Soviet Union had spoken of "peaceful coexistence" and had repeatedly denied any intent to attack the United States.[38] And, in 1956 at the 20th Party Congress, Premier Khrushchev denied the inevitability of war for those that might have missed the message earlier. It appears that at first the Soviet Union rejected the ability of nuclear weapons to be decisive in a new war; then they gradually began to realize that no one would "win" the next war.[39] This debate in the Soviet Union, as in the United States, continues to this day, but no civilian Soviet leader since World War II believed in the efficacy of an atomic surprise attack to meet Soviet national goals. Suffice it to say that behind the bomber gap was the underlying American assumption that the Soviet Union was preparing a first strike against the United States, and this was not true. Likewise, the Soviets had really given no indication that this was the case.

The belief in the bomber gap was not destroyed by comparative data on American and Soviet bomber forces. The bomber gap was simply submerged and replaced by the panic that accompanied the first Soviet testing of an ICBM in August 1957 and then by the successful orbiting of an earth satellite by the Soviet Union in October of the same year. The myth of the bomber gap and the danger of a bomber attack on the United States was replaced in 1957 by the myth of the missile gap and the imminence of a Soviet missile attack sometime around 1961.

III

THE MISSILE GAP: A Study in Myth Creation

(1957–1961)

The period of the "missile gap" (1957–1961) is a classic illustration of myth creation by forces within and outside of the United States government, and serves as an excellent example of the assumptions and forces at work in the development of American defense policy. The components in the American system which produced the missile gap were not new and certainly have not disappeared as of the 1980s. Therefore, if this complex and difficult process can be explained and understood it should aid in an understanding of the problems facing American defense policy makers, not only at present, but also in the future. Many of the lessons to be learned from a detailed study of the missile gap can be of value in an assessment of the SDI, MX, B-1, and SS-20 debate presently taking place and of the ULMS (undersea long-range missile system) debate which is assured for the future. Therefore, substantial detail will be devoted to the missile gap in the hope that by using this as a basic case study some light can be shed on previous and future arguments that inevitably surround a given weapons system.[1]

The basic assumptions of those who accepted the myth of the missile gap are fairly simple. In August 1957 the Soviet Union successfully tested the first ICBM, and in the following October they placed the first earth satellite in orbit. From this point on, it was the commonly accepted belief by many in the United

States that the Soviet Union would mass produce ICBMs, so that by about 1961–1962 they would have roughly 1,000–1,500 missiles (to less than 100 American ICBMs), which could then be used in a surprise attack to destroy the strategic power of the United States.

Whether intended or not, the creation of the missile gap accomplished the following:

(1) It led to a drastic increase in the budgetary allocations for the military, particularly for the Air Force.

(2) The Democratic Party gained substantial advantages, particularly in the 1960 elections, from the illusion that the Republicans had allowed the missile gap to occur.

(3) The belief that the Soviet Union was the avowed enemy of the United States, prepared to attack at any time, was perpetuated and strengthened.

(4) The NATO Alliance was shaken by the weakening of American nuclear credibility and the other forces released by the belief in the missile gap.

(5) American intelligence system was reorganized (DIA).

(6) Relations between the Soviet Union and China were considerably weakened by Mao Tse-tung's belief in the missile gap myth.

(7) The United States military was given an excuse to place IRBMs and MRBMs on the periphery of the Soviet Union (particularly in Turkey, Germany, Italy, and Great Britain).

Once the missile gap myth had been destroyed (1961), it became possible to attempt to answer some of the perplexing questions raised by this controversial period in the history of American defense policy and the arms race. The creation, perpetuation, and eventual destruction of this myth raised serious questions concerning the fundamental assumptions of American military planners and the means by which these individuals attempted to gain a given weapons system or budget allocation.

Due to the complexity of these questions, this analysis is divided into three major parts:

(1) Soviet strategy, American intelligence, and the missile gap

(2) Budgetary, partisan, and military effects of the missile gap

(3) The impact of the missile gap abroad

SOVIET STRATEGY, AMERICAN INTELLIGENCE, AND THE MISSILE GAP

Well before the intercontinental ballistic missile became a reality, the psychological foundation for believing in Soviet strategic superiority had been laid. The surprise attack on Pearl Harbor had left an indelible imprint on American strategic thinking and led to what can be called a Pearl Harbor psychosis. Coupled with this fear was the definition by American leaders of the Soviet Union as an enemy so cunning, so inherently evil, so antithetical to the "American way of life" as to be desirous of launching a surprise thermonuclear attack on the United States the instant it thought this could be accomplished at a level of "acceptable" damage.

It was believed that this situation would exist when the Soviet Union possessed a first-strike nuclear force strong enough to destroy the United States nuclear retaliatory forces. It was also believed that this was the ultimate goal of the Soviet Union and that it was pursuing this goal with all the technological and natural resources at its disposal. This alleged Russian doctrine was based on the belief that the Soviet Union was pursuing a "counterforce" strategy. Those who accepted this interpretation as the basic military philosophy of the Soviet Union tended to overestimate Soviet missile programs and to accept (or create) those missile projection figures which appeared to substantiate their position.

The fear that the Soviet Union is preparing for a surprise attack on the United States still exists, but at no time during the missile gap period did the Soviet Union fully mobilize its production capacity for bombers or missiles. The Soviet Union apparently produced only those weapons it felt were needed to deter an attack on Russia by the United States. In fact, it would appear that between 1957 and 1962 the Soviet Union built less than 4 percent of the ICBMs and only 20 percent of the heavy bombers that American intelligence estimated its economy could have sustained. In its relations with the United States the Soviet Union apparently pursued the policy of minimum deterrence, threatening an all-out blow only in retaliation for use of nuclear weapons against Russian territory.[2]

An analysis of the weapons production of the Soviet Union, including some "official" Pentagon figures indicates that the Soviets were pursuing a minimum deterrent strategy.[3] The Soviet Union possessed a limited number of long-range bombers and a large conventional military force to meet less than all-out nuclear aggression. With these conventional and nuclear forces, Russia could protect its land mass from a conventional attack and deter a United States nuclear attack by possessing a large enough striking force to threaten the *possible* destruction of American population centers. The Soviet Union did not have to possess enough deliverable nuclear weapons to create the *absolute certainty* that it could destroy major American metropolitan areas; Russia only had to create an element of *uncertainty* among high American officials to prevent an attack.[4]

Apparently Soviet leaders believed that this strategy not only guaranteed their military security, but also offered an additional advantage: by not building a large operational nuclear delivery system, Russia could wait for the development of the next, more sophisticated, weapons generation before beginning large-scale production, and therefore scarce Soviet resources could be channeled into other facets of the economy.[5]

However, in the long run this advantage was reduced, if not destroyed, by the Russian leaders (especially Khrushchev) who attempted to take maximum diplomatic advantage of the American belief in the missile gap. The Russian boasts of missile superiority and "rocket rattling" reinforced this belief. It is probable that the United States would have engaged in large-scale missile building anyhow, but the Soviet statements certainly did nothing to weaken those forces in the United States intent upon another escalation of the arms race—an escalation that the Russian leaders were either unwilling or unable to compete with on equal terms.

The apparent fact that the Soviet Union had adopted a minimum deterrent strategy was not believed by those responsible for formulating American military policy. The basic assumption throughout the period of the missile gap was grounded on the belief that the Russians were utilizing the maximum capability credited to them by U.S. intelligence. This assumption was changed only when "hard" information become available which indicated that the Soviet Union was not using its maximum capability, and even then it was not accepted by all agencies of the intelligence community.

The threatened bomber gap, the successful Soviet ICBM test, and the Sputnik earth satellite caused many American officials to raise their estimates of Soviet capabilities and added a strong element of uncertainty within government circles in the calculation of Soviet strategic nuclear power. This American lack of certainty caused serious alarm, and efforts were made by the United States government to obtain accurate information on Soviet missile and bomber programs, but the exact extent of these intelligence efforts were not known to the public. However, numerous public reports have reflected an awareness of at least two of the major sources of information on Soviet missiles available to American intelligence.

The first source appeared in various public reports indicating that in July 1955 the United States had installed missile tracking stations in Turkey which could monitor Russian long-range missile tests. These radar stations reportedly could track Russian missiles up to a range of 4,000 miles.[6]

The second major source of intelligence information was not known to the public until May 1960. The U-2 photo reconnaissance aircraft began flying its high altitude photographic missions as early as June 1956, and was reported to have found the Soviet ICBM testing center at Tyura Tam (near the Aral Sea) before the first Soviet ICBM test in August 1957.[7]

At the time, the most authoritative statement on the value of the U-2 photographs was made by Secretary of Defense Thomas Gates:

From these flights we got information on airfields, aircraft, missiles, missile testings and training, special weapons storage, sub-

marine production, atomic production and aircraft deployment. . . .
These results were considered in formulating our military programs.[8]

Later, Allen Dulles stated that the U-2 photos had given "hard"
intelligence to American analysts and claimed: "The intelligence collected on Soviet missiles has been excellent as to the
nature and quality of the potential threat."[9]

Various other claims have been made with respect to the
accuracy and value of the U-2 photographs, but perhaps the
strongest and, if true, the most significant was the claim that
the U-2 could photograph all of the operational first-generation
Soviet ICBMs, which were installed along the Trans-Siberian
railroad route since their large and cumbersome size prevented
their emplacement far from a major railroad.[10] If this was the
case, then the U-2 had only to fly along the railroad route periodically and photograph new missile sites or those under construction.

However, the classified nature of the American radar stations
in Turkey and the U-2 photographs did not make it possible for
the American public to determine the comprehensiveness and
accuracy of the intelligence sources available to the U.S. government. The possibility also existed that the Eisenhower Administration had other sources of intelligence that still have not
been made public.[11]

But from the published information during the missile gap
period, the Eisenhower Administration apparently had valuable
intelligence sources upon which to base estimates of Soviet
strategic delivery means.

The debate over the missile gap constantly reverted to the
confusing question of the numerous intelligence figures that
appeared, indicating that a number of different assessments existed on projected Soviet missile strength. The reasons for the
confusion within the government were numerous and could not
be traced to one source. However, upon analysis, certain basic
interrelated reasons for the emergence of the missile gap appear.
The first of these is that there were numerous sets of intelligence
estimates available within the United States government at any
given time during the period 1959–1961. The exact number of

estimates available at any given time is impossible to determine, but the following possible situation existed at times: (1) The CIA annual estimates that contained figures based on an "orderly" (low estimate) Soviet missile building program and an estimate based on a "crash" program (high estimate); (2) An Air Force estimate based on its own intelligence sources and its own interpretations of the U-2 photographs; (3) An Army-Navy estimate based on their own sources; and (4) The existence of the previous year's estimates that were still accepted by some even though they had been replaced with more up-to-date estimates. Added to this inherently confusing situation was the secrecy that surrounded the whole debate and the willingness of the military services to selectively "leak" their own estimates to the press in order to strengthen their case for a given weapons system or force level.* It is to an analysis of this complex situation that we will now turn.

Initially, the CIA resisted the pressure from the Department of Defense to provide intelligence projections on Soviet missile strength. In the past, when estimates had proved faulty, the CIA had borne the brunt of public criticism and was not eager to assume responsibility again. But the Department of Defense persisted, saying that it had to have this information to compensate for the long "lead times" needed to produce a given missile system (at least 18–30 months). Finally, the CIA admitted that they were the agency that should do this job and began work on this project.[12]

The CIA believed that the Soviet ICBM test in 1957 had shown a high degree of competence in this field. But the basic question that faced the experts was to determine as closely as possible how the Soviet Union would allocate its total military effort. Obviously, Russian emphasis on heavy bombers, fighter

---

* The reader who is dubious about the power or influence of the individual military intelligence service efforts should be reminded that even in 1970 it was revealed that the three services would spend $2.9 billion on intelligence. This money did not include any CIA operations, nor the tactical intelligence operations of the services in Vietnam. *The New York Times,* May 19, 1970, quoting Assistant Secretary of Defense Robert F. Froehlke in testimony before the House Appropriations Committee.

planes, or conventional weapons would cut down on the funds available for missile programs. Therefore, the early CIA estimates on projected Russian missile strength were based on a combination of proven Russian capabilities, "our view of their intentions," and an over-all assessment of Russian strategy.[13]

With these essential guidelines established, the CIA began to collect information on the Soviet missile effort (presumably from the U-2 flights and the radar stations in Turkey). As "hard" facts became available, the intelligence experts attempted to estimate the actual programming of the Russian missile system. As more evidence was gathered, CIA estimates were revised downward since "hard" intelligence indicated that the Soviet Union had not engaged in a crash missile production program. However, the continued existence of the earlier, more pessimistic, estimates for a given year meant that there were several different projections in existence, produced at different times, but for the same year in the future. As will be seen below, these downward revisions by the CIA were not necessarily accepted by the Air Force or by spokesmen friendly to this military service. The resulting confusion deserves some attention.

The first evidence during the missile gap period of confusion within the United States intelligence community apparently occurred in 1957 concerning the so-called Gaither Report. In 1965, President Eisenhower admitted that this report indicated that United States retaliatory forces would become vulnerable to Soviet missile attack by about 1959, but that he had "other information" on American strategic posture and therefore did not accept the conclusions of the Gaither committee.[14] The former President never explained the source of his "other information" or what it was. In view of the fact that the Gaither committee supposedly had access to all essential classified information needed to conduct their study, it appears that some intelligence information was not turned over to this committee (possibly the U-2 interpreted photographs or an even more sensitive source).

In the summer of 1958, Senator Symington offered the first concrete evidence that there was more than one set of intelligence figures on Soviet missile programs in circulation within the United States government. He sent a secret letter to President Eisenhower and charged that the United States was lagging unjustifiably behind the Soviet Union in missile development and gave "as his authority his own intelligence sources." He further claimed that the full extent of the danger had not been accurately estimated by the CIA.[15] Senator Symington's "own intelligence sources" were never disclosed, but before the missile gap debate was over evidence indicated that his source was the Air Force. (Senator Symington was a former Secretary of the Air Force.)

This secret Symington letter to President Eisenhower was not made public until 1959 when it became apparent that the CIA had made its first downward revision of projected Russian missile strength. No definitive evidence was found as to exactly when the CIA made its revision; however, when the public statement was made early in 1959, it appeared to be based on the assumption that the United States and the Soviet Union had both reached the same negative conclusion concerning the value and efficacy of mass-producing large numbers of first-generation intercontinental ballistic missiles.[16]

By 1959, at the latest, the United States government had decided that first-generation liquid fuel ICBMs were not worth the investment required to produce in large numbers. The Atlas ICBM was heavy, cumbersome, and expensive. In addition, it took thirty minutes to prepare, fuel, and launch, making it highly vulnerable to surprise attack and therefore primarily a first-strike weapon. It was decided to produce a limited number of them and move on to the development and production of the more sophisticated and cheaper second-generation Minutemen. The same reasoning applied to the substitution of the Polaris for the Regulus.[17]

The government had decided to rely, temporarily, on its superiority in manned bombers, plus a limited number of first-generation ICBMs as the major strategic military instrument to implement its foreign policy until the second generation of American missiles became operational.[18]

Secretary of Defense McElroy appeared to confirm this policy when he testified early in 1959:

It is not our intention or policy to try and match missile for missile in the ICBM category of Russian capability *in the next couple of years*. Our position . . . is that our diversified capability to deliver the big weapon [nuclear warheads and bombs] is what we are going to count on as our ability to deter general war.[19]

The Secretary of Defense also admitted that in a year or two Russia could have more ICBMs than the United States.[20]

Evidently, early in 1959 the Soviet Union also had decided not to produce first-generation ICBMs in large numbers. Like the American decision, it was not possible to determine exactly when this became official policy. However, according to the United States Defense Department, by 1961 the Soviet Union had produced only a "handful" of ICBMs and even by 1964 was credited officially with less than 200.[21] If the Soviet Union had embarked on a "crash" missile production program in 1959, they certainly would have had more than a "handful" in 1961 and far more than 200 by 1964 (in 1964 the United States had 750 operational ICBMs and 192 Polaris missiles). In spite of the claim by Khrushchev that Russia was producing missiles in "serial production" and that one factory produced 250 missiles per year, the Soviet Union decided upon a very limited production program for first-generation ICBMs.[22]

Early in 1959, the CIA accepted the possibility that the Soviet Union was not engaged in a large build-up of first-generation ICBMs. Therefore, the first downward revision of intelligence estimates of projected Soviet missile strength was made. This fact came out during the *Joint Hearings,* 1959, when Senator Symington stated that during 1958 he had been briefed by the CIA four times, and that although he disagreed with their estimates based on "other information I had," the CIA figures had been the same all four times. Then he claimed that even lower estimates allegedly from the CIA had been given by Secretary of Defense McElroy in an earlier secret hearing before a different congressional committee.[23]

Simultaneously, the United States government purposely produced two sets of figures in the National Intelligence Estimate based upon different assessments of the number of ICBMs the

Soviet Union *could* produce. Due to a lack of certainty on the part of the intelligence community as to exactly what programs were being pursued by Russia, the National Intelligence Estimate for 1959 attempted to cover two possible contingencies. The smaller projected number represented an "orderly" Soviet missile program based on the missile production capacity credited to the Soviet Union. The larger, second figure attempted to cover the possibility that the Soviet Union might use this capability to engage in a "crash" missile program.[24]

Later in 1959, Secretary of Defense McElroy publicly implied for the first time the possibility of two sets of figures. He stated that the missile gap arose only when the number of missiles the United States actually planned to produce were compared to the number the Soviet Union "could" produce. The Secretary further stated that it was impossible to overemphasize the importance of the word "could" in this "type of estimate," and that United States estimates were not intended to mean that the Soviet Union actually would produce this large number of missiles. To support his argument, he referred to the bomber gap and the fact that at the time of this supposed gap, the American estimates said the Soviet Union could produce 600 to 700 Bisons, but it chose not to do so.[25]

The existence of two official sets of intelligence figures produced in 1959 did not become public until 1960. When they were openly discussed they caused a great deal of confusion, even after it had been explained that official American estimates had rejected a "crash" Russian production program and believed that the Soviet Union had adopted an "orderly" program.[26]

By the end of January 1959, there was a real possibility that there were three sets of secret intelligence figures being discussed within government circles—the two sets in the National Intelligence Estimate ("orderly" versus "crash" production programs) and Senator Symington's "other information."[27]

But the confusion did not stop there. At the same time that the "revised" intelligence estimates were being given to congressional leaders, Secretary of Defense McElroy apparently admitted that by the early 1960s the Soviet Union would have a 3–1 advantage over the United States in operational long-range ballistic missiles. The transcript of the congressional hearing where he allegedly made this statement was never released. But a vast number of reports of this statement were made and it was never denied by Secretary McElroy.[28] The public was never told which set of intelligence figures was used by Secretary McElroy in arriving at his prediction of a 3–1 Soviet missile advantage in the early 1960s.

Politically, whichever set of figures was used by the Secretary was not relevant. This alleged statement gave Democratic critics of the Eisenhower Administration an "official confirmation" of the existence of a future missile gap.

The accuracy of the press coverage of the missile gap controversy is certainly open to question. Claims of "leaks" and of the possession of "official estimates" could not be certified, and even if these claims were true, they could not be admitted by the government officials concerned. The press also displayed many of the political biases and subjective opinions so often found in its treatment of any controversial issue. In spite of these real handicaps to objectivity—and the lack of objectivity—an interesting pattern of reporting on the comparative strategic American-Soviet power appeared in newspaper and periodical analysis.

The earliest public estimates of the missile gap for the year 1962 gave the Soviet Union a projected ICBM lead over the United States of from 8 to 14 ICBMs to one ICBM for the United States. According to these earlier figures, by 1962 the Soviet Union was supposed to have between 1,000 and 1,500 ICBMs while the United States allegedly was programmed to have only 130. Following the first American downward revision of projected Soviet missile strength in 1959, the publicly predicted Russian strength was reduced accordingly to 500 ICBMs. Also, several of these new projections appeared to follow Secretary McElroy's predicted 3–1 Soviet advantage, rather than the earlier predictions of a Soviet advantage of roughly 10–1. It is impossible to determine if the figures in the media were "leaks" from government officials; however throughout the missile gap period many newspapers and periodicals closely paralleled the later figures claimed by the government to be the "official intelligence estimates."[29]

The confusion on estimates that occurred in 1959 took place for the most part in secret; it was not until early 1960 that the almost chaotic situation within the intelligence community became apparent in public sources. This confusion, which continued through 1960 and for most of 1961, was never cleared up in public sources and only disappeared when the missile gap illusion itself disappeared in late 1961.[30]

Throughout this time President Eisenhower attempted to assure the American people of the basic nuclear strength of the United States, while he called for increases in bomber forces and development of missile forces.[31]

Yet while the President proceeded in this manner, his military personnel seemed to be purposely undercutting his effort. The commanding officer of SAC, General Thomas S. Power, gave a speech in January 1960 claiming that the 100 American nuclear launching installations virtually could be destroyed by a limited number of Soviet missiles. General Power stated:

> . . . it would take an average of three missiles in the current state of development to give an aggressor a mathematical probability of 95 percent that he can destroy one given soft target some 5,000 miles away. This means that, with only some 300 ballistic missiles, the Soviet could virtually wipe out our entire nuclear strike capability within a span of thirty minutes.[32]

Needless to say, General Power followed up this warning with a call for a large-scale SAC airborne alert, the production of more long-range bombers, and the development funds for the new B-70 bomber.[33]

In spite of this foreboding prediction of the ability of 300 Soviet ICBMs and IRBMs to destroy the American retaliatory forces, *the fact remains that in 1960 the Soviet Union did not have anywhere near 300 missiles (at the most 10 ICBMs)*, and had only 150 long-range bombers. Arrayed against this force was a large, diversified American deterrent force that even General Power called "the most powerful retaliatory force in the world."[34] This deterrent force consisted of almost 600 B-52's, 1,200 B-47's (with in-flight refueling), and over 200 carrier-based aircraft dispersed on 14 American attack carriers (plus an unknown number of American fighter bombers with a nuclear capability stationed at various American bases throughout the world).[35] No one, not even General Power, questioned existing American security, but the debate continued to revolve around the estimates of future comparative missile strength.

The alarm caused by General Power's speech was demonstrated during the *Joint Hearings, 1960.* According to General Power, the predicted missile gap would arrive when the Soviet Union had the 150 ICBMs and 150 IRBMs. At this time, SAC could be destroyed as an effective retaliatory force. Therefore, the *Joint Hearings, 1960,* concentrated on the question of the predicted Soviet missile strength. This question had to be answered by the American intelligence community, but this community offered "several" conflicting and contradictory answers.

During 1959, a series of unconfirmed reports indicated that the Soviet Union had run into difficulty in its ICBM testing and development programs. There were also indications that the Russian missile program had placed a serious strain on its economy. These reports presaged the second major downward revision of American intelligence estimates in 1960 on projected Soviet missile strength.[36]

This revision occurred early in 1960 when Thomas Gates, the new Secretary of Defense, stated that the Russians had engaged in an "orderly" missile production program and therefore earlier estimates based on a "crash" Soviet missile program were too high.[37] Simultaneously, CIA director Allen Dulles produced a less optimistic, different set of intelligence figures, and the Air Force came up with a third set that was higher than either of the first two. The exact figures used in these estimates were never made public, nor were the reasons for the confusion stated.

It appears now that there were three reasons for the chaotic situation within the United States intelligence community in 1960 and in early 1961. (1) In spite of the continued downward revision of projected Soviet missile strength, several individuals within the government apparently continued to accept the earlier, more pessimistic, projections. (2) The existence of at least two official sets of figures in the National Intelligence

Estimate ("orderly" versus "crash" Soviet programs) until 1960 gave some spokesmen the supposed option of accepting either a "high" or a "low" set. (3) The fact that the military services continued to produce their own estimates of future Soviet missile strength gave rise to at least two additional possible sets of figures—one set from the Air Force and one from the Army-Navy coalition.[38]

In considering these three factors within the intelligence community, logic would indicate the possibility of at least six different sets of figures in 1960 purporting to be the projected number of Soviet missiles for a given year. However, this does not appear to be the case. The real possibility exists that there was a great deal of overlap and duplication within intelligence circles. For example, the "crash" estimates rejected by the Department of Defense could have been the same as the "high" Air Force estimates, while the "low" Army-Navy estimates could have been the same as the "orderly" Department of Defense figures. By the 1980s, confusion was still the rule among the various intelligence services of the U.S.

The almost unbelievable confusion in American intelligence apparently continued until the fall of 1961. At that time, President Kennedy managed to combine the various estimates of the military services under the control of the Secretary of Defense and the newly created Defense Intelligence Agency (DIA). Once this was done, the Air Force apparently accepted the lower figures of the Army-Navy estimates, and the military services finally agreed upon one set of projected Soviet ICBM figures.[39] Even though the creation of the DIA seemed to resolve the differences concerning missile projection estimates, it did not solve the problem of competition between the intelligence agencies.

Once again the mass media appears to have reflected the downward revisions of the United States government. The 1960 downward revision by Secretary of Defense Gates was represented in many periodicals, and showed the Soviet Union with a maximum advantage over the United States of 3–1 by 1961–1962.[40] Early in 1961, the published projections still showed a Soviet ICBM lead, but a reduced lead compared to earlier projections, and by the end of 1961 most published reports claimed either missile parity between the two superpowers or a slight United States lead.[41]

Surprisingly, there have not been many published reports that attempt to explain "where the missile gap went," or to assess the blame for its creation. Spokesmen for the Kennedy Administration attempted to blame statements made by President Eisenhower and his Administration for creating the missile gap illusion.[42] Others claimed that Kennedy's statements were made in "good faith."[43] Still other sources blamed American "politicians," "sensation-seeking journalists," "the Military-Industrial complex," and in some cases the blame was placed entirely on the "bravado" of the Soviet Union.[44]

One of the major personalities involved in the creation of the missile gap, Senator Stuart Symington, came up with his own interesting version of how the missile gap was created and where it went, although he did not deal with why it was created.[45] Senator Symington blamed the CIA and its constant downward revision of national intelligence figures based on Soviet "intent" rather than "capability" as the major cause of the missile gap myth. To prove his point, Senator Symington quoted alleged official figures for projected Soviet missile production for the years 1961–1962. In order to avoid going into the classified number of missiles involved in these secret projections, he used the percentage of predicted Russian missile production as of 1959 compared with the new percentage used in 1961. (See Tables I and II.) According to the figures used by Symington, the official United States government estimates of Russian missile production had been reduced by 96.5 percent from December 1959 to September 1961. So that as of September 1961 the Soviet Union was given credit for the production of only 3.5 percent of the missiles that the United States had said in 1959 the Russians would produce.[46]

When Senator Symington confronted Secretary of Defense McNamara with these figures, McNamara answered rather lamely that those who had discussed the missile gap had based their comments on national intelligence estimates and "were speaking of the missile gap in good faith."[47]

TABLE I

TOTAL HIGH ESTIMATED SOVIET MISSILE PRODUCTION
FOR 1961–1962*

100%	100% (1,500 ICBMs)			
80%				
60%				
40%		34% (512 ICBMs)		
20%			30% (450 ICBMs)	
				15% (225 ICBMs)
0%				3.5% (52 ICBMs)
	December 1959	February 1960	August 1960	June 1961 September 1961

* The figures in parentheses represent the number of Soviet ICBMs projected by public sources for late 1961 to early 1962. The 1959 prediction is used as the base year. The December 1959 figure of a projected 1,500 ICBMs was used here to present the most pessimistic public estimate used at the time.

Due to the fact that Senator Symington had been a major protagonist in the missile gap debate, it was logical that he would attempt to find an explanation for its creation that did not damage his own reputation or political image. Nonetheless, his rationalization of the missile gap appears to be one of the few *public* statements made by anyone who had access to classified information and was connected closely with the development of the missile gap.

TABLE II

LOWER ESTIMATED SOVIET MISSILE PRODUCTION FOR 1961–1962*

	December 1959	February 1960	August 1960	June 1961	September 1961
100%	100% (1,000 ICBMs)				
80%					
60%					
40%		34% (340 ICBMs)			
20%			30% (300 ICBMs)		
				15% (150 ICBMs)	
0%					3.5% (35 ICBMs)

* The figures in parentheses represent the number of Soviet ICBMs projected in public sources using a lower base number of ICBMs (1,000). The projected number of Soviet ICBMs can be found in Appendix A. Both sets of percentage figures were given by Senator Symington in place of classified missile figures. See U.S. Congress, Senate, *Hearings,* January–February 1962, p. 49; Stuart Symington, "Where the Missile Gap Went," *The Reporter* (February 15, 1962), 26:22.

If Senator Symington's percentages are analyzed in an attempt to gain a picture of how the missile gap appeared to those who accepted its existence, the following picture emerges.[48] By using the highest 1959 Soviet ICBM projection for 1962 (1,500 ICBMs) as a base figure and then reducing the number of projected missiles as the estimates were revised downward (according to Senator Symington's percentages), the most pessimistic view of the missile gap seen by those who accepted the downward revision is apparent.[49] (See Table I.) If the lower 1959 prediction of 1,000 Soviet ICBMs for 1962 is used (Table II), then the potential gap is reduced but remains substantial.

From this analysis an interesting observation can be made. A check on the figures presented in Appendix A reveals that the figures in Table II (in parentheses) resemble many of the public estimates presented from 1958 to 1961 in the popular journalistic treatments of the missile controversy.

A comparison of Senator Symington's figures and those presented to the public gives rise to two tentative conclusions. First, the possibility existed that Senator Symington's percentage projections offer enough evidence to create a relatively accurate reconstruction of at least one set of intelligence figures found in the United States government during the missile gap controversy. And, second, the apparent accuracy of published accounts of at least this set of missile projections offers strong evidence that classified information was being revealed to some reporters. These conclusions are tenuous, but there is enough evidence to warrant their serious consideration as a valid reconstruction of how the missile gap appeared to those who accepted a substantial United States missile inferiority. If, in fact, the Soviet Union had possessed between 1,000 and 1,500 ICBMs by late 1961, the missile gap (but not necessarily a deterrent gap) would have been a reality, but the fact remains that at this time the Soviet Union was credited with the possession of less than 100 ICBMs.

At the same time that Senator Symington attempted to explain the missile gap, an Air Force spokesman admitted that the Russians had the "capability" to create the gap, but "they [the Russians] did not do what our intelligence people thought they would do."[50]

The evidence available indicated that the United States government was fairly accurate in determining the Soviet "capability" to produce long-range ballistic missiles, but misinterpreted and exaggerated the "intent" of Russian policy makers in assuming that they would use this capability to its fullest possible extent. And, as far as the intelligence community is concerned, this misinterpretation was the basis of their faulty assessments leading to the belief in the missile gap in the first place. The Soviet Union had the capability to mass produce large numbers of ICBMs, but they had no reason to do this. They simply were not attempting to assume a first-strike posture toward the United States, and to build the missiles would have been a waste of resources. On the other hand, the American willingness to believe that the Soviet Union would maximize this capability once again demonstrated a degree of American paranoia that was not warranted, based on an assessment of either postwar Soviet policies or strategy.

The acceptance of the missile gap by many individuals in the United States had a definite domestic impact on American policies, and this question deserves considerable analysis.

BUDGETARY, PARTISAN, AND MILITARY EFFECTS OF THE MISSILE GAP

The domestic impact of the missile controversy on the United States can be divided into three general, interrelated categories:

(1) Defense expenditures and interservice rivalry
(2) Partisan politics and the missile gap
(3) American military strategy and missiles.[51]

The budgetary procedures of the United States government are difficult to analyze, even for those with access to the classified details on the process of defense appropriations and expenditures.[52] The budget categories conceal the nature of American preparedness for various military contingencies, and the figures available are "written in a jargon that defies comprehension."[53] In addition to these handicaps, the increasing complexity of technological developments in the defense field make the whole process of defense appropriations confusing. As a result, Congress usually allows the major budgetary decisions to be made in the executive branch, and contents itself with minor revisions or, at most, dramatic proposals that still are left to the White House for final action.[54]

These serious difficulties, inherent in American budgetary

procedures, greatly complicate the task of analyzing defense expenditures during the period of the missile gap.

The prime ingredient of the struggle among the military services was the constant fight for a higher budgetary appropriation so that each one could carry out the mission it visualized for itself. In order to justify the requests for these appropriations and to maximize its future role, military doctrines on limited and all-out war were articulated and defined by each of the military services and their business, political, and journalistic allies.

The post–World War II debate over American strategic doctrine cannot be totally attributed to the selfish demands of the military for larger appropriations, but neither can it be denied that this was a significant aspect of interservice rivalry, and it played an important part in the missile gap controversy. It was not a blind search for truth that led the Air Force to believe in a counterforce doctrine (or a variation on this doctrine) and led the Army and Navy to accept a form of minimum deterrent strategy. No doubt it was felt these expenditures would best serve the military interests of the United States. Nevertheless, they added appreciably to the appropriations for the military services.

Along with the constant statements on national security, the military services also mobilized their "independent" organizations and publications to support their position. The Air Force, politically by far the strongest of the three services, presented its case through the Air Force Association and the Air Force unofficial publication, *Air Force* (later renamed *Air Force and Space Digest*).[55] The politically weaker, but still potent, Army and Navy positions were presented by the Association of the United States Army (*Army Magazine*) and by the Navy League (*Navy: The Magazine of Sea Power*), respectively.[56]

The military services also found valuable allies in the weapons industry and among congressmen who represented districts (or states) where weapons industries were located. The industries advertised in the service periodicals as well as in national periodicals with a broader circulation. With huge defense contracts at stake, it was to their advantage to do everything to obtain funds for the development and production of a weapons system in which they were involved. Therefore, for example, in the Thor-Jupiter (IRBMs) struggle, the Chrysler Corporation, under contract to develop the Army Jupiter, and with major plants in Alabama, heralded the ability of the Jupiter and was joined by the Alabama congressional delegation. Simultaneously, Douglas Aircraft supported the Thor missile, and was joined by the California delegation. The same picture emerged from the conflict between the Army Nike-Hercules (antiaircraft missile) versus the Air Force Bomarc systems: Western Electric supported the Nike system and Boeing Aircraft backed the Bomarc antiaircraft systems.[57]

This coalition of military and industrial interests led President Eisenhower to warn of the potential threat of the "military-industrial complex." The same theme has been dramatized and expanded by several authors who came to the conclusion that the pressures for increased defense spending can be traced almost exclusively to this "military-industrial complex."[58]

The mass media is one aspect of the military-industrial complex that has yet to receive adequate examination, and is probably the least understood of the components of American military programs and policies. (Another would be the role of labor unions.) The influence of the press is obviously of prime importance, since many Americans tend to believe everything they read, hear, or see. In fact, the creation of the missile gap and its wide public acceptance was a direct function of the means of mass communication in the United States. Every mass periodical but one accepted and propagated the missile gap myth at one time or another during the period 1957 to 1961. The exception was *The Nation*, but such liberal periodicals as *The New Republic* and *Commentary* joined the more conservative *Time, U.S. News & World Report,* and *Newsweek* in propagating the myth. *The New York Times* also found itself supporting the belief in the missile gap most of the time.

The influence of the mass media is extremely wide, and varies from the journalist who constantly presents a particular military point of view, to the newscaster who will read anything put before him by the Department of Defense; from the special-interest periodicals, to the wire services that present as fact any news release from the public relations establishment in Saigon and elsewhere.

There was a substantial amount of support for the missile gap belief among the nationally syndicated journalists in this country, and a prime example of this was the repetitive sounding of the alarm by Joseph Alsop.[59] These journalists were joined by politicians and scholars,[60] as well as scientists, such as Werner von Braun and Edward Teller, who allegedly provided more scholarly and "scientific" explanations for the existence of the missile gap. It is interesting to note that it would seem that not one journalist, politician, scientist, nor scholar had his reputation even slightly damaged for his part in the creation of the missile gap myth.

During the missile gap period, military appropriations increased but the services continued to obtain roughly the same percentage of the defense budget they had received before the crisis arose. Throughout the missile gap period, the Air Force received approximately 46 percent of the defense budget, while the Navy maintained 28 percent and the Army 23 percent.[61] The one major exception to this unwritten budgetary rule occurred in 1957, when the Air Force received a rather substantial budgetary increase over the Army and the Navy.[62] (See Table III.) However, the crisis atmosphere created by the missile controversy, along with the above-mentioned factors, led to an annual over-all increase in the United States defense budget from 1956 to 1959. When American defense expenditures were reduced in 1960, this reduction apparently was the result of three factors. First, 1960 was an election year and the Republican Administration attempted to create what it believed would be viewed as a favorable economic climate. Second, this decrease in defense spending reflected the earlier decision by American leaders not to mass produce first-generation missiles, but to wait for the more sophisticated, cheaper, second generation. And, finally, the Eisenhower Administration's willingness to

TABLE III

NATIONAL SECURITY EXPENDITURES FOR THE ARMY, NAVY, AND AIR FORCE
1956–1962
(in millions of dollars) *

	1956	1957	1958	1959	1960	1961	1962
Army	8,702	9,063	9,051	9,468	9,392	10,332	11,559
Navy	9,744	10,398	10,906	11,728	11,642	12,313	13,193
Air Force	16,749	18,363	18,435	19,084	19,066	19,816	20,883
Total Defense Budget	40,641	43,270	44,142	46,426	45,627	47,494	51,107

* Not included in total expenditures: Direction and co-ordination of defense, other central defense activities, civil defense, military assistance, development and control of nuclear energy, stockpiling and other defense-related activities. "United States Defense Policies in 1964," The Library of Congress, Legislative Reference Service (Washington, D.C.: U.S. Government Printing Office, June 4, 1965), 89th Congress, 1st sess., House Document No. 285, p. 179.

cut the defense budget may have reflected President Eisenhower's personal belief that United States security would not be seriously affected by this move.

In 1961, American defense expenditures again began to increase. But before these additional funds could have any impact on American deterrent posture, President Kennedy had convinced the American people that there was no missile gap.

The fact that the defense expenditures of the United States did increase during the period of the missile gap is indisputable, and there does not appear to be much doubt that the pressures of the alleged missile gap added to defense costs. However, numerous other factors were working simultaneously to increase the appropriations Congress and the executive branch allocated for security.

One of the factors which created pressure for additional funds was the substantial role played by partisan politics in the missile gap controversy. In theory, a two-party democracy should have a party of the "opposition" and in this case the party of the opposition was the Democratic party. At the national party level, the conflict between the Democratic and Republican national committees continued throughout the missile debate, and the Democratic Advisory Council was the constant critic of the defense policies of the Eisenhower Administration.

At the outset of this discussion, it should be emphasized that although the Democratic party must take the major blame for the creation of the missile gap because it was the party out of power, during other periods of the arms race the exact reverse was true when the Republicans were out of power (e.g., Nixon in 1968—"security gap"). During the first thirty-five years of the arms race, American partisan politics has been completely onesided in the sense that the opposition always called for more defense spending rather than for less.

The politicians who propagated the missile gap thesis appeared to be reacting to at least three interrelated stimuli: prospects for partisan advantage; loyalty to a military service, to a strategic concept, or an industrial friend; and a sincere concern for the defense posture of the United States.

The missile debate was not sufficiently developed in 1958 to play a major role in the congressional elections of that year. When the debate did become an issue in the 1960 presidential elections, it was transformed from the question of a missile gap to one of American prestige, based on United States military and space achievements. Senator John F. Kennedy attempted to exploit this "prestige" issue in October 1960, and during this period public opinion polls showed definite gains in his vote-getting ability. However, with the multitude of issues involved and the impact of the "great debate," it cannot be claimed that the transformed missile gap question proved decisive—only that it was a factor.

The most interesting observation on the long-run partisan effects of the missile gap debate is that none of the major participants was damaged politically by their mistaken advocacy. Senators Symington and Jackson have since been re-elected and Johnson became President of the United States in a "landslide" election in 1964, with hardly a murmur of his past activities in connection with this critical issue of national defense.[63]

Right after President Kennedy's inauguration in January 1961, the House Republican Policy Committee attempted to answer the Democratic charges on the missile gap and submitted a set of figures on comparative United States-Soviet Union military strengths that later appeared to be the official Pentagon figures for January 1961. This estimate of comparative strategic strength showed the following:[64]

UNITED STATES	SOVIET UNION
16 Atlas ICBMs	35 T-3 ICBMs (8,000 miles)
32 Polaris missiles	None comparable
600 long-range bombers	200 long-range bombers

President Kennedy did not believe that the United States had a consistent, coherent, military strategy. He instructed the new Secretary of Defense, Robert S. McNamara, to conduct a special study of defense strategy and weapons systems and to make recommendations to the White House by the end of February.

Almost immediately after President Kennedy announced the establishment of a committee to study United States defenses, an event occurred that presaged the end of the belief in the existence of the missile gap. This event in itself did not end the debate, but it laid the foundation upon which the missile gap myth was eventually destroyed. Early in February 1961 strong evidence indicated that Secretary of Defense McNamara had stated in a "background briefing" to the press that there was "no missile gap." The briefing reportedly was given February 6, and the following day the front page of *The New York Times* carried a lead article entitled: "Kennedy Defense Study Finds No Evidence of 'Missile Gap.' "[65]

The White House reacted immediately; it denied the alleged report by Secretary McNamara that there was "no missile gap," and stated that this report was "absolutely wrong."[66] The next day, in a press conference, President Kennedy was asked to clear up the record on the reported "background briefing" by McNamara. President Kennedy avoided answering the question by simply stating that he had not received the defense report from his study commission on United States defense policy and that "it would be premature to reach a judgment as to whether there is a gap or not a gap."[67]

In spite of the fact that Secretary McNamara later denied he had made a statement negating the existence of a "missile gap,"[68] three major periodicals commented on his February "background briefing" in articles highly critical of President Kennedy and the role he had played in the development of the missile gap thesis.[69] One of these periodicals went so far as to declare that if there was a missile gap, the gap favored the United States and not the Soviet Union, and then listed supposed official intelligence figures to support its case.[70] Even the periodical that allegedly served as the unofficial spokesman of the United States Air Force reported the statement Secretary McNamara was said to have made on the missile gap.[71]

Throughout February and March 1961 the press corps in Washington continued to pressure President Kennedy for a definitive answer on the missile gap question, and each time the President replied that he was waiting for the completion of the defense study he had ordered undertaken by the Department of Defense. On March 1, 1961, President Kennedy said that the study would be completed in several weeks, and at that time he would make his recommendations to Congress. On March 8, the President stated that the study would be completed in several days and then he would indicate "what I believe to be the relative defense position of the United States."[72] But, for some reason, from March 8 until early October 1961 the Washington press corps discontinued its questions on the missile gap and the issue was ignored in presidential news conferences during this period.[73] Why the press let President Kennedy ignore the question during this period is not known. However, any lingering doubts about the possibility of a significant missile gap was finally laid to rest by Undersecretary of Defense Roswell Gilpatric in October 1961. *The New York Times* quoted Mr. Gilpatric as saying that the United States had a *second strike* capability which was at least as extensive as what the Soviet Union could deliver by *striking first* [emphasis added]. In other words, the United States would have a larger nuclear delivery system left *after* a surprise attack by the Soviet Union than the nuclear force employed by the Russians in a first strike.[74] In November, President Kennedy claimed that his statements of American military inferiority had been based on the best information available to him, but that at the present time the military power of the United States was "second to none."[75] Finally, by late 1962, Secretary of Defense McNamara claimed that he was "absolutely confident" that the missile gap was a "myth."[76]

Once the missile gap controversy ceased in early 1962, politically this issue did not appear again until 1964. Then, when it was discussed by the Republican presidential nominee, Barry Goldwater, he did not attack the earlier creation of this myth. Instead he attempted to create a new "deterrent gap" based on his belief that American missiles were not reliable and that the United States should rely on manned bombers rather than on untested missiles.

Any assessment of the total impact of the missile gap debate on partisan politics in the United States is by definition a subjective matter. Although the missile debate raged for over four years and at times assumed an almost completely partisan nature, most of the evidence indicated that it played an important but not a lasting role in the American political process. Evidently the American people and their leaders did not learn much from this experience in myth creation. As a political issue, it helped Senator Kennedy get elected, and in view of the closeness of the 1960 election, a case could be made that it was one of the important factors in his election.

The partisan and budgetary effects of the acceptance of the missile gap were closely related to the impact it made on the development of American military strategy.

An attempt to isolate the missile gap and attribute any basic shifts of American military strategy exclusively to this question would misrepresent the development of American strategy during this period. Such factors as the growing number of nuclear weapons available to both sides, the changing nature of the Cold War, the growth of American economic capacity, shifts in military strategy as it related to the third world, are examples of factors that played an important part in the calculation of American strategy. Nonetheless, an analysis of the missile gap debate in conjunction with these factors does offer some significant insight into the formulation of American military policy during this period.

Once the missile gap illusion was destroyed, the following question was asked by many observers, Was the United States, at any time during the missile controversy (1957–1961), in danger of having the American retaliatory forces destroyed by a surprise Russian attack? The answer to this question was an unqualified no. At no time during this period did any major military or political leader claim that at that moment the Soviet Union could destroy American nuclear power. The "period of maximum danger" of the missile gap always was placed some time in the future, and when this date arrived, a new period was defined. It became apparent that during the ICBM controversy the United States consistently possessed a nuclear delivery system that was far superior to that of the Soviet Union.

Until early 1961, United States nuclear superiority was based primarily on the fact that it had many more long-range and medium-range bombers (with in-flight refueling or foreign bases) than Russia had. As ICBMs became operational, the United States relied on the mixed-forces concept of using missiles and bombers to provide superior retaliatory force. By late 1961, it became apparent that the United States possessed a superiority over the Soviet Union in long-range bombers *and* in intercontinental ballistic missiles.

From 1957 to 1961, officials of the Eisenhower Administration claimed that there was no "deterrent gap," and all the available evidence indicates the truth of this contention. Even if at some time during the 1957–1961 period the Soviet Union had possessed more ICBMs than the United States, a successful surprise attack by the Soviet Union on American retaliatory forces would have been impossible to coordinate. One group of experts estimated that it would take from four to six Soviet ICBMs to destroy one American SAC base.[77] The dispersal of about 100 SAC bases with between 400 and 600 aircraft on ground alert further complicated the Russian task. The Soviet Union also would have had to find and destroy 12 to 14 American attack aircraft carriers with a nuclear capability.

The United States had entered the period of the threatened missile gap with a strategic military approach to deterrence that had evolved from the earlier concept of massive retaliation. As nuclear weapons became more plentiful and their delivery means more sophisticated, this doctrine had been so modified that many observers believed it was obsolete as a strategic concept to meet less than an all-out nuclear attack. By the time the new Kennedy Administration revised American strategic doctrine, it was admitted that the United States had a substantial superiority over the Soviet Union in both missiles and bombers, but even this superiority did not make the doctrine of massive retaliation an effective instrument for preventing limited aggression. A detailed analysis of Secretary McNamara's "second strike counterforce doctrine" will be dealt with in the next chapter. At this point it is sufficient to say that this new doctrine would have been impossible without a recognized American strategic superiority.[78]

The American nuclear superiority over the Soviet Union was the result of numerous interrelated factors. Certainly, the pressures exerted on behalf of the expected missile gap led to an acceleration of the missile program. President Eisenhower decided to produce only a limited number of first-generation ICBMs, but the military critics of his Administration caused the number of these missiles actually produced to be increased. Concurrently with the decision to limit first-generation missile production, President Eisenhower assigned the highest priority to the development and production of the more sophisticated second-generation Minuteman ICBMs and Polaris IRBMs. Therefore, when President Kennedy was inaugurated, the second-generation Polaris was operational and the Minuteman ICBM was less than a year from being operational. The new President's decision to accelerate these two missile programs assured continued American superiority over the Soviet Union.

Militarily, probably the greatest irony of the missile gap debate is the fact that while many American government officials questioned the nonexistent strategic military inferiority of the United States, the real American weakness was a very limited capability to fight a conventional war. This limited capacity was a weakness only when viewed in the light of the almost unlimited American political-military commitments throughout the world to either defend other nations against aggression, or, more important in this case, the American commitment to uphold status quo governments in the face of challenges from their own people. Army and Navy spokesmen had emphasized this fundamental American weakness for several years, but no decisive action was taken by the Eisenhower Administration to correct this deficiency. Thus, when Kennedy assumed office he found that the United States had a scant eleven combat-ready Army and Marine divisions.[79]

The total impact of the missile gap controversy on the budgetary, political, and military situation in the United States proved to be rather large in scope. The missile debate was a factor in the increased American defense spending, the election of President Kennedy, and the misallocation of resources among the military services. In this sense, it was almost an all-encompassing consideration in the development of American policies during this period.

THE IMPACT OF THE MISSILE GAP ABROAD

It would be easy to overestimate the impact of the alleged missile gap on American policy and the policies of the other major world powers. Just as different individuals within the United States accepted or rejected this gap, so various nations (or national leaders) adopted their own attitudes toward this critical question. Also, the distinction should be made between the public attitudes expressed by these leaders and their personal knowledge of existing and future American power and the United States willingness to use this power. Nonetheless, there were three general areas in which the missile gap illusion figures rather prominently: (1) Soviet policy toward Western Europe and the partial fragmentation of the NATO Alliance; (2) the Cuban missile crisis; and (3) the Sino-Soviet dispute.

The fundamental question posed by a possible missile gap to the Western European allies of the United States was, Does the United States deterrent remain credible in the face of Soviet strategic superiority? Or, as was later asked, Even if there was no missile gap, could the United States be relied upon to deter a Soviet attack on Western Europe in the "age of nuclear parity"? The doubts created by the missile gap among Western European leaders hastened the process of questioning American nuclear credibility, but it would appear that even if there had been no missile gap illusion, the increasingly plentiful supply of American and Soviet nuclear weapons and their delivery systems would have created similar attitudes.

Concurrent with the supposed weakened posture of the American strategic deterrent capability in Western Europe was the growing realization by many military experts that tactical nuclear weapons probably would aid a Russian military offense in Western Europe more than the NATO defense of this area. And that in any case, a tactical nuclear war in Europe probably would destroy the very area defended.[80]

If this was the case, then Western Europe would have to be defended with conventional armed forces and this was a capability that few Western leaders believed the NATO Alliance possessed. America's European allies had never met the conventional force requirements agreed upon by the NATO Alliance, and the United States possessed a very limited capability to fight a conventional war.

Thus, the credibility of the American nuclear deterrent to prevent an attack on Western Europe was weakened at the same time that many observers doubted the ability of the armed forces of the NATO Alliance to defend this area without destroying it in the process. The Eisenhower Administration had been too preoccupied with the strategic nuclear balance and increased national defense costs to provide the funds essential for a large number of combat-ready conventional divisions.

The situation during the alleged missile gap presented the Soviet Union with an opportunity that it did not pass up. On numerous occasions, the leaders of the Soviet Union attempted to exploit the unanswered questions that surrounded "deterrence and defense" for Western Europe. The American IRBM bases in Europe, the use of NATO (and other) airbases for U-2 reconnaissance flights, the United States presence in Berlin, and the very existence of the Alliance were all situations that Soviet diplomacy wanted to change. When the opportunity presented itself, the leaders of the Soviet Union had no compunction about threatening America's NATO Allies with "nuclear blackmail" based on the alleged Soviet strategic superiority.[81]

The period of the alleged missile gap had occurred simultaneously with other military, economic, and political changes that led inevitably to a crisis within the NATO Alliance. The role of the missile gap in this crisis appears to be twofold: (1) In Europe, the doubts created by the missile gap helped to reduce the credibility of the American deterrent posture, and (2) In the United States the possibility of a missile gap encouraged the allocation of military resources for development of strategic weapons at the expense of a conventional capability. The former gave rise to the demand for an independent nuclear force by at least one European ally, while the latter eventually led the Kennedy Administration to an increased American emphasis on the development of the capability to conduct limited war (both conventional and unconventional). By 1985 neither of these problems had been resolved, and the NATO Alliance was still in a state of flux.

A second area in which the events surrounding the missile gap and its resultant American strategic superiority appear to have been an important factor was the Soviet decision to place intermediate- and medium-range ballistic missiles and medium-range bombers in Cuba in October 1962. (A detailed analysis of the Cuban missile crisis will be undertaken in the next chapter in the general context of the military-political strategy of the Kennedy Administration.)

The final major area in which the alleged missile gap played an important, though very limited, role was in the field of Sino-Soviet relations. A detailed study of this dispute is far beyond the scope of this book. Nonetheless, the missile gap controversy evidently added an additional element of friction to the developing split between these two Communist nations.

The acceptance of the missile gap thesis by many Americans and the Russian claims of missile superiority caused the leadership of Communist China to accept the existence of a missile gap favoring the Soviet Union. Apparently, Mao Tse-tung incorrectly assumed that the Soviet development of the ICBM in 1957 had brought about a decisive change in the balance of strategic power in favor of the Soviet Union. Based on this belief, the Chinese leader hoped that the Soviet Union would embark on a more militant foreign policy in an attempt to achieve the elimination, or at least the reduction, of American power in Asia. When the Soviet Union did not appear to exploit sufficiently this supposed military advantage, the Communist Chinese resented the cautious foreign policy pursued by the Soviet Union and accused Russia of ceasing to be a revolutionary power.[82]

As has been seen above, the Soviet Union itself added credence to the belief in the existence of the missile gap whenever possible. The boasts and bravado of Premier Khrushchev had been one of the fundamental causes of the creation of the missile gap. However, viewed in retrospect, it appears as though the Soviet Union paid a high price for very little, if any, temporary gains in its attempt to militarily bluff the United States. Diplomatically, during the period of the missile gap (1957–1961), the leaders of the Soviet Union made no solid gains, although negatively it was possible that the Soviet Union had managed to keep the diplomatic initiative. Soviet leadership eventually had to face the consequences for their willingness to exploit the possible missile gap. The Russian statements on Soviet missile strength had added strong impetus to the belief in the missile gap in the United States and therefore helped to encourage an escalation in the arms race which the Soviet Union could ill afford. Soviet claims and diplomacy managed to disillusion Communist China and led to a major diplomatic defeat in Cuba in October 1962.

By 1962, the Soviet Union was faced with a possible "deterrent gap" because of the overwhelming superiority of American strategic forces. The United States had thousands of megatons ready to deliver with superiority in bombers, ICBMs, and

SLBMs as well as an established superiority in tactical weapons. To deliver this megatonnage, the United States possessed over 50 ICBMs (Atlas and Titan), 80 Polaris missiles, about 90 Thor and Jupiter missiles on stations overseas, 1,700 bombers capable of reaching the Soviet Union, 300 carrier-borne fighter bombers with an atomic capability, and approximately 1,000 supersonic land-based fighters with an atomic capability. In contrast, the Soviet Union possessed between 50 and 100 ICBMs and less than 200 long-range bombers capable of reaching the United States.[83] Once this American superiority became known in 1961 it greatly complicated not only Soviet policy, but also laid the blame for Soviet inferiority at the feet of Premier Khrushchev. This American superiority could easily be interpreted as an American preparation for a first strike on Soviet territory and there were still Americans around who thought that this might be a good idea.[84]

Finally, it should be emphasized that even if the Soviet Union had built a large missile force, this would have in no way negated the deterrent force of the United States. With part of SAC on airborne or ground alert and much of the remainder of this force spread throughout the world on American bases, there was no way a surprise attack could have destroyed this force. It was physically impossible for the Soviet Union to find and simultaneously destroy such a diversified force. In addition, the Soviet Union had to find and destroy the fourteen American aircraft carriers with a thermonuclear capability as well as the American Polaris armed submarines. In short, the United States, even had it faced a large Soviet missile superiority, would not have been in danger of the feared Soviet attack.

IV

The Kennedy Administration: Flexible Response
and Second-Strike Counterforce

(1961–1963)

By the start of the Kennedy Administration, American nuclear superiority was firmly established and was to become a permanent reality of the 1960s. The only agency seriously to challenge this was the Air Force and its allies; their challenge and predictions of doom were always for several years in the future, never for the present. As has been seen, the Kennedy Administration, after some initial bungling, managed to destroy the myth of the missile gap without serious political damage to itself or the Democratic party.

As a matter of fact, many accounts of the Administration of John F. Kennedy have claimed that by February 1961 President Kennedy knew America's nuclear strength exceeded its needs for defense, but claimed that he did not dare to challenge Congress on both bomber and missile reduction. So, according to Arthur Schlesinger, Jr., President Kennedy decided to back McNamara in challenging the "vociferous B-70 boys in Congress," while at the same time going along with the supporters of increases in the Polaris and Minuteman programs. And, although the new manned bomber (B-70) was delayed, the United States escalated its missile production.[1] Thus, even in the face of a recognized American superiority in missiles, the Kennedy Administration felt constrained by military and political pressures to escalate the arms race regardless of the comparative strategic power of the United States and the Soviet Union.

President Kennedy's awareness of American nuclear superiority evidently led him to understand partially the very limited diplomatic-military purposes to which this superiority could be applied. It was this awareness of the limited efficacy of nuclear weapons that led Kennedy and his new Secretary of Defense, Robert S. McNamara, to attempt once again a clear definition of American military strategy—the first such effort since the early attempts of the Eisenhower Administration.

It should be emphasized that the amount of military strength needed by the United States during any given period of this study depends upon how American policy makers viewed the role of the United States in the world and the extent of American commitments to its allies and to the maintenance of the status quo throughout the non-Communist world. It was the growing exaggeration and distortion of the perceptions of this role that led the United States increasingly to escalate the arms race in the face of what it believed was a sustained, planned form of aggression from Moscow (and then China). During the Eisenhower years, the common belief was that the United States could fulfill its role in the world with a superiority in thermonuclear weapons and a stated intent to use them. It was only with the advent of the Kennedy Administration that American leaders came to believe that this massive amount of strategic power was of no avail in such complex situations as had developed in such diverse areas as Hungary, Iraq, Cuba, and Indochina. Thermonuclear weapons were of absolutely no value in the Hungarian crisis of 1956, and they had failed to stop either Ho Chi Minh in Vietnam, Kassem in Iraq, or Castro in Cuba.

In order to correct this deficiency in existing United States military forces and to expand the military alternatives available to the United States government, the "two and half war" doctrine was developed by Kennedy and McNamara. McNamara contended that the United States should be prepared for major military actions in Europe and Asia, while at the same time keeping forces available for action in the Western hemisphere. Although this was not clearly articulated at the time, McNamara later put it this way:

> Therefore, we had to provide, in addition to our NATO requirements, the forces required to meet such an attack in Asia [by China] as well as fulfill our commitments in the Western Hemisphere.[2]

As is well known, by the time Kennedy was assassinated the United States still had a large number of troops committed to NATO and had begun to develop the force levels necessary to place over 500,000 men in Vietnam, with American reserve strength still available for the Dominican invasion.

Therefore, it should have come as no surprise that immediately upon assuming office, Kennedy moved to increase American military spending. If the liberals, who had been mainly responsible for putting Kennedy into the White House, had any illusions about his willingness to tackle the influence of the military-industrial alliance, they were sadly disillusioned, for less than three months after assuming office, Kennedy sent a special message to Congress requesting an additional $650 million for the Defense Department for the Fiscal Year 1962.[3] (It should be noted that this spending was requested over five months before the crisis surrounding the building of the Berlin Wall in August 1961.)

By the time the new Administration had completed its requests for additional funds for Eisenhower's original 1962 fiscal budget, President Kennedy had added $5 billion to the earlier requests.[4] After fourteen months in office, the Administration was proudly proclaiming the addition of over $9 billion in defense funds. Only one third of this additional funding went to nuclear striking power, and the remainder had gone for increases in the flexibility of the United States to respond to perceived limited military aggression.[5]

The rationale for the additional spending was not hard to find. Kennedy stated that the object of the additional budget funds was to insure that:

Any potential aggressor contemplating an attack on any part of the Free World must know that our response will be suitable, selective, swift, and effective.[6]

But the articulation of the new strategy of the Administration was left to McNamara. This strategy consisted of two parts—on the tactical level the doctrine endorsed a "flexible response"; on the strategic level it invoked a "second-strike counterforce" doctrine (see Glossary). It was hoped that with the development of a "flexible response" capability the United States would have a nonnuclear alternative to what it defined as aggression. The second-strike counterforce was supposed to give the United States a "rational" use of atomic weapons in the event of an attack on the United States or some close ally (e.g., Western Europe). The doctrine of massive retaliation was officially discarded[7] and replaced by one which was intended to give the United States a larger number of alternative responses to various types of "aggression."

In spite of later claims that the United States was following a policy of Mutually Assured Destruction (see Chapter 5), the dual doctrines of second strike counterforce and flexible response were the official rationale for the arms race during the 1960s. Therefore, it is imperative that a clear understanding of these doctrines be gained in order to analyze critically their efficacy and relevance in today's world. For the purpose of analysis, we will temporarily separate the two doctrines, studying the concept of flexible response first and then the second-strike counterforce strategy. The two halves can then be reunited and an effort can be made to see how the Kennedy (and later the Johnson and Nixon) Administration applied this definition of American power and its uses to the various situations that faced the United States.

FLEXIBLE RESPONSE

In its simplest terms, the military problem perceived by Kennedy was one of finding a doctrine which would bring American military power to bear on the rest of the world without the use of nuclear weapons; the doctrine of a "flexible response" was the answer. Like all shifts of American military doctrine, indications of this change had appeared in the years preceding its formal announcement in 1963.

Throughout the Eisenhower Administration the Army had felt that it was being shortchanged in the fight for military appropriations. This frustration had peaked in 1959 with the retirement of General Maxwell Taylor and the publication of his book *The Uncertain Trumpet*. In this work, General Taylor strongly criticized American defense policies, especially the United States failure to develop a conventional capability and to establish a large Army force capable of carrying out this type of mission. The following year, Lyndon Johnson's Senate Preparedness Investigating Subcommittee conducted an investigation into Army modernization and found, not surprisingly, that the Army had fallen far behind its Soviet counterpart in modernization and re-equipment in the post-World War II period.[8] In a strict military sense, these charges appear to have been well founded. The United States Army in 1960 did have a limited combat capability—both in Europe and in the rest of the world. In the 1956 Hungarian crisis, the United States had no conventional options in the face of the Russian suppression of the Hungarian revolution. Likewise, the Lebanon crisis in 1958 had placed great strains on the Army and Navy capacity to land and maintain a relatively small number of troops in that country; this was done only at the expense of the reserve forces of both the Sixth Fleet in the Mediterranean and the Seventh Army in Europe. Although the estimates vary, it would appear that when Eisenhower left office, the Army had somewhere between eleven and fourteen divisions and the Marines had approximately three.[9] Of these divisions, the United States had five committed to the Seventh Army in Europe and two committed to the Republic of (South) Korea. Therefore, at this time, the combat reserves available to the Army were somewhere between four and seven divisions, some of doubtful combat effectiveness. One member of the Kennedy Administration contended that the United States had only three divisions in reserve.[10]

Kennedy came to the White House determined to change what he perceived to be this fundamental weakness in American power and the military alternatives available to the American President. He increased the budgetary allocations for these services and brought General Taylor out of retirement as special adviser to the President for military affairs. From the start of the Kennedy Administration the major change in military policy was the strengthening of the American ability to engage in limited conflict.[11] Thus, by 1965, on the eve of the Vietnamese escalation, Johnson had sixteen active Army divisions and six National Guard and reserve divisions to work with in his contingency planning for Vietnam.[12]

The rationale for the doctrine of "flexible response" was set forth by Secretary McNamara in the clearest possible terms:

> Suppose you were to start from the premise that nuclear war is unthinkable and that you are not capable of fighting a nonnuclear war. If that is true, then you have no military foundation at all for your policy.[13]

But the doctrine of "flexible response" went beyond the abstraction of offering a nonnuclear alternative and served notice on Communist or Communist-defined forces that in the future they would be confronted with American military power. Secretary McNamara made this clear in testimony before Congress when he stated:

> Our Communist opponents have greatly extended the range of conflict to cover virtually every aspect of human activity. And we, together with our allies, must carefully allocate our defense effort to insure that we can meet the challenge on every front and at every level.[14]

McNamara continued in his testimony: "We must be in a position to confront him [the enemy] at any level of provocation with an appropriate military response."[15]

In order to be in a position to "confront him at any level" Secretary McNamara established the United States Strike

Command by placing the Strategic Army Command (regular reserves of United States Army) and the Tactical Air Command of the Air Force under joint command. This force was to provide an:

> . . . integrated mobile, high combat ready force, available to augment the unified commands overseas or to be employed as the primary force in remote areas.[16]

This was no vague threat of massive retaliation; it was a specific statement of American intent to engage in conflict "on every front and at every level." After the events in Cuba, Laos, Cambodia, Vietnam, and the Dominican Republic, nobody can say that the United States public was not warned of the intentions of the Kennedy and then the Johnson administrations.

The American decision to develop a conventional alternative in the conduct of its foreign and military policy should be understood for exactly what it was—an American decision to engage in this type of conflict whenever the leaders of this country perceived a "Communist" or "Communist-inspired" form of aggression. It seems safe to assume that the Kennedy-McNamara willingness to develop the capacity to fight a conventional war meant a willingness on their part to fight just such a war if they felt American interests demanded it. Obviously, the very existence of the capacity to fight a nonnuclear war increased the chances of one.

SECOND-STRIKE COUNTERFORCE

At this point in the arms race, the American decision to develop a conventional capability could have had at least one positive effect if the United States had decided simultaneously to reduce its massive nuclear striking force to a minimum deterrent posture. Or, put another way, if the United States had reduced its strategic striking force to approximately the same low number of delivery vehicles possessed by the Soviet Union, no longer would the possibility have existed of a surprise attack on the Soviet Union. If this had taken place, the United States would have then been following roughly the same strategic doctrine that the Soviet Union had followed since 1955, that is, the possession of enough nuclear delivery power to deter an attack on its homeland and a large conventional army capable of defending and patrolling the periphery of its empire. In Pentagonese, this translated into a doctrine of minimum deterrence.

However, the Kennedy Administration did exactly the opposite. Instead of reducing the number of American delivery vehicles, it increased them. It not only promised to be able to withstand a Soviet first strike, it promised to be able to absorb such a first strike and still be able to destroy not only Soviet cities, but also the remaining Soviet nuclear force. This "second-strike counterforce" doctrine accepted the existing American superiority in delivery systems and promised an escalation of the arms race for the maintenance of this superiority. There was no system of logic or reason known that could prevent the Soviet Union from perceiving this force as being a potential first-strike force against the Soviet Union; the only way for them to end this potential threat was for the Russians to increase their own nuclear delivery system.

Secretary of Defense McNamara demonstrated his awareness of American nuclear superiority when he announced the new doctrine in the most precise and rational-sounding terms:

> Our nuclear strength . . . makes possible a strategy designed to preserve the fabric of our societies should war occur. The United States has come to the conclusion that to the extent feasible . . . principal military objectives, in the event of nuclear war . . . should be the destruction of the enemy's military forces, not of his civilian population.[17]

Later, he continued his explanation of the forces necessary for such a policy:

> Such a force should have sufficient flexibility to permit a choice of strategies, particularly the ability to 1) strike back decisively at the entire Soviet target system simultaneously, or 2) strike back

first at the Soviet bomber bases, missile sites, and other military installations associated with their long-range nuclear forces to reduce
the power of any follow-up attack—and then if necessary, strike back
at the Soviet urban and industrial complex in a controlled and deliberate way.[18]

But "such a force" as could be left over *after* a Soviet attack
would by definition be large enough to be viewed as a potential
American first-strike force by any objective observer.

An essential corollary to the new doctrine was the perceived need of a substantial American civil defense program.
Official reasoning was that to accept a first strike, you must
have shelters for the population. Or, in the vernacular of the
time: "The United States could have more confidence in its
Sunday Punch if it were associated with some capacity to
absorb punishment."[19] Therefore, one of the first moves of the
Kennedy Administration was to start the process of alerting the
American public to the need for shelters and the allocation of
$207 million in the first six months of his administration for a
shelter program.[20] After an initial period of success in galvaniz-
ing the public (and industry) to build shelters, the program
failed and led mainly to a shelter program for high government
officials, and for the very rich. The not-so-powerful or affluent
gained a number of signs marking "shelter" on public basements
and a growing awareness that the shelter program was completely impractical in the thermonuclear age.

Secretary McNamara's new doctrine was intended to deter
an attack on the United States. But the fact remains that less
American power would have accomplished the same purpose
even if the Soviet Union had been planning a surprise attack
on the United States. In the process, the McNamara strategy
of continued American superiority was perceived as a threat
to the security of the Soviet Union and inevitably led to a *needless* escalation of the arms race. McNamara had not learned that
in the thermonuclear age an increase in arms may mean a
decrease in national security. The leaders of the United States
have yet to learn this lesson.

At a later date, I. F. Stone succinctly pointed out the folly of McNamara's "second-strike counterforce" when he stated: "The finely spun concepts of deterrence and second strike give a rational appearance to an essentially irrational process, the mindless multiplication of weaponry."[21] And, of course, that is exactly what happened under the Kennedy and then the Johnson administrations. The missile gap debate in the United States had already led to a major American escalation of the arms race, and McNamara's new doctrine demanded even greater increases in military spending by the government of the United States.

Therefore, on the strategic level, the Kennedy Administration began to insure the continued United States superiority over the Soviet Union in delivery systems. The new Kennedy budget submitted in January 1962 called for 13 Atlas squadrons to be operational in 1963 (130 ICBMs); 12 Titan squadrons totaling 108 ICBMs; and funds for additional Minutemen, bringing the total to 850. In January 1963 another 150 Minutemen were added to the existing goals, to bring the total projected Minuteman force to 1,000.[22] In addition to these planned increases, "the increase in the strategic bomber force to fourteen wings of B-52s and two wings of B-58s was completed in 1963." The number of SAC bombers placed on 15 minute alert was increased by 50 percent.[23]

Although all of these goals were not met because of changes in the need for certain systems and the introduction of large numbers of Polaris missiles, the fact remains that this build-up began at a time when the Soviet Union had less than 100 ICBMs and fewer than 300 long-range bombers capable of reaching the United States.[24] By November 1963 the United States plans called for 1,000 Minutemen, over 650 Polaris, and over 1,000 long- and medium-range bombers capable of reaching the Soviet Union. But throughout this period, Soviet strength grew very little in proportion to the American increases, with the Soviet Union holding its strategic forces at approximately 300 ICBMs and under 300 long-range bombers until some time after 1966. And, when the Soviet Union finally did begin its own large-scale missile-building program, it appears to have been in part a reaction against the proposed American ABM, the possible development of the B-70 bomber, and possible MRV (Multiple Re-entry Vehicle) on the Polaris A-3 missile.

At this point, the alert observer will ask, But what about all of the savings by McNamara due to his "cost effectiveness program" and his willingness to tell the generals no? And the answer is that there obviously were substantial savings involved in the refusal of the Kennedy Administration to give the military everything they asked for. Probably the two most important areas of at least temporary savings were Kennedy's decisions to halt development of the atomic airplane and his decision not to spend the funds for the Nike-Zeus ABM system.[25] The atomic airplane had cost the American taxpayers over one billion dollars over a fifteen-year period before Kennedy stopped it. And, as is known, the ABM system underwent various stages from Sentinel to Safeguard and was finally resurrected as the Strategic Defense Initiative (SDI) in spite of U.S. treaty commitments.

The major fight between the White House and the Pentagon during the Kennedy Administration (and the Johnson Administration) was, to no one's surprise, the effort on the part of the Air Force to gain additional funds for more bombers and the development of the B-70 long-range supersonic bomber. This drive for funds followed the now-classic pattern of obtaining funds from a reluctant President or Congress. "How Far Is the Red Air Force Ahead?" ran the title to an article in *Air Force and Space Digest* in September 1961. In this article it was contended that the Soviet Union was ahead of the United States in the field of bomber development, and called for more money for the Air Force so that this deficiency could be corrected.[26]

The early stages of this new "bomber gap" centered around the Air Force claim that the Soviet Union had developed a long-range Mach 2 (supersonic) bomber—the Bounder. Therefore, so the reasoning went, the United States should have such a bomber immediately. This claim was also supported in 1963 by the prestigious *Jane's All the World's Aircraft*, at least to the extent that *Jane's* mentioned its existence. But at a later date it became evident that the so-called Bounder was a Soviet test aircraft, references to it in future issues of *Jane's* were dropped, and the Air Force finally quit speaking of the threat from this nonexistent bomber force.[27]

The reader should keep in mind that the threat of the Bounder appeared simultaneously with reductions in the Air Force budget. Secretary McNamara had cut the development funds for the B-70 bomber from $358 to $220 million and had refused to spend the $525 million for the building of a new wing of 45 B-52 bombers.[28] McNamara's reasons for cutting back on the bomber force were not to slow down the arms race but to conduct it more efficiently. He claimed that to develop and procure a "modest force" of these planes would have cost $10 billion. But the planes were not even bombers in the traditional sense: they would carry no "bombs," but a very complex air-launched missile. "The question was not bombs versus missiles. The debate was about alternative launching platforms and alternative missile systems."[29]

Throughout his term, McNamara continued this running battle with the "bomber generals" and succeeded at least to the extent that he prevented a substantial building program for the B-52 or B-58; he also stopped the Air Force from starting construction of the various names under which the B-70 was disguised. Yet in the long run, like the ABM system vetoed by Kennedy, it would appear that McNamara lost this fight also. By 1970, the Air Force seemed to have gained a commitment from the Congress for $10 billion for the B-70 (later renamed the B-1).

McNamara's temporary success in frustrating the grandiose schemes of the Air Force generals led not only to increasing acrimony between the Secretary and the Air Force, but also laid the foundation for the attempted development of a "bomber gap" theme in the 1964 presidential campaign. In spite of the best efforts of General Curtis LeMay and Republican nominee Barry Goldwater, this issue never really caught on, in part because McNamara released to the press the official intelligence estimates of Soviet bomber strength as of 1964 as less than

300,[30] and hopefully in part because the American people had learned something from the earlier bomber and missile "gaps" and were not quite ready to believe another defense myth.

Paradoxically, the total effort of both Kennedy and McNamara was to save the American taxpayer money while simultaneously increasing the military budget of the United States. Money was saved by McNamara's "cost effectiveness" in the sense that the atomic-powered bomber and the ABM system were not built; nonetheless American military spending increased substantially during the Kennedy Administration. Perhaps Noam Chomsky best summed up the achievements of Secretary McNamara in this field when he said: "No doubt McNamara succeeded in doing with the utmost efficiency that which should not be done at all."[31]

The Kennedy Administration had barely begun before it was confronted with three of the continuing "crisis" areas facing the United States—Vietnam, Berlin, and Cuba. It is these three areas that will now be briefly examined.

VIETNAM, BERLIN, AND CUBA

Like all of the other early problems of the Kennedy Administration, the Vietnam crisis was a continuation of the difficulties of the previous Administration. During the 1950s, American aid to the Diem regime in South Vietnam had averaged over $300 million a year and by 1960 the United States had 685 military men in South Vietnam. After some initial hesitation, President Kennedy acceded to pressure from advisers (primarily General Maxwell Taylor and Walt W. Rostow) to commit American military forces in Vietnam to maintain the status quo. It was hoped that the number could be kept at a low level, but General Taylor estimated that it would take approximately 10,000 Americans to "show them how to get the job done."[32]

Thus, at a very early stage in the Kennedy Administration, the doctrine of flexible response was implemented. By the end of his first year, the President had sent 3,200 men to Vietnam; and at the time of his assassination, there were 16,300. During his first year in office, 11 Americans were killed; during 1963, 78, and 218 were wounded as the American commitment continued to expand.[33]

But Kennedy's major historical role in relation to Vietnam was found not so much in the early escalation of the war as it was in the fact that he decided to build up the Army's conventional and unconventional warfare capability. It was this 1961 decision to dramatically increase the size and capability of the Army that enabled Johnson to increase the number of troops in Vietnam from 23,300 in 1964 to 385,000 in 1966. Had the earlier build-up under Kennedy not taken place, Johnson would not have had this option, because the troops would not have been available. Therefore, although historians may argue as to whether Kennedy intended to pull out of Vietnam after the 1964 elections, the fact remains that it was his policy that made a massive land war in Vietnam possible in the first place.

The 1961 crisis over Berlin was a continuation of the Soviet pressure tactics since the end of World War II. In 1958, in the face of the alleged missile gap in favor of the Soviets, Premier Khrushchev had announced his intention to turn Berlin over to the East Germans. An authority who should have known better, D. F. Fleming, attributed this Soviet move to the reality of the missile gap favoring the Soviet Union and the belief that the Soviets were acting on the basis of their lead in the nuclear arms race.[34] Arthur Schlesinger attributes the 1958 Soviet pressure on Berlin to "the changing balance of nuclear forces."[35] Obviously, this was not the case, although Khrushchev evidently thought that he could obtain some diplomatic goals by bluffing in the face of the American belief in the missile gap, and this appears to be exactly what Khrushchev was doing in the case of Berlin, both in 1958 and in 1961. By early 1961, the Soviet leaders are certain to have known that it was a question of months before the obvious American superiority became common knowledge.*

The last chance for the Soviet Union to use the "missile gap" apparently was at the June 1961 meeting in Vienna between

---

* It is well to keep in mind that the U-2 had been flying over the Soviet Union from 1956 to 1961. Once the U-2 was grounded, the intelligence mission of this aircraft was taken over by equally competent earth satellites.

Premier Khrushchev and President Kennedy. At this meeting Khrushchev made his last bluff based on the alleged Soviet superiority and threatened a separate peace with East Germany unless the Berlin question was resolved. By this time, President Kennedy knew that there was no missile gap and that the United States was superior to the Soviet Union in nuclear forces and would remain so for the foreseeable future. Premier Khrushchev's demands were not met, for they were recognized for exactly what they were—a bluff.[36] Once it became obvious that the United States could not be tricked out of Berlin, the Soviet Union decided that its only other means of closing this exit route to Western Europe was to seal off the city. The Soviet Union proceeded to do just that when it began building the Berlin Wall on August 13, 1961.

The United States feared that another Berlin blockade was being attempted and almost immediately sent a battle group (approximately 1,200 men) down the Helmstead Autobahn to Berlin to establish access rights to the city. The battle group was not challenged, and the fear of blockade lessened. However, President Kennedy used this occasion to augment American military spending, increase the size of the armed forces by 225,000 men, and received authority to call up an additional 250,000 reservists at any time.[37] Access to the allied sector of Berlin continued for the Western powers, and the Berlin crisis subsided.

On the other hand, the continuing crisis surrounding Cuba presented a more dangerous threat to world peace.

The Cuban crisis can be broken down into two related crises, one in 1961—the Bay of Pigs—and the other in 1962—the Cuban missile crisis. The blame for the Bay of Pigs fiasco must be jointly shared by Eisenhower and Kennedy. The successful American-sponsored invasion of Guatemala in 1954 had overthrown the Arbenz regime and led to the establishment of a more pro–United States, pro–United Fruit regime in this unfortunate Latin American nation. Based on this earlier success, certain people in the Eisenhower Administration became convinced that the same tactics would work to overthrow Castro in Cuba and thereby destroy the Cuban Revolution. One of the first Eisenhower spokesmen to advocate some type of invasion of Cuba was Vice-President Nixon in April 1959.[38] Eventually, the idea of a Guatemala-type invasion gained the acceptance of the CIA and some in the higher echelons in the Pentagon. President Eisenhower approved of the invasion plan in March 1960; Cuban exiles were then trained and equipped by the United States in Guatemala and Nicaragua. The invasion was set for Spring 1961. When Kennedy came to office he approved of the invasion plan for April 1961 with the understanding that no United States forces would be directly involved.[39]

The invasion was an abysmal failure. Apparently the Cubans had no desire for a return of an American-supported Batista type of government, and they failed to "rise-up" and challenge the forces of Fidel Castro. The failure of the invasion was a distinct blow to the prestige of John Kennedy, and the new President emerged from this crisis determined not to allow such faulty intelligence and planning to reoccur in the future. President Kennedy attempted to place a buffer between the presidency and the CIA in the form of McGeorge Bundy as a special adviser to the President for national security affairs. And, significantly, a short time later the President ordered the Joint Chiefs of Staff to draw up the contingency plans necessary for the future invasion of Cuba.[40]

After the Bay of Pigs failure, many in the United States were critical of President Kennedy for not salvaging American prestige and launching an American invasion of Cuba. However, at the time of the invasion, it is doubtful if the United States could have mustered the forces necessary for an invasion of Cuba without stripping American military forces of all reserves. As Arthur Schlesinger has pointed out:

> . . . the United States could not even have invaded Cuba after the Bay of Pigs without drawing troops from other parts of the world and thereby inviting communist moves on other fronts.[41]

The Bay of Pigs had demonstrated to Kennedy how limited his conventional military options were in view of his determination to control foreign revolutions and internal conflicts. As has been seen, the President and his Secretary of Defense had already begun to expand the conventional forces of the United States and to extend American alternatives to include the use of large-scale conventional/unconventional operations by the armed forces.

But before this expansion of conventional power could take place, the United States was confronted with another Cuban crisis, this time not directly of its own making. By October 1962 it had become apparent that the Soviet Union was installing intermediate-range ballistic missiles (IRBM—approximate range 1,500–2,000 miles) and medium-range ballistic missiles (MRBM—range 1,000 miles), along with a small medium-range bomber force (Ilyushin 28—1,500 mile range). The exact number is open to question, but the following figures are probably accurate—IRBM, 12–16 missiles; MRBMs, 24 missiles; and 48 IL 28 bombers.[42] This Soviet action was taken in the face of an overwhelming American strategic superiority. The United States had over 1,600 bombers capable of reaching the Soviet Union, compared with less than 300 Soviet bombers that could reach the United States. In addition, the United States had almost 300 missiles that could reach the Soviet Union, while Russia had less than 100.[43]

The attempt to place missiles so close to the United States was obviously a dangerous move and one that Soviet leaders must have thoroughly examined in a detailed manner. The Soviet Union was aware of the American U-2 reconnaissance capability and is certain to have known that the risks of discovery were high, if not certain. Therefore, the question must be asked (and answered) as to why Khrushchev was willing to take such risks in the face of an American nuclear force that could survive a Soviet surprise attack, with or without missiles in Cuba, and then proceed to obliterate the Soviet Union.*

A number of explanations for the Soviet action were put forward in the United States, but there was no simple answer.

* It should be pointed out that only the 12–16 IRBMs were capable of reaching American SAC and missile bases in the north and north central United States. The MRBMs and Ilyushin 28 did not have the range to reach most of these targets.

However, it does appear as though there was *one predominant* reason for attempting to place Russian missiles in Cuba, with other motives playing only a supporting role.

The most simplistic reason given for the Soviet move was the belief that it once again demonstrated the highly aggressive nature of the Soviet Union and its desire to upset the balance of power and threaten a first strike against the United States.[44] In view of American strength at this time this argument hardly deserves comment.

A more logical explanation is that by 1962 the United States had upset what Khrushchev believed to be the balance of terror. As has been seen, at this time the Soviet Union was not only inferior to the United States in ICBMs, but also had decided *not* to build large numbers of first-generation ICBMs, and to wait until they had perfected their version of second-generation missiles. In the meantime, United States strategic forces appeared ominous and threatening to the security of the Soviet Union. Therefore, the logical way to close this perceived deterrent gap was for the Soviet Union to deploy some of their numerous medium-range missiles in Cuba as a temporary stop-gap until the second generation of Soviet ICBMs became operational.[45]

If American and Soviet leaders understood the deadly game of thermonuclear diplomacy and the reality of the accompanying weapons systems, then they knew that the deployment of approximately 42 missiles in Cuba did not upset the balance of terror. The Soviet missiles were not of sufficient range to reach most of the strategic delivery systems of the United States. (At most, 16 had the needed range.) In view of the American superiority in delivery systems, the Soviet move in Cuba might serve to re-establish the *certainty* of mutual annihilation that had been temporarily upset; but it could in no way lead to a first strike on the United States, with its advantage in delivery systems that ran over 4–1.

The decision to place IRBMs and MRBMs in Cuba was greatly facilitated by the fact that the Soviet Union had developed a large number of these medium-range missiles in keeping with their doctrine of being able to defend the entire periphery of the

Soviet Union against attack. This could explain the fact that while the Soviet Union was only building several hundred long-range bombers in the late 1950s and early 1960s, they had produced literally thousands of Mig-15 and Mig-17 interceptor aircraft, and were to later produce large numbers of Mig-21s.[46]

Even a few Soviet missiles in Cuba would vastly complicate any American effort to launch a surprise attack designed to *simultaneously* destroy Soviet delivery systems in Russia and in Cuba. The complexity of timing and coordination of such an attack would in itself be enough to prevent the United States from attempting such a difficult task. Thus, Soviet security would be assured until second-generation missiles (or more first-generation missiles) were available.

On the other hand, some experts have contended that the Soviet missiles were placed in Cuba in an attempt to prevent an American invasion. In view of past American actions, the fear of an invasion appears to have been a real one. And it is possible that one of the main reasons that Castro allowed the emplacement of missiles was to prevent such an invasion. However, it is hard to believe that the Soviet Union would risk its existence *only* to prevent an invasion of Cuba. There would appear to be a reason more closely related to Soviet security.

The precise motives for the Soviet action may never be known. But, Soviet leadership could have rationalized such a risky act along the following lines. At the invitation of a friendly Turkish government, the United States had deployed Jupiter missiles near the Soviet border on Turkish territory. If such an act was legal and justified, then why could not the Soviet government accept the invitation from a friendly Cuban government and deploy missiles in Cuba? Throughout the arms race the United States had deployed medium-range bombers and then missiles on allied territory close enough to the Soviet Union to effect a strike on Soviet territory. This had been done in the name of national security. Thus, in the face of the overwhelming American strategic force, why could not the Soviet Union deploy missiles in Cuba to maintain a balance of terror that it felt had been upset to the detriment of their national security?

Of course, America did not see the logic of the Soviet position.

Either the Kennedy Administration misunderstood the reality of the balance of terror, or, more likely, the President's reaction was based more on domestic political considerations than on the military reality of the existing status of the arms race. Possibly President Kennedy felt that the intricacies of the balance of terror were too complicated to explain to the American people. Whatever the case, Kennedy characterized the Soviet act as a ". . . deliberately provocative and unjustified change in the status quo . . ." that could not be accepted by the United States. Kennedy further contended that the Soviet act was a "definite threat to peace" and that the United States had never transferred missiles to any other nation "under the cloak of secrecy."[47] One wonders if the Jupiter missiles in Turkey and Thor in Britain were not a threat to peace since they had been sent there openly in the face of Soviet impotence.

The President then set up a naval "quarantine" (a peacetime blockade, which under international law is an act of war) and threatened further dire action should the Soviet Union refuse to remove its missiles from Cuba. Within 24 hours, the United States had committed an act of war, bypassed both the Charter of the United Nations and that of the Organization of American States, and taken the entire world to the brink of thermonuclear war.

Premier Khrushchev recognized that he had made a serious error in judgment in assessing the American reaction to his Cuban policy. He also recognized that no possible gain in or around Cuba could justify going any closer to war than the situation already indicated. Soviet missiles were withdrawn, and the United States promised not to invade Cuba. With very few exceptions, President Kennedy's handling of the whole crisis was praised as a diplomatic victory and the height of statesmanship. (Of course, there were some who thought that the United States, at last, had been adequately provoked to justify a war against Cuba.)

And yet, the major lessons of the Cuban missile crisis seemed to have been missed by most Americans, both in and out of the government. For the most part, the fact that the Soviet Union was primarily trying to redress a threatening American superiority in thermonuclear delivery systems was ignored at the time. If this had been understood, it might have generated some pressure for a reduction of current missile production programs; however, these programs continued unabated and the result was an increasingly dangerous American superiority, and, of course, eventually a Soviet missile build-up. The ability of the leaders of the United States to convince the American people that Jupiter missiles in Turkey and Thor missiles in England were defensive while similar Soviet missiles in Cuba were offensive epitomizes the double standard by which the United States has fought the Cold War.

In addition, the fact that the American people had so willingly and uncritically followed the President to the brink of thermonuclear war should have served as an indication of a distinct lack of awareness on the part of the American public of the perils of all-out war. Certainly, such ignorance is a dangerous situation in the thermonuclear age, and efforts should have been made to correct this misconception. Such was not the case.

There was at least one encouraging conclusion to be drawn from the Cuban crisis. If there had been any doubt before 1962 that the Soviet Union understood the informal workings of the balance of terror, this doubt *should* have been removed in 1962. The Soviet Union recognized that it had mistakenly backed the United States into a corner from which it felt it had no alternative but to react in a military manner. Once this was fully realized in the Kremlin, the Soviet Union backed down. Unfortunately, some American observers drew the wrong conclusions from this act of wisdom. Some believed that it was simply an example of foiled aggression, while others were convinced that it demonstrated that all the United States needed to do was to rattle its weaponry and at some future date the Soviets would back down again. There are still Americans who, failing to distinguish the uniqueness of the Cuban crisis, think that this is the solution to problems as diverse as Nicaragua, the Middle East, or Europe.

Many Americans were simply not willing to admit that the leadership of the Soviet Union had progressively rejected total war with the United States as a rational instrument of national policy. As has been seen, Stalin had rejected the inevitability of war between the two superpowers. Khrushchev repeated this in 1956, and by 1960 the Soviet Union specifically rejected the notion that a third world war would lead to the end of capitalism.[48] Khrushchev officially accepted the concept of "mutual deterrence" and claimed that only a "madman" would start a war under the existing circumstance.[49] Just prior to the Cuban missile crisis, the 21st Party Congress in 1961 had not only reaffirmed the Soviet belief in peaceful co-existence but had also endorsed the concept of "different roads to socialism."[50]

After the crisis in Cuba had subsided, Premier Khrushchev clearly announced in the Communist party newspaper *Pravda* the Soviet recognition of the horrors of thermonuclear war:

> According to the calculations of scientists the very first blow [in a thermonuclear war] would destroy between 700 and 800 million people. All large cities, not only in the United States and the Soviet Union, the two leading nuclear powers, but also in France, Britain, Germany, Italy, China, Japan and many other countries would be razed to the ground and destroyed. The consequences of atomic-hydrogen bomb war would persist during the lives of many generations and would result in disease, death and would cripple the human race.[51]

If this rhetoric had been accompanied by a massive building program in bombers and missiles that could have threatened a first strike on the United States, then American leaders could have relegated such statements to the category of propaganda and left it at that. But the statements were accompanied by a distinct lack of a massive Soviet effort to build up its strategic power to the point that it could even vaguely threaten a first strike on the United States. During the 1950s and 1960s, Soviet statements on the undesirability of thermonuclear war underlined their failure to produce weapons systems that could threaten the balance of terror. Unfortunately, American actions were not as consistent with American statements and the United States continued to maintain a threatening superiority over the Soviet Union in strategic delivery systems.

THE TEST BAN TREATY

It is possible that the Cuban missile crisis had one beneficial result—an agreement between the United States and the Soviet Union in 1963 to ban nuclear tests in the atmosphere. The fact that the world had gone to the brink of thermonuclear war over Cuba evidently had a sobering effect on both Kennedy and Khrushchev. The cessation of nuclear testing by the two superpowers was to the credit of both nations. However, the fact that this period of détente and limited good will was not expanded to include nuclear arms reduction represented another opportunity lost to end the insanity of the arms race.

There were numerous ramifications of the Test Ban Treaty, but perhaps the most encouraging was the fact that the two major powers acted in a manner that can be described as enlightened self-interest. Scientists had long known the lethal aftereffects of atomic explosions and as early as 1958 a report by the Federation of American Scientists stated:

> . . . with a stockpile . . . that now exists it is possible to cover the entire earth with a radiation level which for ten years would remain sufficiently intense to prove fatal to all living things.[52]

As evidence increasingly indicated that nuclear testing in the atmosphere was creating danger to human life and future generations, it was logical that the nations with highly developed nuclear technology would attempt to prevent further discharges of nuclear debris into the atmosphere, particularly Strontium 90 and Iodine 131. That the Soviet Union and the United States succeeded in this goal is one of the few encouraging aspects of the arms race.

On the other hand, there was a more insidious motive to be found among some Americans who eventually acquiesced to the Test Ban Treaty. As President Kennedy surveyed the forces working within American society against approval of the treaty, he found that there was substantial opposition from the military, the scientific community, and among some of the political leaders of both parties.[53] In order to reduce the opposition to the treaty and insure its passage by the Senate, President Kennedy had to offer certain "safeguards" to these powerful opponents. It was first pointed out that the treaty insured Soviet "acquiescence in American nuclear superiority."[54] Then President Kennedy promised the Joint Chiefs of Staff the following safeguards:

> . . . vigorous continuation of underground testing; readiness to resume atmospheric testing on short notice; strengthening of detection capabilities; and the maintenance of nuclear laboratories.[55]

In addition, Secretary McNamara guaranteed the Senate that he would move in the near future to raise "the megatonnage of our strategic alert forces."[56]

By promising the "vigorous continuation of underground testing," the arms race merely moved underground,[57] but with one very important exception. The fact that all Soviet and American future tests of atomic weapons would take place underground meant that the nation with the most sophisticated testing and the most generous allocation of resources would inevitably have a distinct advantage over the less technically advanced, poorer nation. In both instances, the advantage went to the United States. Although exact figures on the number of Soviet and American underground tests are difficult to find, it would appear that by 1969 the United States had conducted 186 "announced tests" compared to 28 for the Soviet Union. Likewise, the United States was apparently spending over $200 million a year on underground testing.[58] It was this effort that produced multiple warheads and the antiballistic missile system and led to a continuation of the roughly four-year military-technological advantage enjoyed by the United States.

NATO

Although the United States had received diplomatic support from most of its NATO allies during the Cuban missile crisis, the willingness of the United States to act in such a decisive manner without even consulting with its allies led to further estrangement within the NATO Alliance. American and European perception of the Soviet threat had begun to differ sharply by the mid-fifties, and this continued into the Kennedy Administration of the 1960s.

By 1962 the European tendency to play down the Soviet threat had matured considerably. President DeGaulle openly challenged the two basic assumptions of American NATO diplomacy: (1) that the Soviet Union was preparing or desired to attack Western Europe; and (2) that the United States would risk all-out war in the defense of this territory even if an attack took place. Numerous American efforts to discredit the challenge from DeGaulle or to represent "Gaullism" as an isolated phenomenon had failed in the face of growing restiveness within the Alliance. As shall be seen, this fragmentation of NATO was a gradual process dependent on numerous forces within the dynamics of world politics; but by 1962 the major thrust of the disintegration of NATO had been defined. The strength and unity of the alliance system has progressively deteriorated ever since. (The fragmentation of NATO has been accompanied by a similar process within the Warsaw Pact.)

Until the Kennedy Administration, American military strategy toward Western Europe had been based on a confusing combination of relying on the doctrine of massive retaliation, tactical nuclear weapons, and the claim that Europe could be defended by conventional means. From the outset, the new Administration recognized and admitted that there was no conventional option in Europe and stated its declared intention to correct this error. In McNamara's words: "In Europe, we lack the 'conventional option.' And we are not going to achieve that option in the near future."[59] A little later, McNamara unequivocally declared:

> With regard to Europe, the presently programmed United States forces, together with the present forces of other NATO countries, would not be able to contain an all-out conventional Soviet attack without invoking the use of nuclear weapons.[60]

The Secretary then called for large increases in the budget for the Army to increase this conventional capacity.[61]

In keeping with the new doctrine of flexible response and the increased military budget, McNamara was able to increase the size of the Army from 11 to 16 combat-ready divisions. Ironically, none of these went to Europe.*

Since its inception, many NATO supporters have claimed that the NATO forces in Europe were capable of a conventional defense of Western Europe. Was this true at any time in the past or was it true by 1970? Did NATO have a nonnuclear alternative in the face of Soviet-Warsaw Pact strength should war occur? The answer must be a firm no. That the United States and its allies did not have a conventional capability during the 1950s and early 1960s is admitted by most, but not all, observers.[62] So, the question legitimately has to be asked, what had changed by 1970? And the answer must be that NATO was probably weaker in 1970 than it was in 1960.*

The importance of this question does not so much hinge on the question of whether or not the NATO nations *could* develop a conventional defense should they decide to do so. Obviously, this could be done. The significant point to be made is that while the U.S. government was speaking publicly of a conventional defense, it was planning the first use of nuclear weapons in Europe.

In spite of McNamara's efforts at increasing the conventional capability of United States forces in Europe, the American combat effectiveness in Europe was less in 1970 than it was in 1961—because of very limited troop withdrawals, but mainly because of the progressive reductions in combat effectiveness due to equipment and skilled personnel shortages caused by the war in Vietnam.

However, a great deal has been said and written about the American airlift capacity and its growing ability to re-enforce American NATO forces (especially when the C5A became operational). The American taxpayer sees millions of dollars used to demonstrate that one Army division can be moved from

---

* As a matter of fact, by the time McNamara left office, the United States had withdrawn 34,000 military personnel from Europe. (See U.S., Congress, Senate, Authorization for Military Procurement, Research & Development, Fiscal Year 1969, and Reserve Strength, 90th Cong., 2d sess. (February 2, 1968), testimony by Secretary of Defense McNamara, p. 103.

Texas to Germany under ideal conditions in a short period of time; then the public is told that this demonstrates the fact that the United States can defend Europe with reserve forces stationed in this country. Even as astute and critical an observer as Marcus Raskin seems impressed with the American airlift capability. In his perceptive book (along with Richard Barnet) on NATO, Mr. Raskin speaks of the "spectacular air operation, transporting an armoured division from Texas to Germany in a matter of hours."[63] After leaving office, McNamara claimed: "The United States can more than double its combat ready divisions in Central Europe within several weeks of mobilization."[64] Yet the claim that the United States could adequately re-enforce its NATO strength in time of war is simply not true. Those who speak of an airlift distort the ability of American aircraft (including the C5A) to penetrate a European war zone and land troops under combat conditions. A conventional war in Europe would have to be fought with the forces in being, or turned into a tactical nuclear war that would devastate the Continent and maybe beyond.

If there was a conventional Soviet attack on Western Europe —and it should again be made clear that the writer does not believe the Soviet Union is planning or wants such an attack— the situation would be something like this: the Warsaw Pact nations would immediately assume at least temporary air superiority and destroy all major airfields designed to receive re-enforcements. The reasons for this are fairly simple—in 1969 the Soviet Union had more interceptor aircraft, more light bombers, ground-attack aircraft, and medium-range missiles than the NATO forces.[65]

	NATO	WARSAW PACT
Light bombers	50	450 (400 of them Soviet)
Fight ground-attack	1,500	1,650 (1,120 of them Soviet)
Interceptors	720	3,000 (2,000 of them Soviet)
Medium-range missiles	0	750 (Soviet)

In view of this Warsaw Pact superiority, it was absurd to claim that lumbering American Boeing 707s, 727s, 747s, or even a fleet of C5As are going to land American troops in Europe unhindered. Most would be shot down with the loss of not only the aircraft but also the strategic reserve forces of the United States. Those aircraft not destroyed in flight would have great difficulty in finding a place to land, and it is certain that the Soviets would not leave Rhine-Main Airbase intact to accept these re-enforcements. (Rhine-Main Airbase in Frankfurt, Germany, is the major American airbase in Western Europe.)

Some commentators on comparative NATO-Warsaw Pact strengths have attempted to make a case for their belief that the forces in being could defend Western Europe in a conventional manner, and they cite total troop strengths to prove their point. Thus, for example, McNamara in the late '60s claimed that NATO has about 900,000 troops deployed in all regions of continental Europe, compared with 960,000 Warsaw Pact troops.[66] Yet these figures are extremely misleading. First, McNamara was dealing with total NATO forces (counting, for example, Greek or Portuguese troops). Second, the key area in assessing European defensive capabilities is not southern Europe, or even Central Europe, but the area of the North German Plain, the traditional invasion route into the Low Countries and France. It is this area which would be hit the hardest and hit first. The United States Seventh Army (roughly five divisions) is located south of this invasion route and it is highly improbable that it could be pulled out and then placed on the North German Plain before the Soviet forces had begun to occupy it (that is, in three or four days). If this maneuver was attempted, it would probably result in the destruction of the Seventh Army as it was attacked in force from its eastern flank as it moved north. Therefore, the essential defense of Central Europe rested with the British Army on the Rhine (less than 50,000 men) and less than six German divisions. While fighting a minimal hold-action on other fronts, the Soviets could easily muster a 4–1 division advantage on the North German Plain.* A conservative estimate of the time that it would take a determined Soviet effort

---

* In 1963, Secretary McNamara estimated the number of Soviet divisions at 85, with 40 immediately combat ready. See *The New York Times,* November 19, 1963. Normal Soviet mobilization plans would have meant that the remaining 45 divisions would have been combat ready in less than 30 days. The NATO forces could not match this Soviet mobilization figure in Western Europe.

to break through the northern front would be less than a week. This would place Soviet forces *at the rear* of the United States Seventh Army in about eight days or less and in Antwerp in about ten days. There could be no Bastogne this time; the American forces would be flanked and would be lucky to make it to the Pyrenees safely before they were destroyed by a Soviet "wheeling action" at the base of the Swiss and French Alps.

Obviously this hypothetical situation is not going to take place. The Soviet Union is not about to attack Western Europe, and even if they did, the United States would have to use tactical nuclear weapons, and the exact military effect of these is not yet known. But in this event, a solid argument could be made for the case that not only would the societies of Europe be destroyed, but possibly *both* opposing armies. As pointed out before, the United States had 7,000 tactical nuclear weapons in Europe *alone* and the Soviet Union had about half that many.[67]*

The belief that the United States (and NATO) has a conventional option for the defense of Europe is another classic example of myth creation by those who govern the United States. If this myth can continue to be sold to the American, and to a limited extent European, people, a number of objectives will be accomplished:

(1) The American and European populations can continue to live under the illusion that Europe is defended by conven-

---

* Secretary McNamara claimed in 1966 that the United States had 7,000 tactical nuclear weapons in Europe (see *The New York Times*, September 24, 1966). If this was the case, it seems safe to assume that the Soviet Union had as many atomic weapons available as it believed necessary to defend this area. Thus, a conservative estimate would place the total number of tactical nuclear weapons in Europe at over 10,000. These weapons are in the kiloton range and vary from about 1 to 100 kilotons, with the average being about 20—or the same size as the weapon dropped on Nagasaki. Simple arithmetic will indicate that in Europe then, excluding strategic arsenals, there are approximately 200,000 kilotons stored and deliverable, or roughly 10,000 times the amount of explosive power that destroyed Nagasaki. The use of even a small percentage of these weapons would result in the deaths of millions of Europeans and the destruction of the Continent.

tional forces and therefore the continued presence of American troops all over Europe can be justified.

(2) The United States Army is assured of continued budgetary support for these forces, along with the financial contribution for the supporting naval and air units.

(3) The producers of the overpriced and mismanaged C5A cargo plane stand a better chance of the continuation of the flow of funds into the Lockheed coffers. (Most recent estimates placed the overrun cost of the C5A for 200 planes at over \$2 billion.) Other NATO-related industries will also continue to benefit.

(4) The continued presence of American troops in Europe means that American policy makers have forces near at hand for operations such as the past ones in Lebanon or the Congo, or future ones to uphold the regimes in Spain or Greece. The very presence of these units serves not only to give the American government these options, but also the remote threat of their use for such a purpose is a powerful force for the maintenance of the status quo and a deterrent to revolutionary change.

(5) Finally, the continued presence of American forces in NATO nations leaves American policy makers at the least the vague hope that the policies, and particularly the nuclear policies, of these allies can be controlled.

Thus far, only American policies and perspectives toward NATO have been discussed with European attitudes and policies postponed until the reality of American policy had been defined. As has been seen, since its very inception NATO has been confronted with substantial problems within the Alliance itself. Although these problems existed in all 15 of the NATO nations at one time or another, the major crisis facing NATO centered primarily around two nations—Germany and France. Without the former, the manpower and industrial strength needed for even a semblance of a viable Western European defensive system could not exist. Without France, there was not enough territorial or logistical depth in Europe to conduct defensive operations without violating French territory. For the first six years of the NATO Alliance, the resistance to

German participation was sufficient to prevent effective German participation. At no time since the founding of the alliance system has France met the military requirements of NATO; since the early 1960s France has been either inactive in the Alliance or actively hostile toward it.

The politics and diplomacy of the Atlantic alliance go beyond the scope of this study. Those interested in this aspect of the problem of NATO should consult the excellent work by Richard Barnet and Marcus Raskin, *After 20 Years: The Decline of NATO and the Search for a New Policy in Europe*. For the purposes of this study concentration will remain on the relevant military developments that added impetus to the fragmentation of the NATO Alliance in the 1960s.

It is fairly common knowledge that the policies of France and of Charles DeGaulle were the major manifestation of the shift in European attitudes; but for a number of reasons an attempt was made to make "Gaullism" appear as an isolated phenomenon, not related to the French people and certainly in no way related to the general feelings of Europeans.

Gaullism may have started out as a French reaction against complete dependency upon the policies and power of the United States; but as it has developed and spread throughout the NATO nations, it has become much more than a simple reassertion of nationalism based on a resentment of American preponderance. The efforts to decrease military dependence upon the United States have logically led to a substantive increase in the independent military policies followed by American NATO allies. Therefore, what started under the Fourth Republic (before DeGaulle) in France has now escalated to the effective removal of France from NATO, and the policy continues under a supposedly "non-Gaullist" successor government. But the foreign policy of Gaullism now extends well beyond the borders of France. The reductions in the British Army of the Rhine (in Germany), the threatened British "withdrawal east of Suez," and the reductions of the military budget of Great Britain were manifestations of the same phenomena. The similar announcement of Canadian reductions in Europe and the failure of

Prime Minister Trudeau to endorse the American antiballistic missile system are similar examples.

These developments in NATO have been a gradual and as yet incomplete evolution of European policies and attitudes. First, the move from dependence on the United States was simply a demand on the part of some Europeans for more independence in their own national policies. However, as time passed this demand was joined by a much more potent force— fear that the United States might involve Europe in a world war without its consent. The unilateral American actions during the two Cuban crises and the invasion of the Dominican Republic did nothing to forestall these fears. The coup de grâce as far as many Europeans were concerned took place in 1966. "Rusk Says Pacific Is Flank of NATO," ran the byline in *The New York Times*. Secretary of State Rusk contended that the "western flank" of NATO was in the Pacific and strongly implied that in the event of war between the United States and China, the NATO doctrine of "an attack on one is considered an attack on all" would come into effect.[68] Many Europeans could only view with horror the possibility that American misadventures in the Pacific would be the cause of World War III and the inevitable destruction of Europe.

Above are listed a number of the military problems that faced the NATO Alliance during the 1960s, but one additional military problem deserves special attention; it was this problem and the failure of American policy makers to solve it that greatly accelerated the inevitable fragmentation of NATO. In its simplest terms, the origins of this problem are to be found in the demand by Secretary McNamara that in the event of war "NATO target systems must be indivisible."[69]

In layman's terms, indivisible targeting in nuclear war means that there must be one central planning unit that designates *all* targets in event that nuclear weapons are used. Needless to say, under the various plans put forward by the United States, this planning unit would be the American government.

The demand that the NATO target system must be indivisible was designed to accomplish two purposes. First, and most important, it would prevent the European nations from achieving the status of independent nuclear powers and thus assure a continued American monopoly in this area and likewise a continued European dependence on the United States. Second, an indivisible target system translated as the logical corollary to the American doctrine of second-strike counterforce; that is, the United States must have the sole, final say on when and where nuclear weapons will be used in the event of war. Without this guarantee, America's selective, "rational" nuclear response in the event of war was meaningless.

In order for this strategy to work, the United States had to deal with three basic problems—the three nations of Western Europe that could potentially develop an effective nuclear deterrent force of their own—Great Britain, France, and West Germany. The problems created by these three nations were different, and a formula was needed that would meet the demands of all three. The American answer, submitted with a straight face and in all sincerity, was the multilateral nuclear force (MLF). This plan went through numerous changes, but the sum and substance of the plan was to place all *European* nuclear capacity under either multilateral NATO control or under effective American control by designating the NATO commander (always an American) as the final decision maker. Under multilateral control, all fifteen NATO allies would have had to agree to use atomic weapons simultaneously, an almost impossible task, or the American NATO commander would make the decision. American strategic systems (SAC and American ICBMs) would not be subject to MLF control.

According to American reasoning, this would remove the British need for an independent bomber force equipped with American Skybolt missiles (air-to-surface missiles capable of penetrating Soviet defenses). The independent French force de frappe would no longer be needed and could be replaced with reliance on the NATO system. And, finally, the MLF would serve as a surrogate for those in Germany demanding possession of nuclear weapons. With these problems solved, the American monopoly on control of nuclear weapons and the powerful political-diplomatic instrument represented by this monopoly would be maintained. Many Europeans did not see it that way!

The American advocacy of the MLF and the European rejection of it is of prime importance in understanding the progressively deteriorating cohesion of the NATO Alliance; therefore, a more detailed discussion on a country-by-country basis is necessary.

By 1960, a respected and authoritative British military expert had joined those who doubted the credibility of American deterrent policy. Alastair Buchan wrote in *The Bulletin of the Atomic Scientists:*

> . . . confidence in the ability of the United States to guarantee the security of Western Europe is decreasing as Russia becomes a formidable nuclear missile power.[70]

In the same series, this opinion was shared by the American expert Klaus Knorr and the well-known French analyst Raymond Aron.

By this time, the British felt it necessary to develop their own small bomber force capable of reaching the Soviet Union with thermonuclear weapons. But with the advances being made in defensive surface-to-air missiles, serious doubts were being raised as to the ability of the British Vulcan/Victor bombers to penetrate Soviet defensive forces. The British, suffering under the economic strain of maintaining an appearance as a major world power, had decided to rely on the American Skybolt air-to-surface missiles rather than developing their own penetration system. But at the British-American Nassau meeting in early December 1962 the United States announced its decision not to build the Skybolt, and began to push MLF as an alternative to furnishing the British with Skybolt. Under this plan, the United States would *sell* Polaris missiles to Britain; then Britain would be responsible for producing the warheads and its financial share of the naval vessels needed for the system. At this point, the British had no choice but grudgingly to accept the American fait accompli on Skybolt production. On the other hand, if the United States could get the British to accept the

MLF rather than rely on their own deterrent force, then the "indivisibility" of targeting systems demanded by McNamara would have been achieved.

By 1964, the British had rejected the concept of MLF, and Lyndon Johnson let the system quietly disappear from consideration after Prime Minister Wilson's visit in December of that year. Later evidence indicates that the United States had applied substantial pressure on Great Britain to gain its adherence to the multilateral concept of deterrence for Europe, and that the United States had been willing to "pay a good price" in order to gain British acceptance of this concept.[71] The British still refused to accept the system.

If there ever was any doubt in Great Britain as to the efficacy of the MLF, this was certainly not the case in France. Well before DeGaulle became president of France in 1958, the leaders of the Fourth Republic had begun to carve out an independent foreign military policy including the removal of American nuclear weapons from French soil and the decision to proceed with the development of the force de frappe. This policy was continued and expanded under DeGaulle. However, it should be understood that DeGaulle's contention that the Americans would not meet their commitment to defend Western Europe was not so much an accusation of bad faith, but was based on DeGaulle's belief that "no nation will choose to fight to the death for another. . . ."[72] In conjunction with this conviction was DeGaulle's determination to establish the independence of French policy from that of the United States.

It was this realistic assessment of the limits of American power, along with the fear of an American-provoked world war, that fed the increasing restiveness of the major nations of the NATO Alliance. Perhaps the best summation of the French position came not from France but from a well-qualified British observer, Denis Healey:

> . . . France does not believe there is a substitute for purely national defense systems, and does not intend to be sidetracked from the pursuit of nuclear independence by meaningless formulas for collective deterrence. . . .[73]

The French had decided to follow their own concept of how best to obtain some semblance of security and national prestige in the thermonuclear age. This concept did not include the acceptance of a multinational nuclear force that would be unable to react in time of crisis or would be an American-controlled force.

Therefore, the French continued to develop nuclear weapons and the bomber force (the Mirage series) necessary to create the *possibility* of delivering a small number of thermonuclear bombs on Soviet targets. These French actions made McNamara's concept of indivisible targeting meaningless the moment it was proposed. The possibility that the independent French force *might* be able to drop several megaton-range bombs on Moscow and Leningrad ended the indivisibility of the Western target system and in a very real sense established a balance of terror between France and the Soviet Union.

The situation facing German-American relations was a very different one. The United States bore prime responsibility for not only the rearming of Germany and its participation in NATO, but also for the degree of permanency that has characterized the division of Germany into two states since the early 1950s.[74] Thus, when Germany demanded some say on the control of nuclear weapons, the United States was faced with the very difficult task of devising a formula that would make it look as if Germany had nominally become a nuclear power, but in reality, of course, had not. Of the three powers involved, Germany could have at least gained "symbolic" nuclear status and therefore was not as critical of the MLF as Britain and France. The MLF seemed to be the perfect formula to fulfill this purpose, but it never gained acceptance in Germany for the simple reason that the Germans also recognized that it was an unworkable and meaningless concept.

The attempt to force the multilateral nuclear force on to America's European allies was the last major effort on the part of the United States to change substantially its European military policy. Once the MLF had joined the other myths of American defense policy in oblivion, if not ridicule, the United States settled down under Johnson and then Nixon to an acceptance of the status quo in NATO. By 1970, the United States, in the face of a distinctly not expansive, conservative Soviet Union, had decided to place over 7,000 tactical nuclear weapons in Europe, go through the motions and rhetoric of the possibility of a conventional defense, and leave the situation substantially as it had been ever since the 1950s.

V

Johnson-Nixon: Logic Fulfilled

(1963–1970)

The policies of the Johnson Administration were a continuation of the past. President Johnson carried the assumptions and policies of the Kennedy Administration to their logical conclusion. The results have been an unmitigated disaster for the conduct of the foreign and military affairs of the United States. The Dominican invasion, massive land war in Asia, major escalations of the arms race, increased fragmentation of the NATO Alliance, and a general weakening of the world-wide moral position of the United States were the major results of the administration of Lyndon Johnson. What John Kennedy had continued, Lyndon Johnson escalated.

The difference was one of the degree of power committed to a given policy, not to a different policy. Where Kennedy had supported a Cuban emigré invasion during Bay of Pigs and failed, Johnson landed Marines in the Dominican Republic in sufficient strength so as to preclude the possibility of military failure. Where Kennedy had committed up to 15,000 Americans to help a pro-American Saigon government maintain itself in power, Johnson committed 500,000 Americans to fight a war that the Saigon government had already lost. Where Kennedy went through the motions of supporting self-determination, following the Dominican invasion in 1965 Lyndon Johnson approved of the Seldon resolution in the House of Representatives justifying the unilateral use of American troops in Latin

American nations that considered themselves threatened by "international communism, directly or indirectly."[1] This resolution, although it was not legally binding, seemed to finalize the establishment of the Johnson doctrine—a virtually unlimited claim of American legitimacy for armed intervention by the United States in internal or external conflicts throughout the noncommunist world.

It appears that Johnson was overwhelmed by the increasing intensity of revolutionary forces throughout the third world and could not operate with the comparative restraint that had characterized the Kennedy Administration. American installed and supported status quo governments were increasingly challenged by the only instrument available to the forces for change in the third world—revolutionary resistance and warfare. And, at home, Johnson did not seem to possess the will, even temporarily, to resist the demands of the military and its allies in the constant drive for more funds and weapons systems. On the whole, Johnson was not as subtle or as restrained as Kennedy; this was the major difference between their administrations in the conduct of American foreign policy.

In spite of all its liberal rhetoric, the Johnson Administration was in its own way as much a hard-line, fearful, anticommunist administration as that of Eisenhower-Dulles. This fear and uncertainty was best represented by Johnson's statement:

> There are 3 billion people in the world and we have only 200 million of them. We are outnumbered 15 to 1. If might did make right, they would sweep over the United States and take what we have. We have what they want.[2]

In case there was any doubt as to the identity of these billions, Secretary of State Dean Rusk defined the challenge in a press conference in the following manner:

> Question: Why do you think our security is at stake in Vietnam?
> Answer: [Rusk] Within the next decade or two, there will be a billion Chinese on the mainland, armed with nuclear weapons,

with no certainty about what their attitude toward the rest of Asia will be.[3]

But the Chinese threat to American security was not limited to a billion Chinese: the threat was extended to all those forces demanding change in the socioeconomic structure governing their nations. Therefore, by implication, either Moscow or Peking must be involved in revolutionary efforts in the Third World. In Secretary Rusk's words:

> But what the Communists, in their upside down language, call "wars of liberation" are advocated and supported by Moscow as well as Peiping [sic]. The assault on the Republic of Vietnam is a critical test of that technique of aggression.[4]

With this perception of the world facing the United States, it is no wonder that American leadership was willing to take great risks to prevent being overrun by the masses of the world. These "risks" were defined as being unlimited. W. W. Rostow, Johnson's Henry Kissinger, probably said it best in an article entitled "The Test: Are We the Tougher?" Mr. Rostow claimed that "credible deterrence in the nuclear age lies in being prepared to face the consequence if deterrence fails—up to and including all out nuclear war."[5]

But a very important distinction in theories of deterrence is missing in this question. Simple deterrence of a Soviet attack could be accomplished with several hundred Polaris missiles. But more limited military actions for which the Soviet Union or China might be conveniently blamed, although not responsible, could not be deterred or stopped by threatening them. For example, it is highly doubtful that no matter how willing the United States was to go to all-out war against the Soviet Union to prevent Castro from coming to power, no matter how vehement the threats, he would have still assumed power in Cuba. The Soviet Union simply did not control Fidel Castro. The same point can be made for Ho Chi Minh's revolution in Vietnam. Rostow recognized the differences of the tactics of the challenge, but he, like the Administration he served, insisted on holding

Russia or China responsible for all challenges to the status quo throughout the world.

Two points should be emphasized: first, American policy makers viewed the world as billions of people hammering away at the edges of the American empire, rather than as peoples trying to develop their own nations without American intervention. Second, these policy makers saw these challenges as directed from either Moscow or Peking (or both) and therefore national suicide could be contemplated as a last-ditch policy to counter these challenges. It is within this context that American policy was made and must be analyzed if it is to be understood. It is then easier to comprehend United States behavior in the Dominican Republic and Vietnam; and why the United States has insisted on escalating the arms race despite massive strategic superiority.

By the mid-1960s, United States military policy had distinguished between the perceived threat from the thermonuclear power of the Soviet Union, and the different threat to American interests posed by alleged Russian (or Chinese) supported and controlled revolutions aimed at destroying the status quo that the United States wanted to preserve. McNamara calculated the changing nature of the challenges to American interests in the following manner:

> In the eight years through late 1966 alone there were no less than 164 internationally significant outbreaks of violence, each of them specifically designed as a serious challenge to the authority or very existence of the government in question.[6]

He went on to claim that only 15 of these 164 challenges were military conflicts between states, with the remainder (by implication) being indigenous in nature. McNamara also recognized the escalating nature of the insurgency forces demanding some kind of domestic change. In 1958 there ". . . were 23 prolonged insurgencies going on around the world. As of February, 1966, there were 40."[7]

This changed perception of threats to American interests produced a dichotomy in American military planning and weapons systems. To a limited extent, each challenge demanded its own military doctrine and its own weapons system or military force-levels. A large part of the history of the Johnson Administration centered around these questions.

At the strategic level (Soviet or Chinese direct threat), arguments flourished over the Sentinel ABM, the Soviet Tallinn Line, the B-1 bomber, and the Multiple Independent Re-entry Vehicle (MIRV). While on the tactical level (revolutionary challenges), the controversies surrounded more limited systems such as the C5A super transport aircraft, fast deployment logistic ships (FDLS), the TFX (FB-111) mixed-mission aircraft, and the nuclear aircraft carrier. One set of systems was designed for strategic reasons against the Soviet Union and to a limited extent China, while the other represented further preparation for the future Vietnams inevitable in a revolutionary world should United States policy remain unchanged.

For example, the pressures to build the C5A cargo plane and to deploy the fast deployment logistic ships (FDLS) were closely related and reflected future American strategy toward conflicts such as had taken place in the Dominican Republic or Vietnam. The C5A was designed to carry over 500 soldiers long distances (as well as military equipment if needed). The FDLS were designed as floating "barges" with equipment and supplies sufficient to equip two American divisions. The Pentagon scenario might read as follows. There is an attempted rebellion in Liberia against the pro-American government of President Tubman. A small, mobile American military force secures a beach head and an air field on the Liberian coast. At this time, the men from the air fleet of C5As are matched up with the equipment from the FDLS located in the Gulf of Guinea. By that time, a fleet of 80 C5As has placed 40,000 American military men in Liberia to suppress the rebellion and maintain President Tubman in power. With complete American air superiority in local regions of the third world, this operation could be done swiftly, and there are few revolutionary armies outside of Vietnam that could successfully withstand this preponderance of American power so rapidly brought to bear on a local revolution. The very existence of this force and its threatened use would be a major bulwark for pro-American status quo government throughout the world.

Although we will distinguish between strategic and tactical weapons systems, the reader should not be misled into believing that functions of these systems were completely separate. American strategic power was certainly used in the narrow sense as a deterrent against attack on the United States; but this same system and American superiority were also designed in an attempt to neutralize any Soviet and Chinese military responses to American conventional and unconventional military actions throughout the third world. For example, the willingness of the United States actively to expand the Indochina War in 1970 to Laos and Cambodia was based on the belief that American thermonuclear power would forestall any Soviet or Chinese military response.

Before discussing these two types of systems, the reader should be reminded of the fact that the B-1, the C5A, the TFX, and the Minuteman MIRV are Air Force systems. The Sentinel and Safeguard systems, along with the Cheyenne helicopter and the new super tank were Army systems, while the Navy was pushing during this same period for nuclear carriers, fast-deployment logistic ships, Poseidon, and their own carrier-borne version of a new aircraft. The importance of these facts will become apparent below.

AMERICAN STRATEGIC SUPERIORITY

As has been seen, on a strategic level, the United States entered the period of the Johnson Administration with at least a 4–1 advantage over the Soviet Union in the number of deliverable warheads, and by the end of the Johnson Administration, this same ratio remained, although both sides had engaged in substantial building programs during the interim.[8]

McNamara has claimed that this American superiority was "greater than we had planned" but this is hard to believe in view of the fact that McNamara learned almost immediately upon assuming office that the Soviet Union was not engaged in a large-scale missile-building program and that the missile gap was a fiction. Yet he not only continued but escalated the American missile-building program even after he had learned of the Soviet refusal to build large numbers of first-generation missiles. As seen above, Arthur Schlesinger has argued that the early Kennedy Administration felt that it would not fight the forces of the Pentagon on both missiles and bombers, and therefore chose to resist building a replacement for the B-52 (renamed the B-1 in 1970), but felt compelled to proceed with its escalation of the Minuteman and Polaris building programs in spite of the known limited Soviet activity in missile-building programs. If these are the facts behind America's missile build-up of the 1960s, then it serves not only as an excellent illustration of the power of the military and its industrial allies, but it should also serve as a dire warning of the almost unlimited power exercised by the political/economic/military coalition that governs the United States.

However, it must be admitted that to the very end, Secretary McNamara resisted the forces pushing for the various versions of the B-1 supersonic bomber. General Thomas S. Power had supported this aircraft as early as 1960, and by 1962 the B-1 had the support of the Joint Chiefs of Staff. It is to McNamara's credit that he fought the production of this airplane until he left office.[9] Yet even after such effective resistance, by 1969 Congress had appropriated the initial funds for the production of the B-1. In 1969, the costs of the B-1 were dramatically underestimated at $10 billion for 200 aircraft.[10]

This first B-1 bomber was to be operational by 1977 with an approximate speed of 1,500 miles per hour and a 10,000 mile range. This aircraft went through various designations by the Air Force and at times it was variously called the RB-70, RS-70, the B-70, the Advanced Manned Strategic Aircraft, and finally the B-1. For the purposes of this study, it will be referred to as the B-1.

Significantly, by the time the B-1 received congressional and executive backing, even its most ardent supporters no longer contended that it could function effectively as a bomber—its only function in the 1980s was to be as an additional platform from which to launch air-to-surface missiles. This would mean that the United States was going to spend $30 billion for an additional set of platforms to supplement the over 1,500 existing Minuteman and Polaris-Poseidon platforms.[11]

It should be noted that the major effort by the Air Force for a new platform was accompanied by an Air Force demand for a brand new missile to be launched from this platform. The so-called SRAM, short-range attack missile, which was to replace the now obsolete Hound Dog air-to-surface missile, became a priority item for the Air Force. (The SRAM is the latest in a long list of Air Force air-to-surface missiles, including Crossbow, Rascal, Skybolt—with costs totaling $962.6 million.)

The Air Force drive for the B-1 and SRAM was simply another case of a military service bringing all its substantial influence to pressure the executive and Congress for a given weapons system —a weapons system that was not too significant either in the strategic balance of terror or, except temporarily, as an escalating factor in the arms race. However, if the importance of the new manned bomber was primarily monetary, this *definitely was not* the case in the debate over the ABM-multiple warhead question. These two closely related systems and the continued effort to build them led to an immense escalation of the arms race; maybe even more important, it is possible that with the deployment of these two systems even the slimmest hope for arms limitation agreements may disappear. This debate broke into the open in 1967 and really reached its first crescendo with the decision to provide the funds for the Sentinel and eventually the Safeguard ABM system.

As with all major weapons systems, discussion and argument about them had been taking place at higher government levels years before the public became substantially aware of the major problems involved (if the public became involved at all: it normally does not).*

The significance of the ABM-MIRV debate and the eventual decisions concerning them cannot be overestimated in any assessment of the arms race and the continued development of the strategic doctrine of the United States. These two systems

* This analysis of ABM-MIRV will cover both the Johnson Sentinel system and the Nixon Safeguard system due to the complete overlap in the nature of these systems and the debate that concerned them.

represented an eventual potential expenditure of well over $100 billion and thus were the richest set of potential contracts ever dangled by the Pentagon before the corporations of the United States. In addition to the commitment of resources in such gargantuan amounts, there were also those who believed that the military efficacy of the ABM was of the utmost significance if the United States was to control the world. In the words of Senator Richard Russell (Dem.-Ga.):

> I have often said that I feel that the first country to deploy an effective ABM system and an effective ASW (anti-submarine warfare) system is going to control the world militarily.[12]

The debate over MIRV-ABM systems dominated the late 1960s, and American actions during this period led to another massive escalation in the arms race. Therefore, it is important to understand the exact steps in this escalation. The best place to start is to first look at the comparative strategic weapons systems of the United States and the Soviet Union from 1960 to 1969. Once this is done, an attempt can be made to clarify where the major escalations of building programs came from on both sides. In looking at these comparative figures, the reader should keep in mind that throughout the 1960s, both the United States and the Soviet Union possessed enough stored megatonnage to destroy the entire world several times over and could have built more if they desired to do so. The combined megatonnage of the United States and the Soviet Union was well over 15,000 megatons by the end of the 1960s.

Even a cursory look at these comparative figures leads to several basic conclusions concerning the nature of the arms race during the 1960s.

One, at no time did the Soviet Union maximize its ability to build long-range bombers; they never had even half the number possessed by the United States. Two, at no time did the Soviet Union attempt to maximize the in-flight refueling capacity of its large force of medium bombers so that they could reach the United States. Three, at no time did the Soviet Union build any type of aircraft carrier that would pose a threat to the

COMPARATIVE STRATEGIC STRENGTH—THE
UNITED STATES AND THE SOVIET UNION 1960–1969[*]

1960   At this time neither the United States nor the Soviet Union
had more than a handful of ICBMs.

	UNITED STATES	SOVIET UNION
Long-range Bombers	585 B-52s	150
Medium-range Bombers (in-flight refuel or at foreign bases)	1,100	None capable of reaching the United States
Carrier-based Bombers	400	none
	2,085	150[13]

1962   Vehicles capable of reaching opponent's territory.

	UNITED STATES	SOVIET UNION
Long-range	650 B-52s 55 B-58s	70 Bears Less than 200 Bisons
Medium-range	1,000 B-47s Could reach Soviet territory	1,000 Badgers— Could not reach United States
ICBMs	100 Atlas	Less than 100 ICBMs
	54 Titans	
	20 Minutemen	

[*] The figures cited are taken from official United States government statements, *The New York Times,* and the Institute for Strategic Studies (London). After a number of years of surveying comparative weapons systems
and comparing estimates with official United States government releases,
the author has found the latter two sources to be the most consistently
reliable. The figures listed below are not complete in the sense that they
do not always reflect *all* American delivery systems, and therefore the total
number of delivery vehicles at any given time tends to vary according
to which delivery systems are included in the calculation. The totals
listed below include only those vehicles capable of reaching an opponent's
homeland.

1962   (continued)

	UNITED STATES	SOVIET UNION
Polaris	80	none
Vehicles capable of reaching opponent's homeland	1,959	300[14]

1964	UNITED STATES	SOVIET UNION
Long-range Bombers	540	270
ICBMs	750	200
Polaris	192	60
Thor (being phased out)	45	None near United States
Jupiter (being phased out)	60	None near United States
Vehicles capable of reaching opponent	1,587	530[15]

1966   These figures do not include the Polaris A-3 Multiple Re-entry Vehicles that became operational in 1963–1964.

	UNITED STATES	SOVIET UNION
Long-range Bombers	540	270
ICBMs	800 Minutemen	300
	80 Minutemen II	
	54 Titan	
Polaris	400 (possible MRV missiles)	125
Vehicles capable of reaching opponent	1,874	695[16]

1967   Official figures given by Secretary of Defense McNamara.

	UNITED STATES	SOVIET UNION
ICBM Launchers	1,054	720
SLBM Launchers (submarine-launched ballistic missiles)	656	30
Intercontinental Bombers	697	155

1969   (continued)

	UNITED STATES	SOVIET UNION
Total force loadings, approximate number of warheads	4,500	1,100[17]

1969	UNITED STATES	SOVIET UNION
ICBMs	1,054	1,000
Polaris	656	125
Long-range Bombers	500	150
Aircraft Carriers	23	none
	2,610	1,276[18]

1969   Projections of American missiles with Multiple Independent Re-entry Vehicles or MIRV. (In addition to much of the above firepower.)

UNITED STATES	
170 Minuteman III @ 3 each	510
Minuteman I & II	700
31 subs, 16 missiles @ 10 each	4,960
Single-warhead Minutemen	830
B-52s	500
Total	7,500[19]

security of the United States. Four, at no time during the period under consideration did the Soviet Union deploy more than one third of the Polaris-type missiles deployed by the United States. And, five, until 1966 the Soviet Union appears to have settled for a distinctly inferior position vis-à-vis the United States in the number of ICBMs. But by 1966 they had begun a major building program in ICBMs that would allow them to approach parity with the United States in ICBMs by 1969.

But, obviously, these figures and the above conclusions do not tell the whole complex story behind the arms race of the 1960s. Three fundamental questions remain unanswered. Why did the Soviet Union engage in a large-scale missile-building program in 1966 after accepting missile and bomber inferiority since the inception of the Cold War? What exactly did the Soviet anti-bomber and antimissile programs consist of during this period? And what is the state of development and mission assigned to the Soviet SS-9 and the fledgling Soviet MIRV program for the 1970s? Although these three questions are interrelated, they will be treated separately here in order to clarify an extremely complex set of problems.

Before going into a detailed analysis, it should be emphasized that as the arms race progressed through the 1960s and into the 1970s, the technological advances in weaponry and the complexity of the so-called strategies became even more difficult to understand, and the jargon surrounding these questions almost defies comprehension.

SOVIET ATTITUDES

Early in the decade of the 1960s, the leaders of the Soviet Union began to repeat the mistake they had made earlier during the missile gap period—they started to brag about weapons systems that they did not have and did not plan to build in the immediate future. In 1961, Marshal Malinovsky of the Soviet Union boasted of a Soviet solution to a defense against a missile attack.[20] This claim was followed less than a year later by Premier Khrushchev's famous statement that the Soviet Union had an antimissile missile that "can hit a fly in outer space."[21] These claims were later followed by various Soviet boasts on the capability of their antimissile missiles.[22]

The critical observer can legitimately ask why the Soviet Union would make such claims in view of the predictable American reaction to Soviet claims of superiority in *any* weapons system. And, although no definitive answer can be given, a logical conclusion would be that during this period the Soviet leaders knew that they were far behind the United States in strategic bomber and missile forces and that their bravado was an attempt to create some uncertainty on the part of American leadership as to the ability of the United States to destroy the Soviet retaliatory forces by a surprise attack.

There does not appear to be any doubt that the Soviet Union knew that it was far behind the United States in the arms race in 1962. Published Soviet figures of that year indicated that the United States had 162 ICBMs, 96 Polaris missiles, and projected American strength in 1966 to 1,040 ICBMs and 656 Polaris missiles. Therefore, when Khrushchev admitted in Berlin on January 19, 1963, that the Soviet Union only had 120 missiles capable of reaching the United States, it became obvious that the Soviets realized their inferior position.[23] (At this time, American superiority in numbers of bombers was an accepted fact.) In spite of this recognized inferiority, the leaders of the Soviet Union reduced their military budgetary expenditures for 1963–1964. The military budget was again reduced from 1964 to 1965 from 13.3 billion rubles to 12.8 billion rubles.[24] It was becoming obvious that Soviet leaders were willing to engage in the tricky game of bluff and bluster, but were not willing at this time to allocate a large portion of their resources for ICBMs, much less ABM production—this would come later under even stronger impetus and pressure from the United States.

It would appear that by 1964 the Soviet Union clearly grasped the realities of the balance of terror in the face of a 4–1 American advantage in deliverable warheads. By this time the Soviet Union specifically had rejected thermonuclear war as self-destructive; Mikhail Suslov, party theoretician, had stated that the "task of averting war has become especially urgent." Mr. Suslov, allegedly a "hard-liner" in the Soviet hierarchy, freely admitted that "if a thermonuclear conflict arose, it would be a most terrible tragedy for mankind and would, of course, be a heavy loss to the cause of Communism."[25]

The removal of Premier Khrushchev in 1964 did not substantially alter the belief among Soviet political leaders that there was no chance of "victory" in the event of thermonuclear war. In addition, by 1965, at least temporarily, statements by Soviet spokesmen seemed to reflect a more realistic assessment of the difficulties in producing an effective ABM system. One Soviet spokesman, G. Gerasimov, in the official *International Affairs,* claimed that the development of an ABM system capable of making victory possible would be a discovery ". . . bordering on a miracle." This same author contended that there is "no absolute defense against a missile salvo."[26] A Soviet general, N. Talenskii, wrote in the same journal a year later that it was a "dangerous illusion" that "it is possible to find acceptable forms of nuclear war."[27] The above statements are not intended to demonstrate that the debate over nuclear strategy had ended in the Soviet Union; it did not end in the 1960s and continues to this day. There are still advocates of the "hard-line" and the "soft-line" in the Soviet Union ("hawks" and "doves" in United States terms).

ABM AND MIRV

On the American side, the debate over an antimissile missile had been going on inside the high confines of the government for several years in the late 1950s.* As early as 1957, the United States government had given a contract to Western Electric to develop the Nike-Zeus antimissile system.[28]

In 1959, President Eisenhower conducted the first successful resistance to mounting pressure to install a $14 billion Nike-Zeus system that would have been obsolete before it was operational. When John Kennedy came to office, the pressure continued for the deployment of the Army Nike-Zeus system. This early debate took place before the massive Army build-up for Vietnam, and the ABM seemed to offer the Army a means of obtaining a large chunk of the defense budget that it felt had been denied by the Eisenhower Administration. There does not appear to be any doubt that the Vietnam build-up had the effect of reducing and delaying Army pressure for the ABM.

With the impetus offered by the original Malinovsky and Khrushchev statements, the ABM debate became public for a short time during 1963. Senator Strom Thurmond of South Carolina (at that time a Democrat) contended that the Soviet

---

*Under the Eisenhower Administration the decision had been made to give the Army the mission of air defense in the United States. Until 1958, this mission had been performed by interceptor aircraft and the Nike-Ajax system. By 1959, the Nike Hercules was operational, with an atomic warhead and range of 50–75 miles at altitudes up to 100,000 feet.

Union was building an ABM system around Leningrad and had "a lead of at least several years in the development of an active defense against ballistic missiles."[29] This alleged ABM system around Leningrad was later named the Tallinn Line. At the same time, Edward Teller was using this alleged Soviet ABM system as a reason to oppose the nuclear Test Ban Treaty. Teller further contended:

> An effective defense against ballistic missiles is one of the developments which can upset the strategic balance between the U.S. and the Soviet Union. In this the Soviet Union is at present ahead of us.[30]

In 1963, Dr. Teller did not indicate the unbelievable technical problems involved in the construction of an effective ABM system, nor did he indicate just how distant in the future, if at all, such a development might lie. Reports of the Soviet ABM system around Leningrad continued, and pressure mounted for an American ABM system.[31]

The conviction that the Soviet Union was building an ABM system around Leningrad was one of the most significant and misunderstood aspects of the arms race of the 1960s, and the continued impetus given to the arms race by this belief is still being felt. It was this belief, in part, which gave the rationalization for the American decision to equip the Polaris submarines with Multiple Re-entry Vehicles (MRV) when they became available (see below), created stronger pressure for the development of a more sophisticated American bomber, and led to demands for an increase in American ICBM and ABM programs.

By 1966 the pressures on the President to build an ABM in response to the Soviet Tallinn Line were increasing. The Army claimed that their ABM system (now the Nike X) would definitely work and would cost *only* about $8.5 to $10 billion. For this investment, the Army claimed that 25 American cities would be protected.[32] The Army claims for the Nike X were incorrect, and President Johnson successfully resisted these initial pressures for the Nike X. Three years later under President Nixon it would be admitted that American cities could not be defended against a Soviet missile attack. Yet this did not prevent the Army and the new President from successfully renaming the ABM system and claiming that it would protect American Minutemen sites. But, once again, if these sites were really as *vulnerable* as Nixon and the Army claimed, then they were obsolete and would eventually be replaced by Poseidon launchers or some other invulnerable system. Though not then named, this was to be the so-called window of vulnerability.

By 1967, Nixon and the Republicans increased the demands for an ABM system; this pressure promised to play an important role in the 1968 Presidential campaign, reminiscent of the missile gap in the 1960 election. President Johnson could not stop his critics: the easiest way to silence them was to go ahead with the deployment of a limited ABM system—the Sentinel. In November 1967 this decision was made by the Johnson Administration, and a reluctant McNamara attempted to sell the Sentinel system to the American people. It is interesting to note that even this effort by President Johnson did not prevent Nixon from developing a "security gap" theme in the 1968 campaign.[33]

Nonetheless, by the mid-1960s the American belief that the Soviet Union had begun to deploy an ABM system around Leningrad had given an added rationale to the following developments:

(1) Increased demands for the B-70 bomber
(2) Increased demands for a larger American ICBM program
(3) Increased demands for an American ABM system
(4) And, finally, demands for the deployment of Multiple Re-entry Vehicles (MRV) on the Polaris A-3 missile.*

---

* At this point the distinction between a multiple re-entry vehicle (MRV) and a multiple independent re-entry vehicle (MIRV) must be made. In both cases a single missile carries multiple warheads; normally the multiple warhead has three or more nuclear weapons. Also, the number of weapons in a given warhead varies from three to fifteen.

Multiple Re-entry Vehicle (MRV)—The multiple warhead on this type of system is *not* independently targeted. For example, a MRV with three warheads aimed at New York City would hit the city in the same manner

There was a fundamental fallacy in the American decision to increase its offensive or defensive strength in the face of the alleged Soviet ABM system around Leningrad. *The Tallinn Line was not an ABM system, but a new antibomber system* being built by the Soviet Union in response to increased sophistication of American bomber penetration devices and the very real possibility that the United States was going to enter into large-scale production of a new intercontinental, supersonic bomber—the B-1. (The Soviet Union had no comparable bomber.)

By 1967, the American intelligence community was split over the exact mission of the Tallinn Line—with the CIA claiming that it was antibomber and the DIA (Defense Intelligence Agency) still claiming that the system was an ABM system. (The DIA was created by President Kennedy to avoid confusion in the American intelligence community.) By 1968, Secretary of Defense McNamara officially admitted that the Tallinn Line

---

as a shotgun blast sprayed over a target, with each warhead striking somewhere in the general New York metropolitan area, but not specifically aimed at any given section of the city. Needless to say this type of attack would destroy New York as a functioning metropolis. The MRV is a technologically primitive system in that it is much easier to develop than the more complex multiple independent re-entry vehicle. It should be emphasized that although the MRV is an extremely effective weapon to destroy cities, it is not accurate enough to destroy an underground, hardened missile silo; therefore it is a counter-city weapon and is of little use in a first-strike surprise attack.

Multiple Independent Re-entry Vehicle (MIRV)—In this system, each warhead can be targeted independently. For example, a Minuteman III missile has three warheads per missile with an explosive power of 200–400 kilotons for each warhead. If New York was attacked with this system, an attacker could program the three warheads to strike Manhattan, Queens, and Brooklyn and be certain that they would strike their target. However, as this system's accuracy is further refined, it will be possible to aim one of the three warheads at the Empire State building and be assured of hitting within 500 feet of the building, with equal accuracy for the other two warheads. A system this accurate could obviously be used to try and destroy an underground missile silo. Therefore, the real danger of MIRV is that it is a potential first-strike weapon that could destroy an enemy's capability to retaliate. As the United States deployed this weapon, it was certain to appear as a threat to Soviet retaliatory systems.

was not an ABM system but an antibomber system.[34] This very fundamental mistake on the part of American intelligence analysis has passed almost unnoticed during the major debates on the arms race of the 1960s. The only authority this author knows of to correctly assess the importance of this mistake has been I. F. Stone. (*See I. F. Stone's Weekly,* June 16, 1969.)

By 1966, the Soviet Union had almost stopped its deployment of strategic weapons at approximately 250 ICBMs, roughly 200 long-range bombers, and 150 submarine-launched missiles. At the same time the United States had reached its goals of 1,000 Minuteman ICBMs and 650 Polaris missiles, along with 500 B-52 strategic bombers.[35] If both sides had stopped here, it is possible that the Soviets would have accepted American superiority in view of the guaranteed destructive power represented by the Soviet second-strike system. But this was not the case.

The belief in the Tallinn Line, the increased tensions brought about by the expansion of the American war in Vietnam, and the normal economic-military forces at work in the United States seemed to dictate another major escalation of the arms race, in spite of the guaranteed security of the United States from a surprise attack due to its overwhelming superiority. There was no way that the inferior Soviet system could threaten to destroy the dispersed and hardened American delivery systems with a 4–1 American advantage. It was technologically impossible.

Nonetheless, in the mid-1960s, the United States decided to build the F-111 (TFX) with its mixed tactical and strategic mission,[36] work continued on the B-1, the commitment to the development of ABM-MIRV was solidified; and most important, somewhere between 1963 and 1964 the Polaris submarine-launched A-3 (MRV) missile had been deployed.

The decision to deploy MRVs on submarines has been one of the best kept secrets of the United States government, but deployment apparently took place sometime in 1963–1964. The reasons for the secrecy are fairly obvious. First, the American government could not be sure if Soviet intelligence was aware of this deployment or not. Since the United States was increasing a superiority that already verged on a first-strike capacity, there was no reason to further frighten the Soviet Union by informing them of this threatening increase in American power. Likewise, in the face of the American superiority, the deployment of such a system might have raised questions in the United States as to the wisdom of such needless escalation of the arms race. It is this writer's opinion that it would be unwise to underestimate the ability of the Soviet intelligence activities; the Soviet Union probably knew of the deployment of MRV. If so, then the major reason for keeping the deployment of MRV secret was to prevent Congress and the people from learning of this escalation of the arms race.

I. F. Stone claims that the United States deployed MRV by the mid-1960s.[37] By 1969, there was a substantial amount of evidence to indicate that at least ten Polaris submarines were equipped with MRVs.[38] To the best of the author's knowledge, the United States government never did indicate the exact date American submarines were equipped with MRV missiles. However, the apparent fact that the United States has already put multiple re-entry vehicles on at least ten of its submarines is significant in itself. Even if each of these MRV missiles has only three warheads instead of the 10 warheads per missile scheduled for the Poseidon, this still represents an increase of from 160 to 480 warheads for ten submarines.

But the real significance of the U.S. development of an operational MRV goes far beyond the quantitative number of warheads the United States can deliver on Russia or China. The real significance is in the technology itself. It is known that the MRV is much easier to develop and produce than the more sophisticated MIRV. By June 1970, the United States operational MIRVs on the Minuteman III and, by October, MIRVs were operational on Poseidon-equipped submarines.[39] As the United States deployed MIRV, it became more and more apparent *that the Soviet Union was just beginning to test MIRV warheads and was at least 24 to 48 months from deploying its first operational MIRV missile.*[40] (Deployed in 1977.)

If, in truth, the Soviet Union had just begun to test MIRV, then Russia was from five to seven years from the deployment of an independently targeted multiple warhead. If so, and there is substantial evidence that it is so, then the American decision to deploy MIRV in 1970 was not only the most recent massive American escalation of the arms race, but the United States was also guilty of purposely sabotaging the Strategic Arms Limitations Talks (SALT).

THE SOVIET REACTION

There is no doubt that the United States purposely escalated the arms race by putting MIRV into operation seven years ahead of the Soviet Union and at a time when the Soviets had just begun MIRV testing. And, there can be no doubt that the combination of American military programs and actions in the mid-1960s could not fail to produce a reaction on the part of the Soviet Union. No major thermonuclear power, faced with what it perceived as an implacable and strategically superior enemy, could afford to ignore the development of the F-111 supersonic fighter-bomber, the introduction of MRV into the American arsenal, the planned introduction of MIRV, and the decision to deploy an ABM system.

In addition to the challenge to the Soviet Union represented by the development of these American weapons systems, the massive escalation of the war in Vietnam in 1965–1966 raised serious questions in the minds of Soviet leadership as to the rationality of American leaders in the conduct of their foreign policy. This point has been well substantiated by William Zimmerman in his book, *Soviet Perspectives on International Relations, 1956–1967*. As early as September 1965 this feeling began to appear in Soviet thinking, and by 1966 A. N. Shelepin stated: "The events and facts of recent years show that the American imperialists are conducting themselves increasingly irrationally. . . ."[41]

In the face of an American arms escalation and of perceived American irrationality, the leaders of the Soviet Union could repond in only one manner consistent with the security requirements of the Soviet Union—build up their strategic forces to the point where there was *no chance* of them being destroyed by an American first strike; this is exactly what they proceeded to do. Starting in 1966, the Soviet Union possessed only 250 ICBMs (opposed to over 1,000 for the United States), but by mid-1967 they had increased this force to 570, and by 1968 they were credited with having 900 of these missiles. By 1969, the Soviet Union was given credit for having achieved "parity" with the United States in ICBMs, but *not* in the area of long-range bombers (United States, 500; Soviet Union, 150), *not* in Polaris-type missiles (656 to 125), and *not* in carrier-launched fighter-bombers (United States approximately 400; Soviet Union, none). Soviet "parity" existed only in the field of ICBMs, and in all other areas the United States maintained a distinctive superiority.[42]

Earlier, the question had been asked, Why did the Soviet Union engage in a large-scale missile-building program in 1966 after accepting missile and bomber inferiority since the inception of the Cold War? It appears that the answer must be that by 1966–1967 the United States had not only maintained a substantial nuclear superiority but also that reasonable projections of planned or anticipated systems would lead an objective observer to the conclusion that the future strength of the United States would be so great that it *might* destroy the entire retaliatory force of the Soviet Union in a single, surprise attack.

It is also necessary to point out the nature of the Soviet ABM effort during the 1960s. By 1968, it had been firmly established that the initial Soviet system around Leningrad (the Tallinn Line) was an antibomber system and not an ABM system as claimed throughout most of the decade. By 1969, it appeared as though the *entire* Soviet ABM system which had caused such a strong reaction on the part of the United States consisted of the Soviet Galosh system around Moscow with nothing around Leningrad. This system consisted of 67 obsolete Nike-Zeus-type ABMs that apparently even the Soviet Union had realized were worthless (evidence indicated that they had ceased building this system). By this time the United States had abandoned the Nike-Zeus system and was working on Sentinel, and was clearly ahead of the Soviet Union in ABM technology.[43]

The final question asked earlier in this chapter concerned the highly complex nature of the American and Soviet developments in the evolving technology of multiple warheads. Apparently, the United States had begun to deploy the simpler MRV around 1966. As early as 1965, the contract for MIRV had been given to Boeing, and in August 1968 the United States had tested its first MIRV. This placed the United States at least two years ahead of the Soviet Union in MIRV technology. (The first Soviet MIRV test did not occur until 1970, at the earliest.) Quietly and unobtrusively, the Johnson Administration had deployed an operational MRV system and had placed the initial contracts for MIRV before the public was even aware of the existence of these weapons systems.[44]

NIXON AND LAIRD

Thus, by the time the Nixon Administration assumed office, the United States had a demonstrable superiority over the Soviet Union in missiles and bombers. Likewise, the United States had an undetermined but substantial technological "lead-time" advantage over the Soviet Union in the development of ABM and MIRV systems.

In the face of this known Soviet inferiority American escalation of the arms race continued without regard to political party, personal philosophy, or White House occupant.

The election of Nixon in 1968 did not upset or change the Pentagon's plans for the future of the arms race. Nixon had attempted to gain campaign mileage in 1968 from a nonexistent security gap, and if there were any doubts as to where he stood on defense spending, these were immediately dispelled by his attempt to make super-hawk Senator Henry Jackson (Dem.-Wash., location of Boeing Aircraft) his Secretary of Defense. When Jackson refused, he appointed Melvin Laird. For any who might have had any doubts about the attitudes of this Wisconsin member of the House of Representatives, a brief look at his book—*A House Divided: America's Strategy Gap*—served to quiet any fears that a critic of the Pentagon had been made Secretary of Defense.[45]

There is a curious, tragic logic to the appointment of Laird to the position of Secretary of Defense in the Nixon Administration. Since World War II a number of very different men had held this post—sensitive men, ardent businessmen, and a plain systems manager. But with the appointment of Laird, the first military man in civilian clothes was made Secretary of Defense —a man whose career has epitomized what the Pentagon and the Department of Defense have come to represent. At a time when the balance of thermonuclear terror was becoming obvious to all but the most obtuse, this man stated:

> Step one of a military strategy of initiative should be the credible announcement of our determination to strike first if necessary to protect our vital interests.[46]

However, the appointment of Laird was not so strange. He joined a chief executive who during the campaign had promised to put together just such a mythical first-strike force when he stated: "I intend to restore our objective of clear-cut military superiority."[47]

Lest there be any doubts as to the definition of America's "vital interests," Assistant Secretary of Defense Robert Moot defined them in the now traditional immodest terms:

> Our national interests extend across the North Atlantic in Western Europe, and the Mediterranean, south into the Caribbean and Westward in the Pacific countries bordering thereon.[48]

With a promise to "restore" American military superiority and a rather broad definition of American national interests, the Nixon Administration began by picking up where Johnson had left off on the development of ABM and MIRV systems.

The first military appropriation fight faced by the Nixon Administration was the effort to get through Congress the initial appropriation for Phase I of the newly named Safeguard ABM system. It was contended that this system was needed to protect about 350 Minuteman sites from a surprise Soviet attack that might destroy the missiles in their silos. Initial cost was estimated at $12 billion. The fact that the United States had a 4–1 delivery advantage over the Soviet Union was discreetly ignored by the proponents of the Phase I Safeguard or rationalized by some vague future Soviet threat. Likewise, the fact that the ABM (even if it worked) would in all probability be defending empty holes in the ground was also not extensively discussed. Nonetheless, although the fight for the funding for Safeguard was the most intense debate in the history of the arms race, the Senate finally voted the initial appropriation for Phase I Safeguard in 1969.

In 1970, it was predictable that the Nixon Administration would want to expand the Safeguard system. The Administration made the decision to proceed with Phase II of Safeguard. Phase II called for a partial shift of the fundamental rationale for Safeguard from primary protection of American Minuteman sites to the eventual protection of American cities against a Chinese missile attack. Phase II called for a third ABM complex to protect another Minuteman complex near Whiteman Air Force Base in Missouri and planned for five additional ABM sites across the country.[49]

There are serious doubts that an ABM system will work at all, but even if it did function with a relatively high degree of efficiency, *an ABM system would not be needed to deter a Soviet attack on American Minuteman sites* and would be useless against a determined Soviet attack on American cities. The very existence of a large, dispersed, and hidden American Polaris fleet with over 650 missiles means that no matter what happened to American Minuteman sites, the Soviet Union would be destroyed (100 Polaris missiles would be a sufficient deterrent). This submarine missile force could not be simultaneously found and destroyed by Soviet antisubmarine warfare methods or systems known at the present time or predicted for the future. As the director of Navy Strategic Systems Projects, Rear Admiral Levin Smith, has stated: "The Russians have no specific new antisubmarine warfare methods the Navy knows of that would make the Polaris fleet vulnerable to attack. . . ."[50] Likewise, even as the Soviet Union developed the SS-9 missile and MIRVed it in large quantities, as the American government predicted,

Minuteman silos would then be obsolete because of their vulnerability—if the Minuteman missiles were intended to "ride out" a
first strike. In the face of this obsolescence, the United States
would simply escalate the arms race one more step. One example
of this would be deployment of an Underwater Long-range
Missile System (ULMS—$44 million was requested for this
system by Secretary Laird for 1971) under the Great Lakes or
within the twelve-mile limit. Thus, it would appear that the
deployment of an ABM system to protect Minuteman sites
simply did not make sense.

But in moving from Phase I to Phase II, Mr. Nixon's confused rhetoric also indicated that Phase II would be designed
also to protect American cities from a Chinese attack. Mr. Nixon
claimed that such a thin defense was "absolutely essential" if
the United States was to have a "credible foreign policy" in the
Pacific.[51] He further contended that such an American system
would be "virtually infallible" against a Chinese missile attack.
And it is here that is found the real significance of the decision
to escalate the American ABM system. By claiming that the
American Safeguard system would be designed and built (at
least in part) for the protection of cities against a Chinese
attack, not only are the past assumptions of the Cold War arms
race revealed, but also the future nature of this conflict are
made crystal clear. In effect, Mr. Nixon revealed:

(1) That in the future the Chinese would be considered a
threat to American security;

(2) That in order to keep American policy in the Pacific
"credible," the United States would attempt to practice nuclear
blackmail on China for as long as possible;

(3) That in the future the arms race would be conducted with
the Soviet Union and China and that American domination of
the Pacific area would be accomplished by "absolute" protection
of the United States from Chinese attack. By the mid-1980s this
was becoming an impossible task.

(4) And, finally, that the acceptance of the belief that the
Chinese would commit national suicide by attacking the United

States with 25 or 100 missiles indicated that either the Administration believed that the government of China was completely irrational or that the Administration was willing to perpetuate this myth to achieve its desired goals* (in this case, obtaining the funds for Phase II of the Safeguard System).

At this point, it appeared as though the United States was in the process of defining a new major "enemy" in the Cold War and the arms race. China had intervened in Korea. And, as the United States prepared to escalate the air war in Indochina, there was considerable uncertainty as to whether the Chinese would intervene in the Vietnam War. By raising the specter of a Chinese threat, the Nixon Administration could obtain funding for its ABM programs and at the same time warn China of the nuclear dangers of intervention into the war. The message was clear: American dominance in the Pacific could not be challenged without serious nuclear risks to China. As will be seen in the next chapter, the Chinese did not intervene in Indochina and seem to have been willing to sacrifice their interests in the Vietnamese revolution in order to obtain a rapprochement with the United States government. Nixon's 1972 trip to China assured Chinese nonintervention and, at least temporarily, China was no longer touted as an enemy of the United States.

In 1970, the Chinese thermonuclear threat to the United States could not be made credible; at the same time, the Soviet Union still possessed a formidable thermonuclear capacity. A potential lull in the arms race loomed, and it appeared essential to keep the Soviet threat alive for the foreseeable future. Thus, Mr. Nixon's protection of the Minuteman sites, and even more important, the American decision to deploy MIRV on the Minuteman III and the Poseidon. Since there was no way that MIRV could be explained as an answer to the nonexistent Chinese intercontinental delivery system in early 1970, the only

---

* In 1968, Secretary McNamara stated: "We estimated, that a relatively small number of warheads detonated over 50 Chinese cities would destroy half of the urban population (more than 50 million people) and more than one-half of the industrial capacity." See U.S. Congress, Senate, *Authorization for Military Procurement, 1969*, 90th Cong., 2d sess., February 2, 1968, p. 113.

possible justification for this system was the Soviet threat. For forty years American leadership has predicted huge Soviet arms-building programs and imminent Soviet attacks. These false predictions had evidently deadened many congressmen and Americans to the reality of the Soviet willingness to annihilate itself by attacking the United States.

The proponents in the United States government of installing the ABM-MIRV systems followed the new classic pattern of making a case for their multibillion–dollar system. Obviously, it was assumed by these advocates that most Americans would have forgotten the earlier fiascos of the bomber gap, the missile gap, and the Tallinn Line.

First, key officials projected the Soviet Union as a reckless and dangerous opponent that might strike at any time. For example, in 1969 Senator Henry Jackson (Dem.-Wash.) characterized the Soviet Union as "a dangerous, unpredictable opponent" with a "growing military capability."[52] This common liturgy of the Cold War is so well worn and unchallenged (at least until recently) that the cold warriors of America have only to pay it basic lip service to trigger an almost Pavlovian reaction among some Americans.

In the second stage, American leaders invoked the great strength of this "dangerous, unpredictable opponent" and cited the unbelievable *capability* of the Russians to do whatever they say the Soviet will do. Thus, Secretary Laird claimed that the Soviet Union had deployed more than 230 SS-9 missiles and that they had the *capability* to build 420 by 1975.

In Laird's struggle for more funds for the B-1, the Underwater Long-range Missile System, the ABM system, and others, the Secretary of Defense released classified information on the Soviet SS-9 missile. This new terror weapon could carry approximately 20–25 megatons and was capable of carrying MIRV. But what Secretary Laird did not indicate was that the SS-9 was not much more powerful than the American Operational Titan missile (10 megatons) and that the SS-9 with its roughly 12,000 pounds of thrust was almost insignificant when compared with American Saturn Rocket (1,500,000 pounds of thrust). If the United States had wanted larger rockets for MIRV or higher yield warheads, the technology for them had been available since the early 1960s. The United States had simply decided that the destructive power of a number of low yield weapons spread accurately over the same area would accomplish more destruction than one large warhead. Likewise, American rockets were more accurate than their Soviet counterparts and therefore did not have to deliver as heavy a payload to accomplish the same mission.*

Mr. Laird claimed that these SS-9 missiles would be equipped with "multiple warheads" but failed to distinguish between MIRV and MRV—or put another way, between whether this system was a counter-city MRV and therefore not a first-strike weapon or a counter-force MIRV and therefore capable of a first strike.[53] The director of research at the Pentagon, Dr. John S. Foster, joined his boss and predicted that by 1975 the Soviet Union would have the *capability* with 500 SS-9s to destroy 90 percent of the American ICBM force.[54] (This 90 percent figure

---

* The problem of whether to emphasize missile accuracy or high yield warheads is basically a question of the technology available. Due to the fact that the United States has always led the Soviet Union in missile accuracy, the United States chose to emphasize this characteristic rather than developing high yield warheads for its missiles. The official rationale for this decision is offered below by Secretary McNamara:

> Gross megatonnage is not a reliable indicator of the destructive power of an offensive force. For example, one missile carrying ten 50 kiloton warheads (a yield of ½ megaton) would be just as effective against a large city (2 million people) as a single 10 megaton warhead with 20 times the total yield.

Mr. McNamara continued:

> Even against hard ICBM sites, the ten 50 kiloton warheads would (*given the accuracy we anticipate* [emphasis added]) be more effective than a single 10 megaton warhead. And, of course, it would take 10 times as many ABM interceptors to defend a city against ten 50 kiloton warheads as it would against a single 10 megaton warhead.

See: U.S. Congress, Senate, *Authorization for Military Procurement, 1969,* 90th Cong., 2d sess. (February 2, 1968), p. 114. The above statement by Secretary McNamara goes a long way toward explaining the official reasons why the United States government decided to deploy massive numbers of MIRVd missiles.

was roughly the same figure used during the missile gap for the destruction of American deterrent forces.)

The congressional testimony of the Department of Defense left some disturbing questions unanswered:

(1) The Minuteman missile can be fired sixty seconds after the decision is made to fire it. The Ballistic Missile Early Warning System (BMEWS) and reconnaissance satellites guarantee between 15 and 20 minutes warning time in the event of an attack. If the United States received warning of an attack that would destroy 90 percent of the existing Minuteman force (well over 2,000 incoming warheads), why should not the United States launch some of these Minutemen (leaving empty holes to be attacked) and save the Polaris system as a reserve?

(2) Or, conversely, even if a majority of the Minuteman forces were destroyed, there is no known method by which the Soviet Union could track and destroy the 41 subs carrying over 650 Polaris missiles. This force alone is a more than adequate deterrent to a Soviet attack on any part of the United States.

But such questions did not prevent Secretary Laird from persevering in his attempt to gain the funds he wanted for the ABM and MIRV systems. The tried and true method of accomplishing this goal was to frighten the American people, and the best way to do this was to invoke the fear of a Soviet surprise attack on the United States. That is exactly what Secretary Laird did when he stated that there was no doubt that the Soviets ". . . are going for a first strike capability."[55] To support this position, Mr. Laird pulled out the stops before the Senate Foreign Relations Committee and claimed that:

(1) The Soviet Union was going forward with a new sophisticated ABM system.

(2) The Soviets were outspending the United States on strategic weapons by a 3–1 advantage.

(3) The Soviets were undertaking a crash program to overtake the United States in atomic submarines by 1974.

(4) The Soviet Union was deploying Fractional Orbiting Bombardment system (a counter-city, not counter-force system).

And, for good measure, Mr. Laird assured the committee that the Chinese would test fire an ICBM in the next 18–20 months and would have an imposing 25 ICBMs by 1974–1975.[56]

Along with Laird's decision to "release" secret information on the existence of the SS-9 and the American projections of the future numbers of these missiles, could anyone doubt that the United States was indeed in dire peril of surprise attack by Soviet Russia? The basic difference between Mr. Laird's approach and that of earlier advocates of "American superiority" was the degree of paranoia and hysteria that characterized Mr. Laird's attempt to sell his weapons system to the United States Congress and the American people. If Mr. Laird had ever faltered in his earlier ideas expressed in *America's Strategy Gap,* he had obviously returned to them. He believed that the only way to deal with the Soviet threat was based on "American superiority" and that to even allow "parity" would eventually lead to the "military occupation of the United States."[57]

While this standard Cold War perception of the Soviet Union was once again outlined by the Nixon Administration, simultaneously it was allegedly attempting to negotiate in good faith at the Strategic Arms Limitation Talks (SALT) in Vienna. In spite of strong congressional pressure, the Administration refused to freeze deployment of either the Safeguard system or MIRV system. But, as opposed to the initial deployment of Safeguard, the decision to proceed with the Minuteman III and Poseidon systems represented an immediate and serious threat to the balance of terror and world peace.

The United States decision to proceed with the MIRV system once again raised the specter of America preparing for a first strike against the Soviet Union. Once accurate multiple independently targeted warheads were placed on Minuteman and Poseidon, it would be impossible to tell exactly the number of warheads that the United States could deliver. Before the American deployment of MIRV, the United States had a delivery capability great enough to strike *each* Soviet missile and bomber site roughly three times, with enough left over to destroy all major Soviet cities. After the United States deployed its MIRV missiles, the threat of an American first strike did increase immeasurably.

Further complicating the picture was the basic fact that the early MRV system was fundamentally a counter-city system with limited accuracy. The independently targeted warheads (MIRV) were approaching a counter-force weapons system, and there is no doubt that the planned ARV (Advanced Reentry Vehicle) with its own propulsion system and preplanned evasive action against possible ABM defense could definitely be used as a first-strike weapon on Soviet missile sites.

The Union of Concerned Scientists of MIT concluded:

> The tremendous effort being expended to improve the accuracy of the guidance system of the Poseidon and Minuteman III missiles suggests that the mission of these weapons is for silo busting, not for deterrence.[58]

Mr. Nixon's contention in early 1970 that no efforts would be made to improve the accuracy of the American MIRV system was hard to believe. That the American military services would stop improving the accuracy of weapons they were testing anyhow seemed improbable. But even if this were the case, it would take a high degree of gullibility on the part of Soviet leaders to believe this without firm evidence to the contrary.

The situation was further complicated by the fact that the United States was simultaneously undertaking an extensive project of re-enforcing its Minuteman sites to withstand 900 psi (pounds of pressure per square inch). This increase in psi represented the capability to withstand three times the pressure of the earlier re-enforced silos to withstand 250–300 psi. The new Minuteman sites required almost a direct hit by a four megaton weapon to be destroyed. Likewise, the command center for the Minuteman (each controlling 10 missiles) were re-enforced to withstand pressure of up to 7,000 psi. This project was begun under the Johnson Administration and continued under Mr. Nixon.[59]

Along with the increased hardening of Minuteman silos, evidence appeared of increases in the American intelligence effort over the Soviet Union. Ever since the downing of the U-2 aircraft in 1960, the United States had relied on the use of satellites for intelligence information concerning the Soviet Union, including the location of Soviet airfields and missile sites. By 1970, the United States had launched 280 military satellites compared to about 160 launched by the Soviet Union.[60]

Likewise, the United States had been engaged in a much more extensive underground nuclear testing program than had the Soviet Union since the signing of the Test Ban Treaty in 1963. The Atomic Energy Commission reported that since the test ban, the United States had conducted 186 "announced tests" compared to 28 for the Soviet Union—six and one-half times more than the number of Soviet tests.[61]

As evidence began to mount on the American capability for a possible first strike against the Soviet Union, it became apparent that the next phase of the Safeguard system (Phase II) would be designed, if it worked, to prevent a second strike by the Soviet Union on American cities. And, as Ralph Lapp pointed out, "Anything that erodes Soviet second-strike capability must be viewed as very provocative."[62]

But the final and most frightening aspect of the MIRV system was the actual increase in the number of warheads the United States would be able to deliver accurately on Soviet targets by missiles alone. In February 1968, Mr. McNamara issued his final "posture statement" on the defense position of the United States. In 1968, Mr. McNamara claimed that the United States had more than a 3–1 lead over the Soviet Union in the ability to deliver thermonuclear warheads, and by 1973 the United States would increase the number of deliverable warheads by five times. Mr. McNamara's 1968 figures did not include the American fighter-bombers in Europe and other locations, or the aircraft on American aircraft carriers. His figures for deliverable warheads in 1968 were as follows:

	UNITED STATES	SOVIET UNION
ICBMs	1,054	720
Submarine-launched Missiles	656	30
Intercontinental Bombers	697	155
Total force loadings, approximate number of *warheads*	4,500	1,000[63]

According to Mr. McNamara, once the MIRV system was complete in 1973, the United States would have:

> 3,000 Minuteman Warheads (three 300 kiloton warheads per Minuteman III)
>
> 4,960 Poseidon Submarine-launched Missiles (31 submarines, with 16 missiles each at 10 MIRVd warheads per missile)
>
> 160 Polaris Submarine-launched Missiles
>
> 54 Titan II

Total warheads 8,174

In addition, by 1973, the United States was scheduled to have 281 B-52 bombers and 253 FB-111 (fighter-bombers).[64] The Nixon Administration continued all of these programs.

By 1970, the Soviet Union had only 50 cities the size of Hiroshima and only 200 cities with a population over 100,000. According to Secretary McNamara the delivery of only 400 single megaton warheads on the Soviet Union would be enough to destroy over one third of the population and over three fourths of Soviet industry.[65] If this is the damage that 400 megatons could do to the Soviet Union, then it seems pointless to speculate as to the

SOVIET POPULATION* AND INDUSTRY DESTROYED

Number of Single Megaton Delivered Warheads	Total Population Fatalities†	Percent	Industrial Capacity Destroyed
100	37,000,000	15	59 percent
200	52,000,000	21	72
400	74,000,000	30	76
800	96,000,000	39	77
1200	109,000,000	44	77
1600	116,000,000	47	77

* An urban population of 116 million is assumed for the year 1972.
† Fatalities are calculated on the basis of "prompt response"—i.e., death within 24 hours.

effect of the delivery of the 10,000 megatons that the United States had stored and ready to deliver. Nonetheless, below is Secretary McNamara's estimate of what the delivery of up to 1,600 warheads would do to the Soviet population and its industrial capacity.[66]

When the above weapons system and projections for the future are analyzed, at least one major question emerges in the mind of either a Soviet or American analyst. If 100 warheads would kill 37 million Soviet citizens within the *first* 24 hours of hostilities, and if 400 warheads would increase this toll to 74 million Russians, why did the United States feel compelled to increase the number of deliverable missile warheads from 1,700 to over 8,000? This type of overkill does not represent a deterrent force, it represents a potential first-strike system, and it would be illogical to assume that the Soviet leaders would believe anything else.

In view of Soviet inferiority and the past history of the arms race, the argument that the Soviet Union had the capability to build comparable ABM-MIRV systems and therefore would build these systems simply does not hold up. That the Soviet Union had the *capability* to build toward a bomber gap or a missile gap has never been denied. The simple fact is that they chose not to maximize production of these systems, but to build only those forces felt essential to deter an attack on the Soviet Union. When the Soviet Union finally did engage in large-scale missile production, it was in response to a threatening American superiority in *all* strategic weapons systems. Likewise, the fact that eventually the Soviet Union could build some type of ABM and MIRV systems is not the question. The United States proceeded with its deployment of MIRV missiles and by 1975 had nearly 8,000 warheads in operation, while the Soviet Union was only in the initial stages of deploying its early version of MIRV warheads. Once again the impetus and initiative for a major escalation of the arms race had come from the United States.

The leaders of the Soviet Union had to consider the possibility that the American arms programs were geared for a future surprise attack on the Soviet Union, or at a minimum aimed at nuclear blackmail of Soviet diplomacy throughout the world.

As of 1970, Soviet leaders were faced with an American military posture that included:

(1) The large number of increasingly accurate American MIRV missiles would constitute a real threat to the Soviet ability to retaliate.

(2) The continued improvement and effort in the American intelligence effort could pinpoint all Soviet military targets for destruction.

(3) The large number of American underground nuclear tests could give the United States an important advantage in nuclear technology.

(4) The hardened American Minuteman missiles could survive any Soviet retaliatory strike and then hold Soviet cities as hostages should the Soviet Union fail to surrender.

(5) The American attempt to build an effective ABM system *might* endanger the certainty that the Soviet Union deterrent force could get through on a second strike.

(6) The continued American military efforts in Vietnam to win an unwinnable war.

Faced with increasing American superiority, the Soviet Union was forced to escalate its own arms program. During the 1970s, the Soviet Union developed and deployed MIRVs. Then, just as the leaders of the United States had cited the 1970 Soviet achievement of ICBM "parity" as proof of their wisdom in the 1960s, the Soviet MIRV program of the 1970s was cited as further evidence of their inherent wisdom. There has never been a better example of a self-fulfilling prophecy.

VI

The 1970s: Turbulence in American Foreign Policy

The 1970s was a difficult and frustrating time for those Americans who believed that the United States should be able to control the world. The war in Vietnam shattered the United States' omnipotent self-image. Periodic oil crises (the first in 1973) seriously challenged U.S. control of Third World raw materials. Diplomatic turmoil and military confusion increased in Europe. And the Soviet Union appeared to challenge American nuclear superiority.

In 1968, President Nixon had inherited a professed strategic doctrine of mutually assured destruction (MAD) that called for only the minimum level of nuclear forces necessary to deter a Soviet attack on the United States. At the same time, however, the United States had continued to improve its nuclear forces. By 1970, it was beginning to deploy multiple independent re-entry vehicles (MIRV) on its missiles at a time when the Soviet Union had just begun to test MIRVs. By the end of the decade the United States held its advantage over the Soviet Union in deliverable warheads despite the Strategic Arms Limitation Agreement and a Soviet ICBM modernization program. But without a conventional interventionary military force and, more important, the willingness to use this force, the United States could not translate its superiority in nuclear hardware into real global power.

The major problem facing American policy makers during the 1970s was the impact of the loss of the Vietnam War. The national consensus that had dominated American foreign policy since the end of World War II had disintegrated. This "Vietnam syndrome" undermined the former automatic and bipartisan support for American adventurism abroad.[1] Although widespread disagreement on the means used to implement American policy emerged after the Vietnam War, the underlying goals of American policy were never challenged. Ten years after the end of the war, a Gallup Poll indicated that 63 percent of the American people still thought that American involvement in the war had been a mistake, and 75 percent favored a more cautious use of military force overseas.[2] Yet during these years, opportunities to retreat from interventionism and to redefine the goals of American foreign policy were ignored. American policy makers simply attempted to reconstitute the national consensus lost during the war without changing the policies and assumptions that had led to the war in the first place. So powerful were the forces released by the war in Vietnam that by the end of the 1970s the United States was just beginning to reassert its national power and to launch an aggressive foreign policy based on the threatened use of nuclear and conventional military power.

VIETNAM: THE FAILURE OF AMERICAN FOREIGN POLICY

Probably no other event in recent American history has caused as much controversy or has been as divisive as the war in Vietnam. It is important to recognize that the war in Vietnam was not a mistake or an isolated error committed by a single political administration or party. The war in Vietnam was the logical outcome of policies pursued by the U.S. government through every administration since the end of World War II. Responsibility for the war in Vietnam belongs, therefore, to Democrats and Republicans, liberals and conservatives, the executive branch and the legislative branch of the U.S. government. The war was designed to demonstrate to the world that the United States would use whatever power was necessary in the Third World to stop revolutionary and nationalist movements that challenged American hegemony.

American involvement in Vietnam began as the last shots were fired at the end of World War II. Even before the Japanese had been completely disarmed, the United States was involved in assisting the French to restore colonial rule in Indochina, which prompted Ho Chi Minh to begin the war for national independence.

Events over the next ten years showed that no amount of French blood or American wealth could prevent the forces of national revolution from destroying the colonial empire in Indochina. The French Union forces lost 50,000 men and the United States contributed over $2 billion—approximately 80 percent of the cost of the entire French military effort.[3] On May 7, 1954, the Vietminh finally defeated the French in the Battle of Dienbienphu. The French had expected to force the Vietminh into a fixed battle and defeat them at Dienbienphu.[4] But France underestimated the determination of its opponent. Despite its advanced technology and officers trained in its elite military college, France was no match for the people of Vietnam. The colonial policies pursued by the French after World War II had only reinforced the determination of the people of this part of the world to be free of colonialism, no matter how long it took or how great the sacrifice.

The United States witnessed the defeat of the French forces with considerable concern, and negotiations for additional assistance took place throughout the spring of 1954. The doctrine of "massive retaliation" had been announced in January of this year, but was of no assistance to the French. The French and Americans considered the use of tactical nuclear weapons, but reached no agreement on a way to use them.[5] The doctrine of "massive retaliation" and the threat of nuclear weapons could not prevent the "loss" of Indochina. In 1954, there did not appear to be a way to bring the power of the United States effectively to bear on events in this part of the world.

The French defeat in Vietnam should have given the United

States a fundamental understanding of the powerful forces behind national revolutionary movements in the Third World.
Nationalism had emerged as the most potent ideology of the
twentieth century, and for the next twenty years, the leaders of
the United States were to be taught this lesson repeatedly at a
phenomenal cost of lives, money, and social disruption.

The United States simply could not bring significant military
pressure to bear on Southeast Asia. American conventional forces
were limited under Eisenhower. The 1954 doctrine of "massive
retaliation" was not designed to deal with insurgencies in the
Third World. The meaningful application of force by the United
States required military forces that were not available to U.S.
policy makers until Kennedy's presidency.

At the outset of his administration, the Bay of Pigs fiasco had
made Kennedy realize that the United States did not possess
enough conventional military power to invade Cuba, and it was
decided to dramatically strengthen this aspect of the American
military. The 1954 doctrine of "massive retaliation" had proved
useless in the case of Cuba, and American policy makers turned
to developing a doctrine that would allow the use of military
power. The doctrine of "flexible response" was the result. "Wars
of national liberation" were to be met with limited war and
counterinsurgency warfare, and Vietnam was to become the testing ground for the new theories developed by the Kennedy
Administration. By June 1962 there were 9,000 Americans in
Vietnam. At the time of Kennedy's assassination the United States
had over 16,000 troops in Vietnam. In 1963 489 soldiers died.
The buildup continued after Kennedy's death, reaching 180,000
by 1965, and 485,000 by 1967. On April 30, 1969, U.S. forces in
Vietnam reached their highest number—543,000.[6]

The new doctrine of "flexible response" could leave no doubt
about U.S. determination and willingness to do whatever was
necessary to defeat those forces defined as enemies. No matter
what the costs, the United States would affirm the credibility of
American power to stop destabilizing revolutionary movements,
"modernize" Third World societies in its image, and thereby
restore an order favorable to American interests. That this pol-

icy failed was not because the United States did not make a supreme effort; it failed because the United States could not control 4 billion people in 140 nations. Recognizing this reality could prevent a considerable loss of lives and misallocation of resources in the 1980s.

Vietnam was to become the testing ground not only for the doctrines of counterinsurgency and limited war developed by the Kennedy Administration but also for the question of whether American nuclear superiority could be used to assure inaction by the Soviet Union and China (a policy that, in fact, had not succeeded in Korea).[7] Although it had been claimed that the United States was following the minimum deterrent doctrine of mutually assured destruction (MAD) at the time of the war in Vietnam, this was not true. American nuclear superiority in the latter part of the 1960s was represented by approximately 4,500 American warheads compared to 1,200 Soviet warheads.[8] A conscious effort was made throughout the decade to use the dramatic American strategic nuclear advantage to protect the United States in the war in Indochina from the threat of Soviet or Chinese intervention. The public announcement by McNamara of a mutually assured destruction (MAD) policy in no way changed the fact that the United States continued to build weapons systems far beyond the strategic requirements of a minimum deterrence. The United States continued to expand its lead over the Soviet Union in deliverable warheads (reaching an all-time high of 32,000 nuclear weapons and bombs by 1967) and developed more devastating and accurate weapons systems (MRV, MIRV, ABM, Poseidon, B-1).[9] If the United States were in truth following a policy of mutually assured destruction, the relatively inaccurate SLBMs of the 1960s would have sufficed, and none of these new systems would have been necessary.

Again, if the United States had adopted MAD, the targeting system, the supersecret Single Integrated Operational Plan (SIOP) would have been aimed at inflicting "assured destruction" on the cities and industry of the Soviet Union. But this was not the case. Although there are several targeting systems set up in the SIOP, SIOP 62 as revised by President Kennedy and Secretary of Defense McNamara called for the destruction of Soviet military targets first and required the Joint Chiefs of Staff to destroy 90 percent of the Soviet military capability.[10]

The gap between the theory of mutually assured destruction and the reality of the weapons being built for the SIOP is enormous and illustrates that a strategic doctrine is not defined by words—but by actions. In this case, the weapons systems and targeting policies of the U.S. government were a clearer statement of American doctrine than were the words of McNamara.

Although there is no way to ascertain if the Russians or Chinese were interested in intervening directly in Vietnam, the United States did use its powerful nuclear forces as an umbrella under which to fight the war. This practice developed into the strategy of the "sword" and the "shield." According to this doctrine, American nuclear forces are the shield under which American conventional forces operate without fear of intervention by the forces of another major power (primarily the Soviet Union). This was to become the avowed policy of the Reagan Administration and its rapid deployment force.

With this policy in place, the United States proceeded to step up the war in Vietnam in an effort to win. By 1966, the annual bomb tonnage dropped on Vietnam had surpassed that used against Japan in World War II (500,000 tons) and by 1967 the United States had already dropped more tonnage (1.5 million tons) on Vietnam (an area smaller than the state of Montana) than it had on all of Europe during World War II.[11]

The bombing policy of the Johnson Administration and then of the Nixon Administration was to inflict "calculated pain" and "stress" on the people of Vietnam. Some advocates of air power continued to believe in the efficacy of this power to win the war, but most policy makers had recognized that the major function of air power was to "punish" the people of Vietnam.[12] By the summer of 1969, Nixon and Kissinger threatened North Vietnam with a "savage, decisive blow" and "measures of great consequence and force." Plans were made to bomb Hanoi and mine Haiphong Harbor, and discussions began on the possible use of tactical nuclear weapons on the Ho Chi Minh Trail.[13] At a later date, President Nixon clearly indicated this policy when he stated: "What all of us have in mind is that we must punish the enemy in a way that he will really hurt this time."[14] This theme was also clearly stated by Nixon's national security adviser, Henry Kissinger: "I refuse to believe that a fourth-rate power like Vietnam does not have a breaking point."[15]

As we have seen (see page 131), Soviet leaders had begun to suspect the United States of acting irrationally on the issue of Vietnam. It would appear that President Nixon actively culti-vated the "madman theory" in an effort to persuade the Soviets (or Chinese) that he would commit any act to keep them from intervening and to enable the United States to have its way in Vietnam.[16] This approach to a war with a nonnuclear power cer-tainly left the Vietnamese, the Russians, and the Chinese un-certain about what might happen next. It is a dangerous and reckless way to conduct diplomacy in the thermonuclear age.

Nixon's decision secretly to place nuclear forces in their high-est state of alert (DEFCON 1) for 29 days in October 1969 added to his image of unpredictability.[17] This alert was known to the Soviet Union, but was kept from the American people. The Nixon Administration's pattern of keeping information from the nation but not from the "enemy" was to continue throughout the war.

Although by 1971 Nixon believed in bombing Indochina to "punish" America's opponents, he no longer appeared to be under any illusion that the doctrines of limited war and counter-insurgency could work or that the American people were willing to support an extended war. His goal became withdrawing Amer-ican troops from Vietnam, increasing the bombing, and turning the ground war over to the Vietnamese ("Vietnamization"). American troop withdrawals were designed to weaken the anti-war movement in the United States, and escalations of the bomb-ing were to serve as "negative reinforcement" to the Vietnamese who opposed the United States. In spite of increased bombing and the invasion of Laos and Cambodia, the war continued for three more years. There were 15,000 American casualties and no end in sight as Nixon approached his reelection campaign in 1972.[18]

After Nixon's reelection, the United States conducted saturation bombing of North Vietnam in late 1972. But by January 1973 a formal peace had been signed, providing for an end to hostilities, the withdrawal of all U.S. troops, the return of prisoners of war, and the establishment of an international control commission to assure peace. Fighting between the Vietnamese continued until the fall of Saigon in May 1975. Although the exact number of deaths in this war will never be known, it is estimated that in addition to the more than 57,000 Americans who died, more than 400,000 South Vietnamese died and over 900,000 North Vietnamese and Viet Cong died.[19]

The manner of U.S. involvement in Vietnam was repeated in Cambodia. Information about American military operations in Cambodia was withheld from the American people. During 1973, for example, the United States dropped over 100,000 tons of explosives on Cambodia.[20] Since the Russians, the Chinese, and the Cambodians knew about American military operations, from whom were these operations being kept secret? The people of the United States were not to be informed of the extent of their country's involvement in the destruction and mutilation of this land and culture. Although to most Americans Cambodia is an obscure footnote to the war in Vietnam, the bombing continued until August 1973 when U.S. military actions in Cambodia ceased, leaving the chaos and misery that still pervade this hapless land.

The American war in Indochina was a tragedy for all concerned. The people and the land of this region were devastated beyond imagination. The one hope left from this war is that the United States has learned that it cannot police the world. In the short run, American leaders have demonstrated a hesitancy to use American military forces overseas. The unwillingness of many people in the United States to support the war in Indochina demonstrated to American civilian and military leaders the dangers of foreign military intervention without public support.

The immediate result of the Vietnam syndrome and breakdown of American foreign policy consensus was the passage of the War Powers Act, the end of conscription, the Clark Amendment (nonintervention in Angola, 1975–1976), and the restrictions placed on the operations of the CIA. The Nixon Doctrine of Vietnamization and its postwar manifestation of using "surrogate gendarmes" as regional enforcers of American policy (e.g., Iran) reflected this temporary shift in American policy. But by the mid-1980s, the lessons of Vietnam seem to have been forgotten as the American people supported the invasion of Grenada and the U.S. government actively intervened in Nicaragua and prepared to intervene in other parts of Latin America.

SALT I: THE ILLUSION OF ARMS CONTROL

The 1972 SALT I agreements and the trip to China fit well into Richard Nixon's campaign for reelection in 1972. Vietnamization, rapprochement with China, and the illusion of arms control served to defuse the American antiwar and antinuclear movements. As was the case with the partial test ban treaty in 1963, many Americans thought that a significant arms control agreement had been signed and that détente signaled the beginning of the end of the arms race. Yet just as the limited test ban treaty meant that the arms race would be conducted underground, so SALT I meant that future escalations in the arms race would be in missile accuracy and in the number of warheads per missile (along with cruise technology and forward-based U.S. medium-range missiles).

SALT I was a two-part agreement: the ratified treaty, which limited each side to two ABM sites, and the Interim Agreement (in effect for five years), in which both sides agreed not to increase the number of ICBM launchers. Constraints were also placed on the number of SLBMs that could be eventually placed in operation. The distinction between "heavy" and "medium" ICBMs and the exact number of Soviet submarine launchers were the subject of considerable debate within the American defense establishment. The limits on ABM technology were a significant move in the direction of arms control so long as this treaty was honored by both sides. Nevertheless, a close examination of the SALT I agreements and the weapons systems developed afterward indicates that as a means of arms control, SALT I was just one more example of myth creation in the nuclear arms race.

In 1966 the Soviet Union began to build up its ICBM forces to compensate for the enormous U.S. advantage in land-based missile systems (see page 122). At this time the United States not only had superiority but also was moving ahead with other systems that threatened the Soviet Union. These weapons systems—the F-111 supersonic fighter-bomber, the continued work on the B-1 bomber, and further development of American superiority in ABM and particularly multiple warhead technology—reflected the U.S. technological lead over the Soviet Union and were to cause another escalation of the arms race.

American superiority at the time of the SALT I agreements of May 1972 was clearly established. Authorities as diverse as Seymour Hersh and the Committee on the Present Danger agree on the overwhelming nature of U.S. numerical warhead superiority at this stage of the arms race. A mere list of figures might indicate that the United States and the Soviet Union had achieved parity in 1972 in launchers (see Table I), but this would be misleading.

Despite the figures on launchers and bombers, the real comparative strengths were far different when all factors of nuclear delivery systems were calculated. The United States had already begun to deploy MIRVs on its ICBMs and led the Soviet Union in deployed warheads, by 3,500 to 2,350. If the bomber force is added to these delivery systems, the United States had actually over 6,000 strategic nuclear weapons, compared to fewer than 3,000 for the Soviet Union.[21]

In addition, these figures do not include forward-based American bombers, carrier-based bombers, U.S. tactical nuclear weapons capable of reaching Soviet targets, or the nuclear weapons of Great Britain or France—all categories in which the Soviet

TABLE I

	UNITED STATES	SOVIET UNION
ICBM launchers	1,054	1,607
SLBM launchers	656	740
Intercontinental bomber	450	140

Union had no counterpart and all categories that were ignored by SALT I in the final agreements.

Although the Soviets were behind in ABM technology (see page 132), their effort to compensate for their technological backwardness in MRV and MIRV technology represented the greatest single escalation of the arms race since the introduction of the ICBM over ten years earlier. Whereas the United States had deployed MRVs on submarines in 1963–1964, the Soviet Union had just begun testing this first-generation system in 1969.[22] In 1968, a year before the Soviets tested MRV, the United States had tested its first MIRVed missile, and began deploying MIRVed missiles on ICBMs and SLBMs in 1970. The Soviet Union did not deploy its first MIRVed missile until 1975 when the American program was almost completed. Once again, the Soviets found themselves behind in the arms race (and five to six years behind in deployment).

As Nixon was later to say of the Interim Agreement, "under this agreement, the United States gave up nothing because we had no program affected by the freeze."[23] The United States had deployed its last ICBM in 1967 when it brought its total number of launchers to 1,054. The process of MIRVing these missiles was unaffected by SALT I. On the other hand, the Sentinel and Safeguard ABM systems had been successfully challenged as unworkable, and neither the United States nor the Soviet Union could expect to achieve a viable ABM system in 1972 (the United States voluntarily gave up its last ABM site authorized under SALT I in 1975).

Under SALT I, the Soviet Union could not increase its number of ICBM launchers, but it could modernize the ones it had and prepare them for MIRVed warheads when they became available. The Soviet Union did continue its limited buildup of submarine-launched missiles in order to meet the numbers limit agreed upon in SALT I.

One of the ultimate ironies of SALT I was the failure to consider multiple warheads in the offensive limitations of the Interim Agreement. MIRVs had initially been justified on the basis of need in the face of the Soviet ABM system. It was correctly believed that it was easier to "shoot down" a single missile than to destroy 10 warheads launched in flight from a single missile. Theoretically, with the ABM treaty, there was no need for MIRVed missiles, and since the United States held the lead in this technology, U.S. negotiators could have safely included MIRV systems in the limits of SALT I. But they did not. At no time in the history of the arms race has the United States failed to maximize technology and technological advantage over the Soviet Union. Yet it is only by not maximizing technological advantages and by negotiating freezes and reductions that the upward spiral of the arms race can be reversed. So long as every technological breakthrough is maximized, the arms race will continue. There is no indication in the 1980s that the United States is willing to forgo a temporary advantage of superior technology—no matter what the long-range costs may be.

President Nixon claimed that the United States was interested in "sufficiency" and not "superiority" in the SALT negotiations, but he said that he did not want to approach the Soviet Union in negotiations as the "second strongest nation in the world."[24] Yet the United States emerged from SALT I stronger than when it began the negotiations. The ABM systems of both sides were meaningless at current levels of technology. The United States kept its forward-based systems, its three-to-one advantage on delivery systems (missile and bomber force combined), and its ability to continue to MIRV its ICBMs and SLBMs. On the other hand, the Soviet Union had agreed not to increase the number of ICBM launchers for at least five years, thus ensuring that the Soviets could not increase the number of ICBM warheads they possessed until their MIRV systems became operational (1975).

Toward the end of the Nixon Administration, Secretary of Defense Schlesinger clearly stated American policy toward future efforts at arms control when he said he would be against any SALT agreement that did not ensure "an overwhelming American advantage."[25] The American bargaining position has not changed.

At a later date Henry Kissinger was to be attacked for weakening the U.S. position by allowing the Soviets to modernize existing ICBM launchers (as could the U.S.) and for setting up a system of counting Soviet SLBM launchers in a manner apparently favorable to the Soviet Union. These charges (along with unproved allegations of cheating by the Soviet Union) were to be used by the opponents of SALT II and were part of the reason that SALT II failed to be ratified by the United States (see below). Yet the fact remains that by the end of the Interim Agreement in 1977, the United States had not lost ground in the arms race, but had actually increased its lead over the Soviet Union in the number of strategic warheads. In 1977, the United States had 7,200 strategic warheads, compared to fewer than 3,000 for the Soviet Union.[26] Those who attacked the SALT I agreement as unfavorable to the United States ignored the figures of comparative strength for the period covered by SALT I.[27]

SALT I appears to have followed a classic pattern: The military asked for what it wanted, the scientists determined what could be built, and the political leaders rationalized the arms race within these boundaries. The ABM was not technically feasible and more missiles were not wanted; the United States wanted more warheads with greater accuracy. The military got its new weapons and the political leaders achieved the illusion of arms control.

THE COMMITTEE ON THE PRESENT DANGER AND THE TRILATERALISTS

In spite of President Nixon's diplomatic successes with the Soviet Union and China, his presidency was deteriorating under the pressures of the Watergate scandal. By 1974 the power of the American presidency had been considerably diminished. The forced resignation of President Nixon and the final debacle in Vietnam had led to the caretaker administration of President Ford. The Vietnam syndrome had led to a reluctance on the part of the United States to intervene in Angola's civil war, and the confusion in American policy-making circles was revealed in America's lack of response to the continued warfare in the Horn of Africa (Ethiopia and Somalia). President Ford's efforts to save the crew of the *Mayaguez* (May 1975) led to the sacrifice of the lives of 18 marines *after* the crew had been released by the Cambodians.[28]

The early 1970s had not been the best of times for the Soviet Union either. The United States had successfully subverted the socialist Chilean government of Salvador Allende (1973) and the Soviet Union steadily lost influence in Egypt, Somalia, and Guinea. On its eastern frontier, the Soviet Union continued to have difficulty with the People's Republic of China.

Despite the growing number of nuclear weapons available to each of the superpowers, events were proving over and over again that this form of power could not be translated into control of the individual nation-states of the globe. In the immediate future, Poland and Afghanistan would demonstrate this to the Soviet Union, and Iran and Nicaragua would bring this lesson home to those who were paying attention in the United States. Unfortunately, leaders in both countries were unwilling to learn this fundamental lesson of the nuclear age.

The events of 1975 were to have a profound effect on American policy for the next decade. The Central Intelligence Agency (CIA) was accused of underestimating Soviet military capabilities, and President Ford agreed to allow the appointment of an "outside" group to examine CIA estimates. The work done by Team B has been equated with the NSC #68 on the 1950s and the Gaither Report on the 1960s.[29] Chaired by Richard Pipes, Team B also included Paul Nitze, an author of the NSC #68 (see pages 14–16), and William R. Van Cleave. All three became members of the Committee on the Present Danger (CPD), Board of Directors.[30] In their own words: "The intellectual basis for the Committee grew out of the work of the now-famous Team B which presented its view that the CIA had consistently underestimated the massive Soviet military effort."[31]

The Team B report was not unusual. The CIA was periodically taken to task for "underestimating" what the Soviet Union was doing. This had occurred during the debate on the "missile gap" in 1957–1961 and in 1969 when the CIA was pressured to change its estimate of a Soviet MRV test to a MIRV test.[32] In 1985 the CIA and the Defense Intelligence Agency were again at loggerheads, this time over the so-called spending gap, with the CIA accused of underestimating Soviet spending for the entire period from 1976 to 1985. The CIA seems to function well at collecting information but less effectively at implementing policy.

The original focus of the CPD was to warn the United States of the problems of SALT I and the dangers of the current negotiations for SALT II. Once SALT II was withdrawn from Senate consideration in 1979, the CPD continued to function as an influential educational body to warn the United States of the menace of the Soviet Union and the importance of increasing American military budgets. The success of the CPD is a tribute to its ability to manipulate American public opinion.

Any tendency to regard the CPD as just one more anti-Soviet, Cold War organization must be resisted simply because of the importance of the members of the CPD. No fewer than 60 of the original members of the CPD Board of Directors were to serve actively in the administration of Ronald Reagan. A sampling of those on the board who served in the Reagan Administration dramatizes the influence of the CPD:

William J. Casey—Director of the CIA
Richard Allen—Assistant to the President for National Security
Max Kampelman—Chief Negotiator, Geneva Disarmament Talks
Jeane Kirkpatrick—U.S. Representative to the U.N.
Paul Nitze—Chief Consultant, Geneva Disarmament Talks
Fred Iklé—Under-Secretary of Defense for Policy
Richard Pipes—Director of Soviet Affairs, NSC
Eugene Rostow—Director of the Arms Control and Disarmament Agency
Kenneth Adelman—replaced Eugene Rostow, Arms Control Agency
President Reagan also served on the board of the CPD.

The agenda of the CPD was initially adopted before the end of the Carter Administration. The election of Ronald Reagan signaled the committee's ascent to full power. The CPD defined the threat to U.S. security, predicted the consequences if the danger were not met, and offered solutions to specific problems.

In 1977 the CPD claimed that "the principal threat to our nation, to world peace, and to the cause of human freedom is the Soviet drive for dominance based on an unparalleled military build-up." The CPD then went on to claim that "if past trends continue, the USSR will within several years achieve strategic superiority over the United States." The early 1980s was defined as the new "period of maximum danger."[33]

It was alleged that not only were the Soviets attempting to gain military superiority over the United States but also the Soviet Union was designing a pre-emptive strike against U.S. forces while reservng sufficient forces to hold the U.S. population hostage. This would allow the Soviet Union to "prevail while maintaining a post-war preponderance of global military power."[34] This led the CPD to a rather ambiguous conclusion.

> A clearly superior Soviet THIRD-strike capability, under the assumption of clear Soviet strategic nuclear superiority, would undermine the credibility of our second-strike capability, and could lead us, either to an accommodation without fighting or to the acceptance of unmanageable risks.[35]

In this short essay, the CPD demonstrated its commitment to several fallacies of the Cold War.

(1) That in 1977 Soviet or American nuclear superiority had meaning.

(2) That a pre-emptive strike was possible.

(3) That the concept of prevailing in a nuclear war was plausible.

By the 1980s, both Carter and Reagan embraced all three fallacies as the United States called for an American nuclear superiority in order to prevail in a nuclear war.

To meet the perceived Soviet challenge, the CPD called for a restoration of an "allied defense posture capable of deterrence at each significant level and in those theaters vital to our interests."[36] The commitments of the United States in accordance with this policy were defined in traditional grandiose terms.

It appears therefore that no part of the world can be excluded in advance from our security concerns. The globe itself is the strategic theater of central conflict of our time.

It follows that we and our allies need forces in being at all times capable of deterring attack and, if necessary, defending the nations to whose security we are committed.[37]

Finally, the CPD found at least two new "gaps" in American defense policy and began to make them an issue in defense policy debates. The "spending gap" debate continues and will be dealt with in the next chapter. The "technology gap" was only a potential threat and not given much attention.[38] If a "technology gap" even appeared, it favored the United States.

The Committee on the Present Danger was organized during 1976 but decided not to "go public" until after the 1976 election in order to avoid appearing partisan. Yet the impetus behind the organization of the CPD was at work in the 1976 election. The Vietnam syndrome, the legacy of Watergate, and the lackluster leadership of President Ford could be expected to produce a victory for the Democrats. But the close margin of victory in the 1976 election should have warned the Democratic Party that it was heading for future difficulties.

The CPD represented one of two approaches on how to solve the problems created for American policy by the war in Vietnam. The second approach was that embraced by the Trilateral Commission. The influence of the Trilateral Commission and the CPD was not based on organizational strength but on the power of the individuals attracted to the organizations. The differences between the two groups concerned geographical and ideological matters, not the over-all goals of American foreign policy. The power structure of the United States remained committed to the status quo in the noncommunist nations; the question that remained was how best to achieve this goal.

Founded by David Rockefeller in 1973, the Trilateralists wanted to give American policy a European (and Japanese) focus. The Trilateralists were concerned with trade, and perceived foreign policy conflict in terms of North versus South—that is, the industrial, developed nations versus the underdeveloped nations. The Trilateralists wanted to incorporate U.S., European, and Japanese interests in order to guarantee continued access to raw materials, markets, and cheap labor in the Third World. This foreign policy elite comprised approximately 270 members from all three regions, with 76 members from the United States. Members were drawn from the worlds of politics, business, labor, and education, and many joined the Carter Administration.

Harold Brown—Secretary of Defense
Cyrus Vance—Secretary of State
Walter Mondale—Vice President[39]

President Carter was also a member of the commission.

The interests represented by the CPD on the other hand, placed paramount importance on East-West (Soviet-American) antagonisms. Military preparedness on the part of the United States was the CPD's primary foreign policy goal. In the 1976 election, the Trilateralists generally supported Carter, and the CPD backed the Republican Party. In a sense, Trilateralism got its chance in the Carter Administration and the CPD philosophy in the Reagan Administration. The underlying similarities between these two administrations are a tribute to the consistency and continuity of the goals of the men who make American foreign policy. As we shall see, the transfer of American military policy from Carter to Reagan was amazingly smooth, with little disruption of policy or weapons programs.

CARTER AND THE BALANCE OF TERROR—1977

When Jimmy Carter became President of the United States, he inherited the Nixon Doctrine, SALT I, détente, and the Vietnam syndrome. By the end of his first term, the Nixon Doctrine had collapsed, SALT negotiations had failed, détente had ended, and the strength of the Vietnam syndrome was ebbing. Carter's campaign commitment to cut military spending had been reversed by a dramatically increased military budget, and a fundamental noninterventionist policy had been replaced by the Carter Doctrine.

Jimmy Carter was sworn in as President of the most powerful nation in the world in terms of nuclear forces. The United States had almost completed its modernization program and by 1977 the United States had deployed over 9,000 MIRVed missiles and bombers. The Soviets had fewer than 4,000, including a limited bomber force. (See Tables II and III.)[40]

In 1977, the United States maintained its lead over the Soviet Union in every significant category of nuclear power: number of nuclear weapons, number of warheads, "lethality factor," and accuracy. The United States had begun to deploy MIRV on its submarines in 1970, yet the Soviet Union was just beginning to test these submarine-launched systems in 1977.[41] In addition,

TABLE II

TOTAL U.S. WARHEADS DEPLOYED—1977[42]

Missile Name	Number Deployed	Warhead Yield	Warheads per Missile	Total Warheads
ICBM				
Titan 2	54	5–10 MT	1	54
Minuteman 2	450	1–2 MT	1	450
Minuteman 3	550	170 KT	3 MIRV	1,650
Total ICBM Warheads				2,154
SLBM				
Polaris A3	160	200 KT	3 MRV	
		1 MT	1	480
Poseidon C3	496	40 KT	10–14	4,960
Total SLBM Warheads				5,440
Total U.S. warheads deployed in 1977				7,594

The United States also had 330 B-52 bombers in 1977. If each bomber carried 8 nuclear weapons, then the total B-52 delivery weapons would be 2,640. This would give the United States a total delivery force in 1977 of 9,234 nuclear weapons (not counting forward-based systems or carrier-based aircraft).

TABLE III

TOTAL SOVIET WARHEADS DEPLOYED—1977[43]

Missile Name	Number Deployed	Warhead Yield	Warheads per Missile	Total Warheads
ICBM				
SS-7/SS-8 (ICBM)	156	5 MT	1	156
SS-9 (ICBM)	264	18–25 MT	1	
		4–5 MT	3 (MRV)	264
SS-18 (ICBM)	36	18–25 MT	1	
		2 MT	8–10 (MIRV)	288
SS-11 (ICBM)	910	1–2 MT	1	
		500 KT	3 (MRV)	910
SS-17 (ICBM)	20	200 KT	4 (MIRV)	80
SS-19 (ICBM)	100	200 KT	6 (MIRV)	600
SS-13 (ICBM) (Only solid fuel)	60	1 MT	1	60
Total ICBM warheads				2,358
SLBM				
SS-N-4/5	78	1 MT	1	78
SS-N-6	544	1 MT	1	
		? KT	3 MRV	544
SS-N-8	220	1 MT	1	220
Total SLBM				832
Total Soviet Union warheads deployed in 1977				3,190

In addition, the Soviet Union had 100 Tu-95 Bear bombers deployed in 1977 and 35 Mya-4 Bison deployed. Both bombers were intercontinental in range.

the United States maintained approximately 50 percent of its SLBM submarines "on station" (at sea and ready to launch), while the Soviet Union had only 11 percent of its offensive submarines at sea at any given time.[44] American submarine and SLBM technology was still far ahead of the Soviets' (and this has not changed in the mid-1980s). In 1978 the United States also began deploying the new Mark 12A warhead on Minuteman III ICBMs. With a warhead of 370 kilotons and a circular probable error (CEP) of one-tenth of a mile, this warhead would have an 80 percent chance of destroying a hardened Soviet missile silo.

There was one additional, major difference between the strategic forces of the United States and the Soviet Union that continued through the 1970s. In the early 1960s the United States had developed and deployed solid fuels in their missiles. In 1977 the Soviet Union remained dependent on liquid fuels (except for the 60 SS-13s deployed). Solid fuels were easier to handle and, more importantly, were capable of being fired within 120 seconds of the decision to launch the missiles. Liquid fuels were cumbersome and took longer to launch. Although the Soviet Union decreased its liquid fuel launch time for the SS-18 to under 10 minutes, the consequence of using one type of missile fuel instead of another was and is dramatic. Soviet missiles were much more vulnerable to a first-strike attack than U.S. missiles. This vulnerability reinforced the Soviet fear of a U.S. first strike. On the other hand, this very vulnerability led some U.S. leaders to assign a first-strike mission to Soviet missiles and this in turn caused concern on the part of U.S. policy makers. It was obvious that one of the next steps for the Soviet Union in the arms race would be to catch up with the United States in solid fuel technology. (By the mid-1980s, the Soviet Union has not yet accomplished this task, although they are testing solid fuel missiles.)

Even though the Soviet Union trailed the United States in the development of solid fuels and miniaturization, its land-based missile technology was still its most advanced delivery system, and during the 1970s the Soviets did achieve fundamental parity with the United States in land-based ICBMs. This technological lag meant, however, that Soviet missiles had to be larger and have more thrust than was necessary for American missiles to accomplish the same mission. The fact that Soviet missiles were larger than U.S. missiles led some observers to claim that the Soviets had superiority when mere size actually demonstrated Soviet technological inferiority. The Soviet Union, with its clear weakness in SLBM technology, had no choice but to develop its ICBM forces. This heavy reliance on ICBM technology led the Soviet Union to place 70 percent of its nuclear warheads in fixed, land-based silos that faced increasingly accurate American strategic forces, whereas the United States had only 30 percent of its warheads based in fixed silos.[45]

The American lead continued in other ways: The United States had already embarked upon the next generation of weapons systems in each category of the American TRIAD (land-based ICBMs, SLBMs, and its bomber force). Both the Trident I and II submarines were scheduled to replace the Poseidon, the B-1 bomber survived a Carter challenge to its development, and the MX missile showed a durability that defied understanding (see below). All three of these sophisticated weapons were superior to their Soviet counterparts. In addition, the U.S. development of the neutron bomb and advanced cruise missiles were to contribute to further escalations of the arms race.

NATO: "FIRST USE" AND NUCLEAR "COUPLING"

The end of the war in Vietnam and the advent of the Carter Administration led to a shift of emphasis in American foreign and military policy. Europe once again became an area of major American involvement and the power and influence of the Trilateralists assured that NATO concerns would once again be at the top of American priorities. American military policy toward Europe has been consistent since the beginning of the nuclear age. Few believed that NATO conventional forces could defend Europe, and NATO strategy has therefore been to prevent Soviet aggression by "extended deterrence." This means that Europe would be kept under the American nuclear umbrella and that the doctrine of "first-use" would guarantee that any attack on Europe would be met with a nuclear response.

The doctrine of "first use" was connected to the policy of "coupling" the defense of Europe with a U.S. escalation of the types of nuclear weapons used and the targets assigned to these weapons. Initially, this response would be in the form of the first use of tactical (battlefield) nuclear weapons coupled to the automatic use of theater (European) nuclear weapons as the war intensified. If tactical and theater nuclear weapons did not achieve victory, then the United States would further couple its use of nuclear weapons to include strategic (world-wide) systems against the Soviet Union. Thus, ultimately deterrence in Europe would rest on the U.S. commitment to use its strategic nuclear forces, even if this meant the destruction of the United States. Assuming that this doctrine made sense during the 1950s, its credibility declined dramatically as the Soviet Union also placed tactical nuclear weapons in Europe and deployed its own theater nuclear weapons. The doctrine made no sense at all in the era of guaranteed mutual annihilation. Since the policy was rapidly losing credibility, Europe was being "decoupled" from the United States in spite of the best efforts of President Carter and later President Reagan.

Europe could have been completely destroyed by the tactical nuclear forces that were in place in the mid-1970s. The United States had 7,000 tactical nuclear weapons in Europe and the Soviet Union was estimated to have had 3,500.[46] The United States also had the means to deliver these weapons. All of these weapons remained under U.S. control and only the United States could make the decision to use them—a fact that made many Europeans justifiably anxious about their ability to control a European war. In addition, some of these weapons (not to mention the French and British nuclear forces) had the capability of reaching the western part of the Soviet Union. And by 1977 the Soviet Union had begun to modernize its theater nuclear forces and to replace its obsolete intermediate range missiles in Europe with mobile, three-warhead SS-20 missiles. As we shall see in Chapter VII, this Soviet move was to have far-ranging ramifications for the NATO Alliance.

By the late 1970s, it was becoming apparent to many Americans that the first-use doctrine in Europe was founded on the contradictory principal that the best way to defend Europe was to threaten to destroy it. If the American threat to use nuclear weapons in Europe failed to prevent war (no matter who started it), then the only option under this doctrine was to destroy Europe, and there were few Western observers who believed that a limited nuclear war could be fought in Europe without leading to a general nuclear war with the Soviet Union.

Some liberals in the United States began to look for a means of jettisoning the first-use doctrine in favor of another defense strategy. Many of these observers seemed to believe that Europe could be defended by conventional forces in existence in Europe at the time. Conservatives took the position that "first use" was essential, but that a conventional defense might be possible by dramatically building up the forces in Western Europe and taking advantage of new developments in technology that favored the defensive forces in conventional warfare (e.g., antitank technology as demonstrated in the 1973 Middle East War). Interestingly, both the liberal and conservative positions rationalized increased American military spending.[47]

A major unresolved problem arose as both liberals and conservatives called for increased conventional forces. Although these increased expenditures were nominally for the defense of Europe, a substantial portion of U.S. spending on nonnuclear systems was intended for U.S. interventionary forces in the Third World and had essentially nothing to do with the defense of Europe. For example, about half of the Navy's general purpose spending is for sea lane protection and supply functions, and the other half is for Third World interventionary forces—power projection ships, escorts, and logistical support systems.[48] The failure by U.S. political leaders to distinguish between the types of missions assigned to U.S. forces is an intentional ploy designed to enable the United States to intervene militarily throughout the world; whatever forces might be needed are sought under the guise of a conventional buildup to defend Europe. In the 1980s, this deliberate confusion of military missions is still used to increase American spending on interventionary forces.

Despite U.S. expenditures on the military, NATO forces in Europe have never been capable of successfully defending Europe in a conventional war of longer than one month. On this evidence, one can argue that the United States has never intended to conduct a conventional defense of Europe. For example, in 1977 petroleum stockpiles in Europe were counted in terms of weeks of supply and not months by both the United States and the Soviet Union.[49] By 1985, American ammunition reserves were still not adequate for even thirty days of fighting in Europe and such reserves were not expected to be available until 1990. The failure to establish petroleum or ammunition stockpiles capable of lasting more than 30 days conclusively demonstrates the lack of intent to defend Europe with conventional forces.

There is no question that the defensive capabilities of NATO for the Central Front (Germany) had increased by the latter part of the 1970s. The war in Vietnam was over, American defense planning had moved to strengthen Europe, and West Germany was boasting the third-largest defense budget and the third most powerfully equipped land army in the world (France was fourth in both categories).[50] In addition, the dependability of Soviet allies in the Warsaw Pact remained suspect. In the East, China had become a nuclear power with a huge land army, and this also required part of Soviet military strength in a counterforce.

In 1977 NATO officials calculated the forces on the Central Front for the first day of a theoretical war in Europe. (See Figure V.)

Although NATO was stronger in 1977 than in the 1960s, certain basic changes that would offer it a degree of certainty in the conventional defense of Europe had not yet been made. The Soviets have an obvious advantage in numbers. What is less obvious is that the six-division U.S. equivalent, the Seventh Army, which had ended up in central Germany at the end of World War II, was located in the wrong place to defend the Central Front. Because the North German Plain invasion route was to the north of the Seventh Army, the Soviets could exercise a holding action against the army while moving across the North

TABLE IV

U.S.–NATO TACTICAL AND THEATER NUCLEAR WEAPONS–1977[51]

Ground Launched

Name	Number	Range (mi)	Yield (Kt)
Honest John	196	4–25	20
Pershing I	180	95–450	60–400
Lance	43	3–70	1–100
Sergeant	56	2–85	Low
Pluton	24	75	15–25
SSBS S-2	18	1,875	150
M-109 155mm Howitzer	326	9–10	2
M-11 8-inch Howitzer	360	8–10	Low
M-115 8-inch Howitzer	?	10	Low

Nuclear Capable Tactical Aircraft in Europe
(U.S. only)

Type	Number M-Day*	M+30	Strike Radius
F-4	528	888	800 Miles
F-111	72	288	1,700
F-105 D/B	0	158	1,140
F-100 C/D	0	352	680
A-6	24	48	1,020
A-7 A/B/E	60	120	1,020
Totals	684	1,854	

* "M-Day" represents mobilization day, the day of the outbreak of hostilities. M+30 is mobilization plus 30 days.

During the 1970s, the United States had approximately 7,000 tactical nuclear weapons compared to 3,500 for the Soviet Union. With increasing accuracy and sophistication of these weapons, the United States began to reduce the number of tactical nuclear weapons it felt were needed in Europe. Although Polaris and Poseidon systems are not included here, some of these systems were regularly assigned to NATO missions.

TABLE V

CENTRAL FRONT FORCES[52]

	NATO	Warsaw Pact
Troops	823,000	899,000
Tanks	7,000	20,500
Artillery	2,700	10,000
Tactical Air (Ground support)	2,350	4,075
Interceptors (Fighter aircraft)	600	3,050

German Plain, then wheel south behind it, and thus succeed in turning the northern flank of the army (a Soviet Eastern European version of the Schliefan Plan).

But the location of the Seventh Army was not the major problem with the conventional defense of Europe. On the modern battlefield, the loss of personnel and equipment would be exceedingly high in the early stages of combat. Thirty days after the initiation of hostilities (M+30), the Central Front would be destroyed and the losses would be staggering. By that time the Soviet Union would have increased its forces in Europe considerably (in spite of Western nonnuclear *interdiction*). The initial Soviet air superiority and the destruction of military airfields would also have made it impossible to reinforce the Seventh Army in any substantial manner. Even optimistic Department of Defense estimates indicate that it would take 19 days to airlift one American division and its equipment to Europe. With prepositioned equipment, 10 days would still be needed to move one division.[53] In addition, the Soviet Union would have a deep geographical base of several thousand miles, from the front to the Ural Mountains. NATO's logistic base would only be several hundred miles deep and much easier to attack.

In 1977 any conventional defense of Europe would have required forces already in Europe and could not have relied on extensive American reinforcements during the first several months. And it is still true today that no matter what defensive posture Europe assumes, it must rely on those capabilities that are already on the Continent to win a war. As we shall see in the next chapter, the United States can solve this problem if it is willing to "let Europe go" and "decouple" American nuclear response from European security.

But, it was not the conventional defense of Europe that seemed to bother most Europeans. Instead, many Europeans had begun to fear that the United States would involve Europe in a nuclear war, a war that was neither initiated nor controlled by European nations. Their fear of a lack of U.S. commitment to use nuclear weapons to defend Europe, on the one hand, and their belief that the same weapons would lead to the destruction of Europe in a proxy war, on the other hand, set up fundamental contradictions in American and European policy that have yet to be resolved. This quandary clearly represents the difficulties in making nuclear weapons an instrument of foreign policy. A policy of destroying a nation in order to "save" it is a difficult concept for many people to accept or understand, yet this was and is the rationale for American policy on the defense of Europe. This contradiction eventually must lead to a redefinition of American policy on NATO and the defense of Europe.

As the military situation was becoming more complex within the NATO Alliance, diplomatic relations within the Alliance were becoming strained. The Nixon policy of détente and the bilateralism of the SALT negotiations together with the *Ostoolitik* of the Federal Republic of Germany led to a further alienation within the Alliance. European economic needs, strong national feelings, and the growing distrust of the American commitment to defend Europe were contributing to a weakening, if not redefining, of the NATO Alliance. There was a sense among Europeans that they were being omitted from decisions that critically affected their well-being, if not the continued existence of their society and culture. The post–World War II bipolar world defined by the United States and the Soviet

Union was becoming less and less acceptable to the people of Europe.

Two events in October 1973 had underscored the Europeans' dilemma. The Organization of Petroleum Exporting Countries (OPEC) had raised the price of oil on October 16 and had embargoed oil exports to the United States on October 20, to punish it for its support of Israel. On October 25, 1973, U.S. nuclear military forces were placed on a world-wide nuclear alert to prevent Soviet intervention in the Yom Kippur War, which Israel was in the process of winning.[54] This alert was given without any consultation with America's European allies. Thus, in this short period the United States demonstrated both its inability to control the oil of the Middle East and its willingness to move toward nuclear confrontation without consulting its allies.

The United States could have seized the critical oil fields of the Middle East, but they would not have been operational. The vulnerability of the wellhead, pipelines, and pumping stations would lead to their destruction by either a conquering military force or local acts of sabotage.

Many Europeans believed that a major confrontation between the United States and the Soviet Union would also bring war to Europe. In the event of war, the Soviets would not wait to be attacked, but would take the war to their enemies' territory. Similarly, with the American doctrine of "first use" in place, the Soviet Union would attempt to move their troops as close as possible to NATO forces, to reduce the use of tactical nuclear weapons on the battlefield. American support of the state of Israel may have conformed to the Nixon Doctrine of using "surrogate" regional powers to implement U.S. policy, but there was a price to be paid for this policy in Europe, as well as in the Middle East.

The energy crisis demonstrated the limits of American military power and represented a "quintessential trilateral problem."[55] The Trilateralists were committed to a common European and American strategy toward the Third World and to obtaining secure access to world oil supplies. But throughout the 1970s management of the energy crisis was not possible by the Trilateralist approach. The forces of nationalism were gaining the upper hand in the industrial world. And (in spite of the belief that allies should be treated as equals and not as clients) the United States proved incapable of treating the Europeans and the Japanese as anything but junior partners in American foreign policy.

Jimmy Carter did redirect the focus of American foreign policy to Europe and the Middle East after years of attention to the East and Asia. Early in his administration, President Carter had reversed an earlier, less-assertive policy, as well as his original call for reductions in the military budget.[56] During his first year in office, the top-secret Presidential Review Memorandum 10 (PRM 10) was leaked, indicating the U.S. "nuclear tripwire" in Germany would not be automatic but that the United States might be willing to relinquish a large portion of Germany (up to 100 kilometers deep) in order to conduct a conventional defense of the Central Front.[57] This prospect did not find favor in West Germany. Within 100 kilometers of the German border lie the German cities of Hamburg, Hanover, and Frankfurt as well as 30 percent of the population and 25 percent of all industry in the Federal Republic.[58] The U.S. policy clashed violently with the European goal, which was to prevent *any kind of war,* not just nuclear war. According to U.S. policy, Europe would be the battlefield, but the twentieth century had already taught the Europeans that there must be *no* third war fought on their soil.[59]

In addition to general U.S. policy, President Carter caused considerable consternation in Europe by indicating that the range of the cruise missile might be limited in SALT II, so that it could not reach the Soviet Union. The Chancellor of the Federal Republic, Helmut Schmidt, spoke for those in Europe who did not want Europe "decoupled" from American strategic weapons when he said:

> the SALT process may lead to a paralyzation of the Soviet and American central strategic forces and . . . the strategic nuclear component will become increasingly regarded as an instrument of the last resort, to serve the national interest and protect the survival of those who possess these weapons of last resort.[60]

To many Europeans, bilateral talks had come to symbolize the international balance of terror between the two superpowers. But this guarantee of mutual annihilation raised other questions about the defense of Europe and the "coupling" of American strategic weapons with the defense of the Fulda Gap on the eastern border of the Federal Republic.

The American decision to deploy Euromissiles and the neutron bomb in Europe was an attempt to tighten the connection between American nuclear doctrine and the defense of Europe. Both the Euromissiles and the radiation-enhanced neutron bomb met with European opposition, but the Euromissiles were deployed in Europe in the 1980s. The neutron bomb posed a different problem. This was a weapon designed to kill people but preserve property and many Europeans objected to defending Europe with such a weapon. The neutron bomb went into production and was stockpiled in the United States for use in Europe, but its deployment in Europe was delayed indefinitely.[61]

The jostling of the deployment of the neutron bomb reflected the treatment of Europe as a whole. However, major events of 1979 were to push European concerns into the background once again. Iran, Nicaragua, and Afghanistan would become the central concerns of the United States and the Soviet Union, leaving Europe as only a witness to the superpowers jostling each other in other parts of the world.

THE YEAR OF DECISION—1979

The goals of the United States did not change during the 1970s. American political leadership, however, had been divided between those advocating the Trilateralist approach and those supporting the philosophy of the Committee on the Present Danger (CPD). In a very real sense, the debate ceased in 1979. The overthrow of the Shah of Iran, the successful Sandinista revolution in Nicaragua, and the Soviet invasion of Afghanistan combined to produce an overwhelming victory for the CPD position in the ruling circles of the United States.

Jimmy Carter had come to power with the support of the Trilateralists and they were well represented in his administration. In its last two years the Carter Administration completed the shift to a more aggressive and militarized policy. In quick succession, President Carter established the rapid deployment force, committed American nuclear power to the Persian Gulf, and articulated a doctrine of "enduring" a "protracted" nuclear war (Presidential Directive #59).

The overthrow of the Shah of Iran was to have a traumatic impact on the conduct of American policy. In the past, the United States had had limited success in using local regimes to implement American policy. American efforts had put the Shah back on the Peacock Throne in 1953 and kept him in power until January 1979. In the Middle East, the Nixon Doctrine had relied on Iran and Israel to supply the "surrogate gendarmes" to implement American policy. Both nations had been armed with the most modern and effective nonnuclear weapons the United States could provide. With the overthrow of the Shah, the keystone of American policy in the Persian Gulf (Arabian Gulf) had been removed, and American policy in this region began to disintegrate. (American weakness was further demonstrated by the impunity with which the Iranian students took American personnel hostage later in the year.) In the American view the entire region was destabilized. Fears were renewed over the ability of the United States to control the oil supplies from the Middle East. Control over Middle Eastern oil should have been of greater concern to the Japanese and Europeans than it was for the Americans. When the Middle Eastern crisis began in 1973, the United States relied on Middle Eastern oil for only 2 percent of its energy needs, whereas 59 percent of British oil, 72 percent of French oil, and 75 percent of German oil came from the Middle East.[62]

The United States could do nothing to prevent the Iranian Revolution and Iranians blamed past American policies for most, if not all, of the problems faced by this oil rich nation. Instead of attempting to reach a mutually satisfactory agreement with Iran, the United States continued to antagonize the new government. Once again, American leaders had failed to recognize the powerful revolutionary forces at work in the twentieth century. The United States was simply unable to control the events in this part of the world. Instead of recognizing this, the right wing in the United States blamed America's earlier military retreat in Vietnam, U.S. military weakness, and the unwillingness of the United States to engage in a militarily aggressive foreign policy to achieve its goals in the Middle East.[63]

Clearly, American policy makers felt that the Vietnam syndrome was a threat to American global order. How to use U.S. power to maintain the status quo in the face of the failure of this policy in Vietnam had been the central question of American policy makers ever since the defeat of Vietnam. The Iranian crisis helped to consolidate the views of policy makers on this issue. As in the early Kennedy years, policy makers realized that they needed both the will and the means to intervene. The American people had to be prepared for intervention and the military capability to intervene had to be present. Both Carter and Reagan discovered that it was easier to persuade Congress to appropriate the funds for interventionist forces than it was to persuade the American people to use military force.

The Carter Administration's effort to create the means to intervene was publicly announced in June 1979 by Army Chief of Staff, General Bernard Rogers, when he called for the establishment of a "unilateral force" for combating armed insurgencies abroad.[64] The concept of a rapid deployment force (RDF) was not new; earlier, in the Eisenhower years it was called the "fire brigade" and under Kennedy the United States Strike Command (see pages 79–80). What was new was the size and the mission of this command.

In the past, the "fire brigades" had been of limited size and their missions had been modestly defined (e.g., the Lebanese invasion in 1958). In contrast, the new RDF numbered 200,000 men by 1981, and is still growing. Major force units were designated as part of this command, including four army divisions, a marine division, appropriate air support, and three carrier task groups. In addition, the Pentagon was allocated an additional $6 billion to procure 150 new long-range transport aircraft and an additional $3 billion for a fleet of 15 marine prepositioned ships (MPS). It was estimated that this force would need 440,000 men in the event of a Soviet invasion of Iran.[65] In spite of all of this effort, there were lingering questions, about how quickly the RDF could be deployed beyond a token level.

But it was the mission of the RDF as a "special contingent for waging 'brush fire' wars in the Third World" that formalized and explained the role of American military power.[66] These troops were to be used in a "pre-emptive strategy": They would be sent into foreign areas *in advance of enemy action*. This approach was further refined by General P. X. Kelley of the marines (soon to command the RDF) in 1980 when he said:

> A pre-emptive strategy to me means that we get forces into an area rapidly, irrespective of size, because once you get a force into an area that is not occupied by the other guy, then you have changed the whole calculus of the crisis, and he must react to you, and you not to him.[67]

Under this strategy the United States was going to use the troops of the RDF as hostages, at least in the Middle East. Placing a force, irrespective of size, in an area (such as Iran) would either lead to the death of the troops or the use of American nuclear weapons in an attempt to save them. Fundamentally, the pre-emptive strategy was an expansion of the American doctrine of "first use" of nuclear weapons to the Middle East and possibly beyond this area.

The RDF and its proposed use also demonstrated in the clearest possible terms the U.S. policy of intervening with conventional forces under the umbrella of American strategic nuclear forces. Or, to put it another way, the American shield (nuclear weapons) would prevent the Soviet Union from reacting to the American sword (conventional forces). The RDF was a "tripwire" (as were American forces in Europe) for the use of nuclear weapons, from tactical to theater to strategic forces.[68]

This "tripwire" and "first use" doctrine of the United States is predicated upon the U.S. possession of a counterforce targeting system. The first use of nuclear weapons must be backed up by the capability to launch a first-strike counterforce against the Soviet Union. Otherwise, an expanding local war could result in the annihilation of the United States. It makes no sense to use nuclear weapons first in a local war if your homeland is going to be destroyed in the process by strategic retaliation. Thus, an essential corollary to "first use" is a first-strike counterforce to back it up. This connection between a "first use" doctrine and a first-strike counterforce capability does a great deal to explain why the United States continues to stockpile accurate strategic nuclear weapons. This buildup continues under the Reagan Administration even though fewer than 400 SLBMs would be enough to guarantee deterrence. (See Chapter VII and the concept of "escalation dominance.")

As leaders in the United States were planning how to hold the line against the revolutionary forces in the Middle East, American hegemony in the Western Hemisphere suffered another setback in the Caribbean Basin. American concern with the Middle East is a relatively new phenomenon, but U.S. involvement with other countries in the Western Hemisphere began right after the American Revolution and has never slackened. In recent history, the United States has been the dominant force throughout Latin America and particularly in Central America. The Monroe Doctrine was aimed at keeping Europeans out of the Western Hemisphere and the Roosevelt Corollary defined U.S. control over this region. The United States was actively intervening in Latin America long before there was even the remotest possibility of attributing the problems of this region to Communist intervention. During the period 1898–1920, the U.S. Marines had intervened in the Caribbean area no fewer than 20 times.[69]

By American government standards, the policy of intervention had considerable success after World War II. Guatemala in 1954, the Dominican Republic in 1965, and Chile in 1973 are examples of successful U.S. intervention. The American-sponsored Bay of Pigs invasion demonstrated, however, that success was not automatic, and raised questions about using mercenaries in fighting this kind of war.

During the 1920s, the U.S. Marines fought an ongoing war against the rebel Sandino in Nicaragua. In 1934 the American-supported National Guard captured Sandino, and President Anastasio Somoza had him murdered. From 1936 to 1979 the United States armed and trained Somoza's National Guard, 2,969 National Guard officers in the United States from 1949 to 1964. (The United States trained more officers from Nicaragua than from any other Latin American country.) Somoza's corrupt regime ruled a society in which 2 percent of the population owned the land and controlled the wealth of the nation. The stage was set for the "inevitable revolution" discussed at length by Walter LaFeber in his excellent book *Inevitable Revolutions*.[70]

In spite of Jimmy Carter's human rights policies and his desire to dissociate the United States from Somoza, the basic contradiction between the American belief in self-determination and the demand for continued U.S. control could not be resolved. As in the case of Vietnam, self-determination was ignored and the drive for control continued; it continues to this day. The government of Somoza collapsed in July 1979 and the Sandinistas came to power. Initially, there were some efforts at cooperation with the new regime, but these quickly dissolved into suspicion and inaction. American demands for a prominent role in the shaping of the new government were rejected. Forty thousand people had died (the equivalent of four million U.S. deaths) and the Nicaraguans were not going to return to a system of domination that had already produced the tragedy of the Somoza regime.[71]

In the 1980 election, Jimmy Carter was accused of "losing" Nicaragua. Nicaragua thus joined China, Cuba, Vietnam, and other sovereign nations that the United States had somehow "lost" since the end of World War II. No one ever bothered to explain exactly how the United States "lost" something it never owned; but the new administration came into office determined that it was not going to "lose" any more countries. American leaders did not seem to understand the nature of the forces they were dealing with. The same historical forces that had led to revolution in Nicaragua were present throughout Central America and, for that matter, throughout most of the Third World. An awareness of the power of revolutionary nationalism still had not managed to penetrate American military and foreign policy thinking.

The Iranian and Nicaraguan revolutions challenged American interests in two parts of the globe that were considered "vital" by American policy makers. The "loss" in these two areas reduced further the influence of the Trilateralists and set the stage for the assumption of power in Washington by the "hardliners" of the CPD. The accompanying shift of American attitudes and political leaders was reinforced by the Soviet invasion of Afghanistan.

THE CARTER DOCTRINE AND PRESIDENTIAL DIRECTIVE #59

If 1979 was a traumatic year for the United States, it proved to be an equally difficult year for the Soviet Union. By invading Afghanistan in December, the Soviet Union demonstrated that it also was losing control over its empire. In Afghanistan, the Soviet Union was to demonstrate the same ruthless disregard for self-determination that the United States had shown in Vietnam. The major difference was that the Soviet Union intervened in a nation on its border (as they had done before), whereas the United States tended to project its power everywhere in the world except on the Soviet border.

The invasion of Afghanistan on December 27, 1979, was an overt admission of failure by the Soviet Union to control its client states (as had been the case in Hungary and Czechoslovakia earlier). Historically, the Soviet Union had always demonstrated a willingness to take whatever military action was necessary to protect its buffer zone in Eastern Europe. What was new in Afghanistan was the Soviet willingness to expand this policy to Asia. The 1968 Brezhnev Doctrine of not allowing a friendly socialist state to be overthrown by Western influences was extended beyond Europe to Asia (and possibly beyond).

The Soviet Union had "changed the rules" and was accused of taking the initial steps toward domination of the Persian Gulf area and its important oil resources.[72]

The United States and its European allies reacted differently to the Soviet invasion. President Carter reacted strongly and claimed that the Soviet action posed

> a threat to the rich oil fields of the Persian Gulf area and the crucial waterways through which so much of the world's energy supplies had to pass.[73]

George Kennan, America's elder statesman, offered a different interpretation, attributing the invasion to political instability on the Soviet border "rather than some grand design for control of the Gulf."[74] The Europeans, though more dependent on Middle Eastern oil than the United States, viewed the invasion with considerably less alarm. Soviet influence had been predominant in Afghanistan for a considerable period of time and Europeans were not prepared to support the strong economic sanctions taken by the United States against the Soviet Union.

The American response to the invasion was the Carter Doctrine and an effort to cover the Middle East with its "nuclear umbrella." On January 23, 1980, in his State of the Union message, President Carter stated American policy:

> Let our position be absolutely clear: An attempt by any outside force to gain control of the Persian Gulf region will be regarded as an assault on the vital interests of the United States of America, and such an assault will be repelled by any means necessary, including military force.[75]

Despite these words, the United States had *no* conventional military capability in the Middle East. It was a region thousands of miles from the United States with no permanent American military garrisons. The rapid deployment force was not ready, and even if it had been, there were still doubts about the ability of the United States to confront the Soviet Union in the Middle East in a conventional war. At the time, existing estimates indicated that the United States could move an American light division (about 12,000 men) to this area in about two weeks.[76] With a large Soviet force available in Southwest Asia (up to 400,000 men), the American force could be considered no more than a token, destined to perform the role of hostage assigned to the RDF in the Middle East.

The inability of the United States to confront the Soviet Union in a sustained conventional war is even more obvious in the Middle East than in Europe. The basic geopolitical fact is that the United States cannot successfully confront Soviet conventional forces on the Eurasian mainland in a long-term war. This does not mean that local regional forces could not do so. If it is necessary to contain the Soviet Union on the Eurasian landmass, this will be done by the regional forces on the periphery of the Soviet Union. This cannot be done under current American military planning and with conventional forces. The political and economic costs for the United States to build up its conventional forces to this level would be prohibitive.

U.S. leaders believed that the threat of the "first use" of nuclear weapons against the Soviet Union would deter any Soviet move toward the Persian Gulf. By placing the entire area behind this shield, the United States opened other options for limited American military intervention in this area should American "vital interests" be challenged. Although one of the missions of the RDF was to contain the Soviet Union in areas such as the Middle East, the primary mission of this force was apparently to intervene in any area of the world where U.S. leaders perceived a threat to their interests and anticipated military success in overcoming this threat. In the case of the Middle East, this threat could be defined as a coup d'état in Kuwait, war on the Horn of Africa, or a revolution in Saudi Arabia.

If the first victims of the invasion of Afghanistan were the people of that country, then the second victim was the final demise of the SALT process in the United States. On June 18, 1979, Jimmy Carter had signed the SALT II agreement and sent it to the Senate for ratification. The Committee on the Present Danger had done everything in its considerable power to discredit the entire SALT process and probably would have succeeded in defeating SALT II without the Soviet incursion in Afghanistan. But with the Soviet invasion, Jimmy Carter withdrew SALT II from Senate consideration.

As an arms control measure, SALT II possessed the same fundamental weaknesses as SALT I. SALT II also defined what each side wanted to do and could accomplish in the next several years and then approved these plans to escalate the arms race. The CPD objected that SALT II did not cover the Soviet Backfire bomber or the 308 heavy Soviet missiles.[77] Although it limited the number of strategic launchers to 2,400 and the number of MIRVed launchers to 1,320 (with only 820 of these on ICBMs), SALT II did not cover forward-based systems, the actual number of warheads on MIRVed missiles, or the French and British strategic systems that were capable of reaching the Soviet Union.

By 1979 the United States had decided not to build the B-1 bomber. President Carter did not make this decision as an arms control measure, but based it simply on the assumption that the United States could build 100 cruise missiles for the cost of each single B-1 bomber.[78] Even accepting the contention that the Soviet Backfire bomber could reach the United States, the roughly 100 Backfire bombers certainly did not represent a substantial leap in Soviet delivery systems, compared to over 1,000 cruise missiles planned for early deployment. The possible SALT II limits on the range of the cruise missiles deployed would have expired before the planned U.S. deployment of long-range cruise missiles and shorter-range deployment was not limited.

As for the balance between the American and Soviet systems, President Carter best summed it up when he said, "We have more warheads with higher average accuracy, and the Soviets have more launchers with greater total explosive power."[79] Like many others before him, President Carter did not include in his totals the important bomber forces of the United States, which had a clear superiority over Soviet bomber delivery systems. Whenever efforts are made to discuss the American and Soviet military balance, all *three components of the TRIAD* must be included—ICBMs, SLBMs, and bomber forces. (In addition to

TRIAD forces, American forward-based systems [e.g., Pershing II] have assumed increased importance in the 1980s.)

Of greatest significance in SALT II was the failure to place any limit on the number of warheads on the MIRVed missiles and the lack of any effort to prevent the testing of these warheads (or missiles) to increase their accuracy for a counterforce mission. Thus, even if SALT II had been ratified and honored by both sides, the arms race would have continued.

Even conservative 1979 estimates by Paul Nitze of the CPD placed the United States ahead of the Soviet Union in the number of strategic warheads deliverable:[80]

TABLE VI

1979 UNITED STATES–SOVIET DELIVERABLE WARHEADS

	UNITED STATES	SOVIET UNION
ICBM Warheads	2,154	5,820
SLBM Warheads	4,800	1,782
Bombers (bombs/warheads)	2,560	624
Totals	9,514	8,226

Again, this is not a complete list of U.S. strategic systems. The United States had over 500 nuclear capable F-4s in Europe, along with F-15s with a similar capability, and over 600 carrier-based planes with a nuclear capability. Similarly, the Soviet Union could not ignore destructive power represented by the nuclear forces of Great Britain and France. When all these forces were combined, the Soviets faced well over 11,000 strategic weapons capable of reaching their territory.

In conjunction with these systems, the United States was developing the Trident I (operational in 1980) and Trident II submarines, cruise missile technology, and Stealth technology. In all three categories, the American technological lead was clear. In addition, the Soviet Union had no plans for the intermediate nuclear forces to match the planned deployment of the

Pershing II and cruise missiles in Germany. Nor did the Soviet Union have the basing capability of the United States for its cruise missiles in the remainder of Europe. For the United States, the Pershing II and European-based cruise missiles were a strategic system for use against targets inside the Soviet Union. There was no way the Soviet SS-20s in Europe could reach the United States. A comparable Soviet position would have been the deployment of the SS-20 in Cuba—something the United States had disallowed in the early 1960s.

The strategic advantage of the United States over the Soviet Union was confirmed in 1980 when President Carter made a profound shift in strategic doctrine. In the summer of 1980 Presidential Directive #59 (PD #59) was leaked to the press by the Carter Administration as part of the presidential campaign then in progress. This was the first time since the second-strike counterforce doctrine that an administration had made a public statement that the United States should be prepared to fight a "prolonged" nuclear war with the Soviet Union. This Carter Doctrine of a "countervailing strategy" officially introduced the concept of "enduring" in a nuclear war and "recovering" from such a war.[81] The thinking behind PD #59 had been articulated as early as 1977, in the Department of Defense, *Annual Report to Congress for FY 1978*.

> The present planning objective of the Defense Department is clear. We believe that a substantial number of military forces and critical industries in the Soviet Union should be directly targeted, and that an important objective of the assured retaliatory mission should be to retard significantly the ability of the USSR to recover from a nuclear exchange and regain the status of a 20th century military and industrial power more rapidly than the United States.[82]

Let me repeat a word of caution about stated nuclear doctrine. The United States has gone through a number of "strategic theories" for the use of nuclear weapons: "massive retaliation," "second-strike counterforce," "nuclear flexible response," "mutually assured destruction," Nixon's "sufficiency" and "controlled response," and now Carter's "countervailing" strategy and the evolving NUTS (nuclear utilization target selection). Aside from the confusion they can create in the minds of the American people (and the Congress), these various doctrines must always be assessed, not so much according to what is said, but according to what the United States was (and is) prepared to do. That is, strategic theory should not be confused with strategic *targeting systems*. For example, it is one thing to proclaim a MAD doctrine with just enough nuclear forces to guarantee destruction. It is quite another matter to declare MAD while possessing and continuing to build accurate, first-strike, counterforce weapons systems. The weapons needed for MAD are few and not very accurate; the weapons needed for a first-strike counterforce are many and extremely accurate.

Other writers have gone so far as to say that the real danger of relying on an assessment of nuclear doctrines is that "they might be believed" and used as a basis for action. Rather, available weapons and targeting policies, not stated doctrine, determine nuclear weapon use.[83] Based on this perspective, the announcement of PD #59 simply confirmed publicly the U.S. counterforce targeting doctrine that had dominated the American Single Integrated Operational Plan (SIOP) since its inception.

By 1980, SIOP 5 had been amended a number of times. In the Soviet Union, there were only 900 cities with a population over 25,000 people. There were 3,500 key military targets (including 1,398 land-based missile launch control centers and 500 bomber capable airfields).[84] Presidential Directive #59 downgraded economic and industrial targets and increased the counterforce military targets and command, control, communications, and intelligence targets (C3I targets). This announced shift to a public counterforce posture along with more than 10,000 strategic warheads produced an American capability that the leaders of the Soviet Union dared not ignore.

The United States continued to extend its military posture of deterrence throughout the world in an effort to guarantee Soviet inaction. The United States had not changed its policies; it simply had gone public with them and thereby placed pressure on the Soviet Union to acquiesce to them.

In the 1980 election, the American people overwhelmingly rejected the Carter presidency and elected Ronald Reagan. Judged by the goals of both the Democrats and the Republicans, the foreign policy of the 1970s had been a disaster. The legacy of Vietnam, the "loss" of Nicaragua, the Iranian crisis, the OPEC oil policies, and diplomatic difficulties in Europe indicated that the United States faced numerous obstacles in maintaining the kind of world-wide control it had sought for the last 35 years. As in the past, failures abroad led to changes in the means for accomplishing U.S. goals—but not to changes in the goals themselves. Jimmy Carter's RDF and PD #59 were the harbingers of the new tactics of the Reagan Administration.

VII

Ronald Reagan: Myth and Reality in the Nuclear Age

If the Carter Administration introduced the concepts of "endure" and "recover" to U.S. military doctrine, then the Reagan Administration fulfilled the distorted logic of thirty-five years of the nuclear arms race when it spoke of "nuclear superiority," "war-winning strategies," and "prevailing" in a "prolonged nuclear war." In October 1981 fragments of the top-secret National Security Decision Directive #13 were leaked to the press. They confirmed not only President Reagan's acceptance of Carter's Presidential Directive #59 but also added a new credo, that of the "controlled escalation" in a nuclear confrontation that would allow the United States to win the war.[1] Concepts such as "winning" and "prevailing" have absolutely no meaning under any nuclear doctrine except in a first-strike counterforce war plan.

Upon assuming office, the Reagan Administration set three objectives: (1) to escalate the strategic arms race to offset the Soviet Union's move toward parity in the 1970s; (2) to consolidate the American position in Europe by increasing the American commitment to the nuclear defense of the Continent; and (3) to build American nonnuclear forces to a level that would make possible successful American intervention in the Third World. To gain the support of the American people for these

objectives, the Reagan Administration further integrated nuclear weapons into the over-all military posture of the United
States, forging a "deadly connection" between nuclear and conventional military power.

By the early 1980s the U.S. commitment to a counterforce
doctrine aimed at Soviet nuclear installations and command
centers was reflected in the Single Integrated Operational Plan
(SIOP). General Lennie Davis (SAC commander in 1985),
who was in charge of developing SIOP 6, made the following
cogent observation on American targeting systems:

> I think that a fundamental issue here is that most people
> really don't appreciate that the U.S. strategy is one of counterforce.
> That is, it is not a mutually-assured-destruction strategy or a city
> strategy. It goes after the Soviet military-leadership threat and, of
> course . . . the land-based ICBM capabilities.[2]

This doctrine was further elaborated as the administration's
war fighting a doctrine that called for American nuclear forces
to "prevail even under conditions of prolonged war" and to "render ineffective the total Soviet military and political power
structure."[3]

General Davis was right. The American people have never
realized that their government condones not only battlefield
"first use" of nuclear weapons but also a strategic first-strike
against the Soviet Union. The connection between "first use"
and "first strike" doctrine is the essence of the "coupling"
strategy for the defense of Europe (discussed later in this chapter); in the event of hostilities, the United States could not win
a war in Europe but would instead escalate the conflict to all-
out nuclear war.

As early as 1954, General Curtis Lemay (SAC commander from
1948–1957) had said that the United States "would not hesitate
to strike first" if "pushed into a corner far enough."[4] Every
SIOP since the Kennedy Administration has had a first-strike
counterforce option clearly available. Whether this attack is defined as preventive or pre-emptive alters neither the strategy
nor the weapons built to implement it. The current pattern of

the arms race can continue only if the U.S. government can at the same time follow a first-use and first-strike strategy and convince the American people of the "defensive" character of the U.S. nuclear arms buildup. Until the American people understand the true offensive mission of nuclear weapons in the conduct of American foreign policy, there is no way the arms race can be slowed, stopped, or reversed.

Although Secretary of Defense Caspar Weinberger attempted to make the new strategy sound like a modified version of the "second-strike counterforce" doctrine of earlier years, various members of the administration continued to call for what amounts to a first-strike posture.[5] Of even more importance than what was being said was what was being done. The United States embarked on a massive arms buildup to achieve the "superiority" that Reagan and the Republican Platform had called for in the summer of 1980.[6] By the end of the first Reagan Administration, the following strategic weapons were operational: Trident I SLBM, air-launched cruise missiles (ALCMs) on B-52G bombers, ground-launched cruise missiles (GLCMs) in Europe, Tomahawk sea-launched cruise missiles (SLCMs), and Pershing IIs in Europe. On the drawing board and scheduled for deployment before 1990 were the Trident II SLBM, the B-1 bomber, and the MX missile. Finally, the Strategic Defense Initiative was proposed, and research began on this nominally defensive system (labeled "star wars" but referred to hereafter as SDI). Each of these weapons could be used as a first-strike system—or certainly be viewed that way by the Soviet Union.

In addition to developing these new delivery vehicles, the Reagan Administration responded to the alleged "warhead gap"[7] and called for increasing the American nuclear warhead stockpile from 25,000 to 29,000, by building 1,500 warheads a year (over 4 per day). The number of U.S. warheads which had reached an all-time high of 32,000 in 1967, fell to 25,000 by 1982 because of obsolescence and redundancy. By 1983, plans called for a total of 21,000 new warheads to be manufactured in the next decade.[8]

In an age of thermonuclear plenty and an unbelievably complex number of nuclear delivery systems, many experts challenge even the remotest possibility that a surprise first strike could destroy enough of an enemy's capability to prevent effective and devastating retaliation by the other side. That has been the accepted meaning and reality of the balance of terror. The willingness of the Reagan Administration and the U.S. Congress to invest hundreds of billions of dollars in first-strike counterforce weapons in spite of this view appears to mean that the United States is both adopting a first-strike posture and building a superior and threatening nuclear force to deter any Soviet military action or reaction to American operations.

Because the United States was not prepared to settle for deterring a nuclear war, the primary motivation behind American military doctrine (and thus weapons) was to prevent a first strike against the United States. This doctrine meant that the United States would use its nuclear weapons first rather than risk losing them. By defining a first strike doctrine and developing the weapons systems necessary to implement such a policy the United States adopted a dangerous and provocative posture vis-à-vis the Soviet Union. A counterforce posture on the part of the United States gave the Soviet Union no choice but to perceive of this policy as an effort to disarm their nuclear capability in a first strike. This potentially disarming attack could and would be used by the United States to coerce the Soviet Union in world politics.

To deter a Soviet attack on the United States, a first strike doctrine and the accompanying weapons systems were not necessary. Basic deterrence of a Soviet attack would have only required 500 of the 9,000 American warheads available as Reagan again escalated the arms race. If American policy had been simply to deter an attack by the Soviet Union on the United States, 500 forty kiloton Poseidon warheads would have been more than enough. Deterrence did not require a single new delivery system or warhead—it was all in place in 1981.

To induce the American people to go along with such an expensive and dangerous approach to the Soviet Union, American leaders had to claim that American weapons were defensive and the enemy was satanic. Since its inception, the Committee on the Present Danger (many of whose members are in power in Washington) led this effort. Whereas the right wing in the United States has always defined the conflict with the Soviet Union in the absolute terms of democratic capitalism versus Soviet "godless" totalitarianism, Reagan went one step further to label the Soviet Union "an evil empire," indeed the very "focus of evil in the modern world." The conflict between the United States and the Soviet Union was therefore a "struggle between right and wrong, good and evil."[9] Faced with such an enemy bent on world domination, American leaders could justify any means to defeat the Soviet Union. The 1984 Reagan landslide victory was a tribute to the ability of American political leadership to convince the American people of the wisdom of such policies.

US AND USSR STRATEGIC FORCE LEVELS—1982

When Ronald Reagan assumed office he claimed that the Soviet Union had a "margin of superiority" over the United States in nuclear weapons. He further defined a number of new "gaps" that put the United States behind the Soviet Union in the arms race. Soviet superiority was claimed with a "warhead gap," a "MIRV gap," a "spending gap," an "intermediate nuclear force gap," a "mobility gap," and a Soviet superiority in "throw weight." President Reagan used these alleged Soviet advantages as justification for massive increases in military spending and he simultaneously called for the establishment of American nuclear superiority.[10]

Yet, an examination of the comparative strength of the United States and the Soviet Union in Table I clearly demonstrates the U.S. advantage at the start of the Reagan nuclear buildup. By 1982, as a result of the Carter arms buildup, the United States MIRV program was complete and the United States had a substantial lead in the number of deployed strategic warheads (9500 to 6657) (see Table I). The United States did have several hundred fewer ICBM launchers than the Soviet Union. But, in addition to the obvious lead in the number of deliverable warheads, the United States led in the following categories.

TABLE I

THE STRATEGIC BALANCE BETWEEN THE
UNITED STATES AND THE SOVIET UNION—1982[11]

Weapons System	UNITED STATES		SOVIET UNION	
	Number	Warheads	Number	Warheads
ICBM	1,052	2,152	1,398	4,904
SLBM	520	4,768	918	1,494
Bombers	330	2,580*	154	259
Totals	1,902	9,500	2,470	6,657

In addition, the United States had 2,580 strike fighter-bombers with a nuclear capability of delivering 5,060 warheads or bombs on their first mission.

* In 1982, the United States began deploying B-52G bombers with 12 to 24 cruise missiles on each bomber (ALCM or SRAM). By 1984, the American strategic bomber force carried 5,400 warheads or bombs with 30 percent of the B-52 bomber force (over 1,000 warheads or bombs) on a fifteen-minute alert and therefore not vulnerable to a first-strike attack.[12]

(1) *Existing Weapons Systems*—The Trident I SLBM had become operational in 1980; the Soviet Union had no counterpart to U.S. SLBM accuracy or invulnerability. The B-52 was being equipped with 12 to 24 cruise missiles in 1982; once again, the Soviet Union had no counterpart to this in size or accuracy. Only in the ICBM category did the Soviet Union have more warheads than the United States, but as will be seen below, this numerical advantage was dramatically offset by the vulnerability of the Soviet ICBM force and by the accuracy of the American systems.

(2) *Solid Fuel Technology*—The United States had moved from the liquid fuel Titan II missile to the solid fuel Minuteman I in the early 1960s, yet by the early 1980s the Soviet Union was still relying on liquid fuel missiles for all of its ICBMs (except for 60 SS-13s). In 1974, the Soviets developed a liquid fuel that permitted the SS-18 to be fired in 4 to 8 minutes, but even this advance had drawbacks: The liquid fuel was cumbersome

and dangerous. In 1982, over 20 years after the deployment of the solid fuel Minuteman, the Soviet Union tested the SS-X-24 solid fuel ICBM.[13]

(3) *Miniaturization and Compactness*—Throughout the nuclear arms race the United States has led the Soviet Union in both categories. The United States had continually been able to reduce the size of the warheads while maintaining the amount of destructive power necessary to accomplish the mission assigned to a given weapon. This was one of the reasons the United States moved rapidly to multiple warheads (MRV and MIRV) on its missiles six or seven years ahead of the Soviet Union.[14] The American lead in solid fuel technology, miniaturization, and compactness has never been seriously challenged by the Soviet Union.

(4) *Accuracy*—American missiles have always been more accurate than their Soviet counterparts. The American superiority in SLBM technology has never been challenged by the Soviet Union. The American Minuteman III is more accurate than the most accurate version of the Soviet SS-18 or SS-19. The Pershing II and ground-launched cruise missile are at least three times as accurate as the Soviet SS-18 or SS-19. With this greater accuracy, the United States did not need large, heavy warheads on its missiles. The Soviet Union, by contrast, was forced to deploy large, heavy warheads on its missiles as a substitute for accuracy.[15] As General Bruce K. Holloway (SAC commander in 1968–1972) said, "If you can get pinpoint accuracy, then you don't need much yield for most hard targets."[16]

(5) *Throw Weight*—The amount of useful weight a missile can place in trajectory has always been a false issue in the nuclear balance. The United States has always been able to deliver more weapon tonnage by simply increasing the number of heavy bombers, by building more Titan IIs, or by using the heavier Saturn missile. In warhead yield-to-weight ratios, the United States has always sought to produce more power with a lighter warhead in order to maximize the number of warheads a single missile could deliver. Thus, the Mark 12A warhead at 335 kilotons was 97 percent more powerful than its predecessor, the Mark 12 warhead.[17] On the other hand, the Soviet Union

has had to rely on high throw weight missiles in order to compensate for the limited compactness and accuracy of its ICBM force.

(6) *Alert Status*—All U.S. missiles are solid fuel, "quick-launch" systems that can easily be fired in less than two minutes. The United States keeps over 50 percent of its strategic SLBM submarines "on station" at any given time, whereas the Soviet Union has only 11 percent of its force "on station." The American bomber forces can have 68 bombers in the air in five minutes and another 95 bombers in the air in 15 minutes. The Soviet Union appears to have no substantial part of its bomber force on alert of 30 minutes or less.[18]

(7) *Forward-based Systems (FBS)*—U.S. forward-based systems (FBS) supply another 2,200 warheads from cruise missiles, fighter-bombers, and carrier-based aircraft[19] that can reach Soviet targets. The number of forward-based systems is increasing in the 1980s. Since the Cuban missile crisis, the Soviet Union has had no forward-based systems capable of reaching the United States.

(8) *Euromissiles*—The deployment of these intermediate nuclear forces (ground-launched cruise missiles [GLCMs] and Pershing IIs) added substantially to the forward-based systems of the United States. Although the United States claimed that these were theater and not strategic missiles, they were still capable of strategic attacks on Soviet territory. The phenomenal accuracy of the Pershing II meant that western Soviet command and control centers were less than ten minutes from destruction. The Soviet Union had no comparable weapon basing system.

The lead enjoyed by the United States in these eight areas will be enhanced by six weapons systems being developed in the 1980s (see Table II). In each case, the United States already had a substantial lead in technology or basing; each of the weapons systems would be viewed as offensive, not defensive, by the Soviet Union. The extraordinarily accurate cruise missile, whose flight path and destination can remain undetected, was particularly controversial. In the words of Aleksi

TABLE II

UNITED STATES WEAPONS SYSTEMS SCHEDULED
FOR 1980s DEPLOYMENT[20]

System	Warhead (kt)	Accuracy (ft)	First-Strike Characteristics
Trident II	475	480	accuracy, speed
B-1 12–20 (ALCM)	300	300	accuracy, secrecy of target
MX	300	300	acuracy, speed
GLCM	500	61	accuracy, secrecy of target
Pershing II	200	100	accuracy, speed
SLCM	200	304	accuracy, secrecy of target

Obukhov, the Soviet Foreign Ministry representative to the
Strategic Arms Reduction Talks:

> What makes it [the cruise missile] a first-strike or surprise
> attack weapon is how much warning we have that it's coming, and in
> the case of the cruise missile that warning might be a matter of
> minutes. The whole purpose, after all, is to avoid detection.[21]

In short, Reagan's continued claims that the Soviet Union was
ahead of the United States in the nuclear arms race were false.
The American lead in nuclear delivery systems had never been
seriously challenged by the Soviet Union. The Soviet Union had
indeed improved on its substantially inferior position at the
time of the Cuban missile crisis, and by the 1970s the Soviets
had created a system of missiles (primarily ICBMs) that guaranteed freedom from the kind of nuclear extortion to which they
had succumbed in 1962.

The fact that the Soviet Union had a larger number of warheads on ICBMs than the United States (U.S. 2,152 to USSR
4904) was more than offset by U.S. advantages in other categories. That the Soviet Union had 74 percent of its warheads on
ICBMs while the United States had only 23 percent on ICBMs

actually worked against Soviet security as ICBMs became the most vulnerable of the strategic weapons systems to first-strike destruction—ironically even as talk of an American "window of vulnerability" arose in the early 1980s.

But Ronald Reagan's decision to step up the arms race in the 1980s once again threatened to destabilize an increasingly delicate balance, even though it was a balance of terror.

THE ARMS RACE: ESCALATION
OR ARMS CONTROL?

By 1982 the United States had reached another plateau in its nuclear arms buildup. All of the new weapons systems listed in Table II were in the advanced stages of development, but none were operational. The United States was in a position to test the willingness and seriousness of the Soviet Union to negotiate significant arms controls measures. But, by failing to forgo the immediate "modernization" of its nuclear forces, the United States again missed an opportunity to engage in a good faith effort to limit the arms race.

Missing this opportunity was not surprising given Reagan's historical hostility to arms control. Reagan had consistently opposed the 1963 test ban treaty, the 1968 nonproliferation treaty, the SALT I agreements (including the ABM treaty), and the SALT II treaty. During his first Administration, he had suspended the comprehensive test ban talks and scuttled efforts to ratify the threshold test ban treaty (prohibiting explosions over 150 kilotons.)[22] And, as we shall see, Mr. Reagan was ready to violate the ABM treaty with his Strategic Defense Initiative (SDI).

President Reagan's very grasp of arms control issues was suspect. In *Deadly Gambits*, Strobe Talbott examined Reagan's March 9, 1982, speech outlining America's negotiating posture in the upcoming START (Strategic Arms Reduction Talks). The President called upon the Soviet Union to dismantle large numbers of their ICBM force without being aware of the almost total Soviet dependence on this weapon.[23] A few months later, Reagan made his notorious claim that SLBMs could be recalled once launched. And in 1983, the President declared that whereas ICBMs carried nuclear warheads, neither SLBMs nor bombers did.[24] Finally, the man responsible for determining American policy in arms control admitted disingenuously that he had never understood what "this throw weight is all about."[25]

Officials determined early in the Reagan Administration that the START negotiations would not be permitted to interfere with the American Single Integrated Operational Plan (SIOP) of defeating the Soviet Union in a "protracted war." Edwin Meese, an important White House adviser, remarked that START "will be lucky if we let it get away with benign neglect."[26] There was nothing moreover, in the unratified version of SALT II (which the United States was observing) that would hobble the Reagan armament program, and START simply could not prevent this escalation of the arms race. (SALT I had expired in 1977, the ABM treaty was still in force, and the unratified SALT II agreement was scheduled to expire in 1985.)

Accordingly, Reagan's promised prompt and meaningful negotiations with the Soviet Union were neither. By the end of his first term, all talks with the Soviet Union had broken down.

The deadlock imposed by the administration's attitude to START meant that neither arms control nor arms reduction was possible. It could safely be said that the United States was not negotiating in good faith, without which it was impossible to determine if the Soviet Union was sincerely interested in arms reduction. While calling for "superiority" and "victory," the United States wanted reductions in the only areas in which the Soviet Union had even approximate parity with the U.S.—ICBM forces and throw weight. The United States wanted to retain its superiority in SLBM and bomber forces. At the same time, American negotiators contended that cruise missiles, Pershing II, American forward based systems (FBS), and French and British nuclear forces were not subject to negotiations as strategic weapons.

When Reagan introduced the SDI concept of destroying Soviet missiles once they were launched, his demand for reductions in Soviet offensive missiles became theoretically meaningless. The United States was inviting the Soviet Union to reduce the number of ICBMs (and therefore launchers and U.S. targets) in the face of (1) a growing American first-strike ability to destroy these missiles in their silos (Pershing II, cruise missile systems, B-1 and Stealth, Trident II, MX) and (2) America's expressed intent to "shoot down" any missiles that might have been missed in a first strike. Clearly the only possible Soviet response to this threat to its ICBM force would be to increase the number and flexibility of its ICBMs in order to prevent the potential loss of its main deterrent force. Only if the United States reduced its first-strike systems and abandoned the SDI would it make sense for the Soviet Union to reduce the number of the increasingly vulnerable ICBM.

In the early 1980s, the debate around U.S. nuclear strategy concerned three topics. (1) The early Reagan claim of a "window of vulnerability" became closely intertwined with his desire to build the MX missile. (2) The United States alleged there was a "spending gap" between U.S. and USSR military spending. (3) Ronald Reagan proposed a new ABM system—the Strategic Defense Initiative.

The Window of Vulnerability

During the 1980 presidential campaign the "window of vulnerability" emerged as a major threat to American security. Just as candidate John Kennedy had used the alleged "missile gap" effectively against the Republicans in 1960, candidate Ronald Reagan attempted in the 1980 campaign to blame the Democrats for the "window of vulnerability."[27]

In its most basic form, the "window of vulnerability" meant that a nation's ICBM silos were vulnerable to an accurate missile attack by an opponent. By the early 1980s, the advanced ICBMs of both the United States and the Soviet Union were becoming accurate enough to threaten, theoretically, the destruction of the ICBM silos of the opponent. Each additional increment of accuracy in a given weapons system increased its counterforce capability and therefore the possibility that a given system could be used to attack fixed land-based ICBM silos.

By the early 1980s, the controversial MX missile was being

promoted as the answer to the "window of vulnerability." With ten 300-kiloton warheads on each missile and a circular error probable of less than 400 feet at intercontinental range, the MX is technically one of the most effective counterforce weapons in the American arsenal. To justify the deployment of this first-strike weapon, however, scientists had to develop a "basing mode" that made the MX less vulnerable than the other silo-based American ICBM forces. When none of the Carter Admin-istration's plans to make the MX mobile (railroad cars and trucks) proved feasible, the problem of basing was left for the Reagan Administration. After pursuing the possibility of "dense pack" basing, which counted on missile "fratricide," the new administration ultimately decided that silo-based ICBM vulner-ability was not important in the first place, and decided to place the MX in existing American ICBM silos.

In the words of the Snowcroft Commission, which Reagan had appointed to solve the survivability problem:

> Whereas it is highly desirable that a component of the stra-tegic forces be survivable when it is viewed separately, it makes a major contribution to deterrence even if its survivability depends in substantial measure on the existence of one of the other components of the force.[28]

In other words, the "window of vulnerability" had never been of significance because of the size and strength of American bomber and SLBM forces.

With this convenient rationalization for the basing of the MX missile, the administration proceeded to pressure Congress into funding this incredibly expensive weapons system. By 1985, the United States had already spent over $14 billion on the MX and another $27 billion was scheduled to be spent by 1990, for a total of over $42 billion from 1974 through 1990.[29] Since the advanced Minuteman ICBMs were already more accurate than the Soviet heavy missiles, the MX could only be viewed as an-other first-strike weapons system in the American arsenal.

With over 70 percent of Soviet warheads on ICBM missiles, the question can legitimately be asked: If there had been a "window of vulnerability," which side was vulnerable? The United States had only about 25 percent of its warheads on ICBMs, with the rest on SLBMs and bombers. Over 50 percent of U.S. warheads were on invulnerable submarines. Even if the Soviet Union could destroy every American ICBM launcher, it would make no sense for them to leave over 7,000 American strategic warheads intact for the retaliation that would surely follow. Even by 1985, the Soviets were still relying on the liquid fuel SS-18 and SS-19 as their primary ICBM force, with all but sixty of their 4,900 ICBM warheads launched by the liquid fuel missiles, which are less mobile and slower to fire.

Like all other escalations of the arms race, this one prompted the Soviet Union to again try to catch up. By 1982, the Soviets had tested the solid fuel SS-X-24 and by the mid-1980s they had tested the SS-25 solid fuel missile.[30] Even though the Soviets moved toward greater reliance on solid fuels more than 20 years after the United States had, U.S. leaders now began ironically to claim that new Soviet missiles represented yet another "missile gap," again in favor of the Soviet Union.[31]

The Spending Gap

The Reagan Administration may have been forced to relinquish the "window of vulnerability" in order to gain the MX missile, but it had no intention of losing the debate over the "spending gap," which was an effective tool in frightening Congress into spending larger and larger sums on the military.

During the latter part of the 1960s and early 1970s, the Soviet Union, in response to the earlier American ICBM advantage, had indeed increased its military spending in order to complete its missile buildup. (See Chapter VI.) Allegations that the Soviet Union was spending 13 to 15 percent of its Gross National Product (GNP) on the military[32] were not effectively countered, however, by reminders that the Soviet Union's GNP was only half that of the United States. Only 6 to 7 percent of the U.S. GNP was needed to equal in dollars the Soviet expenditure of 14 percent of its GNP. Moreover, the Soviet buildup was essentially complete by 1977, and it was becoming apparent that with the elimination of the missile gap, the Soviets had reduced their annual increases in spending and stabilized their military procurement. A CIA report published in 1984 confirmed this.

> New information indicates that the Soviets did not field weapons as rapidly after 1976 as before. Practically all major categories of Soviet weapons were affected—missiles, aircraft, and ships. . . . the rate of growth of over-all defense costs is lower because procurement of military hardware—the largest category of defense spending—was almost flat in 1976–1981 . . . [and that trend] appears to have continued also in 1982 and 1983.[33]

The following year, Senator William Proxmire (Dem.-Wis.) also claimed that Soviet military spending had increased by only 2 percent in 1982 and that weapons procurement spending had not increased at all. The Pentagon and the Defense Intelligence Agency disagreed with these estimates, insisting that Soviet military spending was growing at an annual rate of 4 to 5 percent. In spite of this evidence, the Reagan Administration was calling for an increase in U.S. military spending of 6.6 percent after adjustment for inflation.[34]

At this point, it is worth noting that *only* the military budget has its increases stated as a percent *after adjustment for inflation*. Increases for domestic social programs are stated in simple increases over the amount of the past year. Thus if inflation for a given year is 5 percent and the military increase is 6.6 percent, the total increase is 11.6 percent for the military. On the other hand, Aid to Families with Dependent Children is calculated as a percent of increase over the past year, with no compensation for inflation. Thus, a 2 percent increase at a time of 5 percent inflation means a decrease of 3 percent for AFDC.

The difficulties in accurately comparing American and Soviet military spending should not be underestimated. One factor complicating this comparison is the American belief that sea power is essential to U.S. security. Behind two oceans of three and five thousand miles and with no enemy on its borders, the fundamental security of the United States has been challenged only as bombers and missiles became intercontinental. Only the nuclear weapons of the Soviet Union, half a world away, threaten the United States directly. On the other hand, the Soviet Union is a "heartland" power, a nation at the center of the Eurasian landmass. Historically, Russia has attempted to expand both east and west and in turn has been invaded or challenged on its eastern and western borders. The enemies of Russia have been more of an immediate threat than those of the United States.

On the basis of geography alone, the real and perceived military requirements of these two nations are different. For example, the American navy is designed to protect the world's sea lanes and trade routes, and to project American military power anywhere in the world, whereas the Soviet navy is designed to disrupt world-wide sea lanes and protect the coastal waters of the Soviet Union. Different missions require different weapons and no case better illustrates this than the 13 large American aircraft carrier task forces, which can project American military power on a global scale. The Soviet navy has no counterpart to such a projection force. Again, in design, function, weapons, and organization, the armies of the United States and the Soviet Union differ according to the specific missions assigned to these military forces.

Another factor complicating the comparison between American and Soviet military spending is that the Soviet Union spends approximately 50 percent of its military budget on areas that have little or nothing to do with the United States.[35] Fortifying the Sino-Soviet border, controlling Eastern Europe, fighting a war in Afghanistan, and maintaining internal control (KGB) require major expenditures and are important to Soviet perceptions of their national security, but are not directly related to the threat of the American military. Money spent on these problems should not be placed in the same category as spending on those forces in direct confrontation with the United States. By contrast, almost all American military expenditures are rationalized as a response to the communist challenge directed by the Soviet Union.

Further complicating the comparison of spending figures is the ruble. The Soviet economy does not operate within the world capitalist market, and the exact value of the ruble is thus extremely difficult to determine in comparison to the dollar. U.S. inflation rates and increases in Soviet costs are not comparable. Moreover, it is worth remembering that the all-volunteer military of the United States is much more expensive than the conscripted armed forces of the Soviet Union. Perhaps most significant is the peculiar practice by which American defense contractors are asked to estimate the cost of a given Soviet weapons system based on their own projected costs for the same system. Thus, for example, the U.S. government might ask General Electric how much it costs the Soviet Union to produce a jet aircraft engine. General Electric then estimates the cost of the engine to the Soviets according to U.S. costs. Since defense contractors want lucrative government contracts, their natural tendency would be to estimate high Soviet costs in order to justify their own high estimates on comparable weapons systems. The information needed to produce accurate comparative estimates is simply not available to U.S. civilians or even to the U.S. government.

All of the questions surrounding the "spending gap" notwithstanding, the Congress and the American people seemed to accept the "spending gap" and American military spending increased dramatically. Over-all, the American military budget was scheduled to rise from a little less than $200 billion in 1980 to almost $400 billion annually by 1990, or an increase of over 90 percent in ten years. During the same period, direct military costs were expected to rise from 23 percent of the federal budget in 1980 to 36 percent by 1990. Weapons procurement costs alone began a decade-long increase from $35 billion in 1980 to a projected $106 billion by 1986.[36] This fundamental shift of American wealth took place at a time of record-breaking budget deficits, extreme shortfalls in the U.S. balance of payments, and drastic restrictions on domestic programs.

This distortion and misallocation of American wealth goes far beyond the scope of this study. Ironically, during this period of massive military expenditures, the United States has grown less secure from the threat of war. Each new generation of nuclear weapons made nuclear war more, rather than less, probable, and led to the inevitable increases in Soviet military programs. By the mid-1980s, it appeared that eventually the "spending gap" would join the "bomber gap," the "missile gap," the ABM gap, and the civil defense gap as another misperception of what the Soviet Union was really doing. And, as in past cases, the "spending gap" myth had performed its function of persuading Americans and Congress to increase the military budget. If forced to do so, the Reagan administration could discard the "spending gap" with no damage to its political credibility. Indeed, new myths were already being created as the Department of Defense introduced the "warhead gap" and the Pentagon issued its *Soviet Military Power* (*1985*), a precursor of the debate on "Star Wars" technology.

The Strategic Defense Initiative

On March 23, 1983, President Reagan announced the new Strategic Defense Initiative (SDI) to be pursued by the United States.

> I am directing a comprehensive and intensive effort to define a long-term research and development program to begin to achieve our ultimate goal of eliminating the threat posed by strategic nuclear missiles.[37]

From this point forward, the United States would pursue a strategy that would "render these weapons impotent and obsolete."[38] With these words, the President of the United States officially announced the American decision to develop an ABM (antiballistic missile) system and thereby to violate the 1972 ABM treaty. Simultaneously, the nuclear arms race publicly entered the realm of outer space, though in reality it had been conducted there since the 1950s.

Earlier "technological fixes" had not guaranteed American security or even increased it. Advanced bombers, ICBMs, MIRVs, ABMs, and a host of other programs had not led to greater American security in the nuclear age; but "Star Wars," as the media labeled it, was going to render all of this weaponry "obsolete." The United States was going to move from the philosophy of deterrence, encoded as mutually assured destruction (MAD) (to which it had never fully adhered), to the policy of mutually assured survival (MAS), an illusion in the nuclear age.

The Reagan Administration again asserted that even in this area the Soviet Union continued to outspend and outbuild the United States, and Secretary of Defense Weinberger and his department claimed that the Soviet SDI effort was "much larger than the United States effort."[39] The Soviet effort, as always, was said to destabilize the balance of terror, whereas the American SDI enhanced it.[40] With the introduction of the new space technologies, U.S. leaders conveniently faced an almost unlimited number of esoteric "gaps" in American defense that could only be closed by larger military appropriations. Space war strategies were a bottomless pit into which to throw the world's resources.

Conceptually, the SDI was an enormously complex system that relied on two basic components. The first was designed to "shoot down" Soviet missiles at some point between the time they were launched and the time they reached the target in the United States. The second component was an antisatellite (ASAT) capability that would "blind" Soviet intelligence operations by destroying its satellites.

As billions of dollars were being spent on this technology, the wrong questions about SDI were being asked. Concerned parties were asking, Can it work? instead of asking, What is the assigned mission of this weapons system once developed? By arguing about the complex technology of SDI, attention was diverted from the fundamental question of the purpose of SDI when it came into operation.

In spite of President Reagan's earlier statement that SDI would make nuclear weapons obsolete, by 1985 the U.S. government had conceded that SDI could not guarantee the safety of American cities from Soviet attack: The Soviets had too many warheads.[41] Thus, the only realistic mission of the SDI was to protect American nuclear delivery systems. Since America's submarine fleet and alerted bomber forces were not vulnerable to Soviet surprise attack, the SDI would theoretically protect land-based ICBMs left in their silos during a Soviet attack. The decision to risk losing these ICBMs or launch them before Soviet warheads detonated would obviously be a conscious one. But since little warning time (less than 2 minutes) was required to launch these solid fuel missiles and since the American military would undoubtedly resist allowing these missiles to "ride out" a Soviet surprise attack, they would most likely be launched rather than left for possible destruction.[42]

Thus in examining the American SDI strategy, a Soviet analyst could legitimately ask: If the SDI could not defend the American population and if the United States would launch its missiles rather than risk that SDI's ABM component could not protect it from Soviet attack, then why develop and build the SDI system in the first place? It would seem that the only logical explanation for this system is one never mentioned by the Department of Defense or the President of the United States: *The Strategic Defensive Initiative is not a defensive system but an offensive system.* Rather than defending against a Soviet attack, it is designed to "mop up" after an American surprise attack. Or, put another way, if a hypothetical first strike by the United States on the Soviet Union destroys 1,200 of 1,500 Soviet missile launchers, 300 launchers would be left for Soviet retaliation. The SDI system would then be responsible for destroying these remaining forces. Thus, this technology would not be called upon or designed to destroy 100 percent of the Soviet attack force, but only the 20 percent left after an initial surprise attack by the United States has reduced the original force and seriously disrupted ("decapitated" in Pentagonese) the command and control systems of the Soviet Union.

The above analysis does not necessarily mean that the United States is going to launch a first strike against the Soviet Union. Rather, it means that the SDI would add credibility to the possible American use of nuclear weapons and would increase the Soviet fear of this possibility. The Soviet Union would be prevented by a fear of this possibility from vigorously pursuing its foreign policy goals or from actively resisting world-wide U.S. actions. The SDI would also increase the probability that the United States would use tactical, theater, or strategic nuclear weapons in an increasingly volatile and revolutionary world. The Strategic Defense Initiative represents a quantum escalation of the arms race and a serious increased threat to world peace.

The debate on the workability of the SDI continues, but money is readily available from a willing Congress. Research costs for the first five years are placed at $30 billion.[43] The technological complexity of attempting to destroy even 20 percent of a Soviet launch force (currently 1,500) is staggering. The entire Soviet missile force would have to be destroyed in less than an hour. The SDI blueprint calls for the vast majority of this destruction to take place during the "boost phase," the first 180 to 300 seconds from missile launch.[44] A major article in *Scientific American* identified four other severe weaknesses of such a system: (1) A defensive force could easily be overwhelmed by an offensive buildup; (2) all offensive systems would have to be subject to attack by the defensive system; (3) SDI would be extremely vulnerable to attack; and (4) an infrared detection system could be easily deceived by decoys.[45] A study prepared for the congressional Office of Technological Assessment by Ashton Carter concluded that the possibility of "a perfect or near perfect defense system is so remote that it should not serve as the basis of public expectations or national policy."[46]

As though the destruction of 1,500 Soviet launch vehicles were not complicated enough, two other components of the SDI strategy made it even more complex. Antisatellite (ASAT) warfare and the military control of space were essential for the SDI antiballistic missile system. The development of ASAT and the militarization of space combined with SDI technology represented future military spending of a magnitude that truly staggered the imagination.

Although neither side possessed deep space ASAT weapons in 1985, the United States had assumed its usual technological lead over the Soviet Union in this dangerous technology.[47] The ability to destroy an opponent's satellites was the ability to "blind" an opponent in the event of an attack and to destroy major components of its command and control systems. In the event of war, the continued existence of American military satellites had to be guaranteed for Reagan's SDI, and the destruction of the Soviet satellite system was an equally important part of this ABM (antiballistic missile) system. In order for the SDI to succeed, the United States would have to increase its ASAT warfare capability. In the mid-1980s the ASAT arms race was escalating as the United States continued development of the air-launched miniature homing vehicle, which would be carried by the F-15 as an integral part of an ASAT system.[48]

The militarization of space by the United States and the Soviet Union began in the late 1950s. As the American public focused on U.S. civilian space accomplishments, the United States achieved and maintained "technical superiority" over the Soviet Union in the military uses of space. The U.S. Air Force recognized space as the "ultimate high ground" and claimed that the United States would continue to exploit "the potential of space to conduct operations as required to further military objectives." A Pentagon spokesperson, Michael I. Burch, stated U.S. policy toward space in the clearest possible terms.

The Air Force will maintain U.S. technological superiority in the Aerospace and ensure a prolonged war-fighting capability by developing the potential for combat operations in the space medium.[49]

The American decision to pursue the SDI and to escalate the arms race in space prompted an immediate and predictable response from the Soviet Union. Yuri Andropov stated in *Pravda:*

All attempts at gaining military superiority over the USSR are futile. The Soviet Union will never allow them [the U.S.] to succeed. It will never be caught defenseless by any threat.

Let there be no mistake about this in Washington. It is time they stopped devising one option after another in search of the best ways of unleashing nuclear war in the hope of winning it. Engaging in this is not irresponsible, it is insane.[50]

In 1984 the Soviet Union had "authoritatively and concretely declared that it unilaterally assumes the obligation not to test and deploy anti-satellite systems."[51] By 1984, the Soviet Union had already unilaterally declared that it would not use nuclear weapons first and called for a "freeze" on nuclear weapons. These Soviet initiatives were not matched by the United States. Development of the SDI and ASAT continues, the "first use" of nuclear weapons remains the policy of the United States, and the "freeze" was never seriously considered by the Reagan Administration. Thus another opportunity to slow the arms race was lost. If the United States had agreed to stop the testing and deployment of ASAT systems, the arms race in space could have effectively been prevented. The effectiveness of the ASAT system in 1985 was limited and required a sustained testing period. The inability to continue testing of this technology would mean the inability to deploy it. Since the "blinding" of satellites is the first step in a nuclear war, a ban on the development of this destabilizing system would seem to be to the advantage of all parties. But the United States refuses to enter into negotiations for banning ASAT because it prefers to pursue its SDI advantage. Once again, the sincerity of U.S. interest in meaningful negotiations with the Soviet Union must be questioned.

NUCLEAR WINTER: CONTROLLING THE DOOMSDAY MACHINE

As the Reagan Administration increased the military budget and devised even more sophisticated ways to fight a nuclear war, scientists in both the Soviet Union and the United States began to articulate a theory of nuclear war that would appear to truly render these weapons "obsolete." The Conference on the World after Nuclear War held in 1983 presented the scientific theory that a nuclear war of even a limited magnitude would result in "nuclear winter."[52]

At an earlier stage of the arms race, Herman Kahn had half-seriously suggested (in *On Thermonuclear War*, 1961) that the perfect deterrent would be a nuclear doomsday machine that absolutely guaranteed world-wide annihilation in the event of any nuclear attack. With such a machine in place, deterrence would become absolute. The superpowers may have inadvertently stumbled over their own version of a doomsday machine in creating the possibility of a nuclear winter.

The estimates of the cost of a nuclear war and then a nuclear winter are numbing. The World Health Organization has estimated that the immediate casualties from a nuclear war would be over 2,000,000,000 people. This would be the casualty figure at the beginning of nuclear winter. Nuclear winter would come more slowly, but steadily:

> Within one or two weeks, the individual plumes of dust and soot would coalesce in an enormous dark cloud shrouding most of the Northern Hemisphere, particularly the mid-latitude belt encompassing most of the United States, Canada, the Soviet Union, Europe, China and Japan. Beneath the spreading clouds, very little sunlight—in the worst cases, as little as a tenth of one percent of the normal light level, averaged over the hemisphere—could reach the surface. Even relatively limited wars could reduce light intensities by 95 percent or more.[53]

Continental temperatures would drop to below −20 degrees Centigrade (below 0 Fahrenheit). It would take over three months to recover, and when the skies did clear, the stratosphere ozone would be destroyed, allowing the penetration of radiation in the ultraviolet range. As one panelist at the conference put it, an attacker would "win" for only about two weeks.[54]

It is estimated that nuclear winter could be brought about by the explosion of as few as 100 megatons in an attack on cities. If the attack were a counterforce strike, then 2,000 to 3,000 warheads targeted on silos would have a comparable result. By the mid-1980s conservative estimates placed the number of stored and deliverable megatons at over 12,000 in the world's arsenals. Less than 1 percent of the world's nuclear megatonnage could induce a nuclear winter.[55]

The concept of nuclear winter was endorsed by the National Academy of Sciences. Soviet scientists also confirmed the findings on nuclear winter.[56] If this assessment of the atmospheric impact of nuclear winter is correct, then theories of deterrence are meaningless and theories of "prevailing" and "winning" a nuclear war are irrational. But many do not understand this.

Although Secretary of Defense Caspar Weinberger admitted that the danger of nuclear winter "might" exist, the Department of Defense did not use this new information to reexamine old policies; rather it used it to justify existing ones. Thus, nuclear winter was used as evidence to support (1) the Pentagon's counterforce doctrine of not attacking cities, but of targeting Soviet nuclear delivery systems; (2) the development of greater accuracy by allegedly smaller warheads on American missiles for a counterforce attack; and (3) the continued development of SDI.[57] Nuclear winter became yet another rationalization for the United States to promote a threatening first-strike counterforce.

In the face of the possibility of nuclear winter, the Reagan Administration's reaffirmation of its counterforce doctrine meant that the fate of the world was being gambled on two basic assumptions: first, that a U.S. counterforce attack would not set off nuclear winter, and, second, that the U.S. attack would be so successful that the Soviet Union could not retaliate against American cities. The stakes of this gamble were no less than the fate of humanity. If the world had lived with a delicate balance of terror in earlier years, the introduction of the concept of nuclear winter increased the terror and further destabilized the balance. The likelihood of nuclear winter made it clear that there was more to be lost in a nuclear war than the experts had realized and a counterforce doctrine brought nuclear war that much closer to reality.

This dangerous doctrine had to meet four conditions to have even the remotest chance of being viable: (1) Under no circumstances could the Soviet Union be allowed to conduct a counter-city retaliatory attack against American cities; (2) there could be no human or machine error; (3) "escalation control" in the event of nuclear war had to be absolute; and (4) U.S. command, control, communications, and intelligence (C3I) systems would have to survive and function perfectly.

Points one and two are relatively easy to deal with. Only a

perfect first strike, with ABM backup, could prevent Soviet retaliation; and human or machine perfection has yet to be demonstrated. Points three and four are more difficult. "Escalation
control" and the survivability of C3I systems represent some of
the most complex and frustrating problems facing war planners
in the United States or Soviet Union.

COMMAND, CONTROL, COMMUNICATION
AND INTELLIGENCE C3I

In its most basic form, the question facing planners is how to
control nuclear war if C3I centers are destroyed. It is estimated
that 250 Soviet warheads (with over 6,000 available) would
effectively destroy C3I centers of the United States within 5
hours of the outbreak of nuclear war. Government leaders in
Washington or Moscow would live less than 8 minutes once
nuclear war began. According to actual exercises, it is impossible to place leaders in a "safe" command center with less than
8 minutes of warning time. The President of the United States
would not survive the first 15 minutes of the war, much less live
long enough to control American nuclear forces.[58]

When Ronald Reagan was wounded by an assassin's bullet, the
American people got a glimpse of the difficulties in dealing with
succession in the American chain of command. Secretary of
State Haig informed the country that he was "in charge" while
many people wondered what had happened to the Vice-
President. In a nuclear war, exactly who was alive and in charge
would be very difficult to determine. In a worst-case scenario,
the Soviet Union would attack Washington during the President's State of the Union address, a time when American military and political leaders would be together in the targeted city,
leaving the government and its defense in chaos.

Let us follow this scenario further. Even if it were clear who
could give the orders to use American nuclear weapons, it is
not clear how these orders would be transmitted once the communications system had been seriously disrupted or even destroyed. The current C3I systems of radars, communication net-
works, satellites, and ground-air control centers are extremely

vulnerable to nuclear attack. The destruction of Washington, D.C., the North American Aerospace Defense Command (NORAD) in Colorado Springs, and SAC headquarters in Omaha, Nebraska, would cripple the command and control system of the United States. Airborne command centers would have limited effectiveness—the airborne command center for the President, Kneecap, would not have the President on board, and SAC's airborne center, Looking Glass, would be vulnerable to the effects of the nuclear attack and "blinded" by the loss of contact resulting from the destruction of NORAD headquarters. General Bruce K. Holloway (SAC commander in 1968–1972) said that "if the enemy struck first—barraged Washington, Omaha, etc.—we'd never recover, never recover control, never recover anything."[59]

Although the C3I systems are vulnerable to attack, the weapons would survive. The alert status of the bomber force, the invulnerability of U.S. submarines, and the ability to quickly fire land-based ICBMs mean that all of these systems could be used in a nuclear war. But they could not be "controlled" under any circumstances other than a U.S. first strike. The alleged dilemma of "use them or lose them" is only true of ICBMs; the real dilemma of nuclear weapons is to use them or lose control over them. Most nuclear weapons could be used even in the absence of the civilian approval allegedly needed for their use. For example, the submarine forces can launch their missiles with no external or civilian control, using only personnel and systems on the submarines. The missiles can be launched by a complex series of actions indicating agreement by critical officer personnel that the missiles be launched. With its tremendous firepower, a single Poseidon or Trident submarine could theoretically roam the oceans for weeks after a nuclear war had begun and then decide to launch its missiles.[60]

American command and control systems work relatively well in peacetime and thus far have worked safely to prevent the accidental launch of nuclear weapons. These systems would theoretically perform well in the event of a first strike by the United States. In spite of all efforts to make these systems secure in wartime, they are still peacetime systems. In 1980, the

United States spent $8 billion on C3I and by 1986 $22 billion will be spent on these systems, representing a 275 percent increase in spending.[61] Yet their continued vulnerability to attack confirms that there must be a basic policy of never allowing these systems to be hit first.

The United States continues to develop and deploy weapons with a "prompt hard target kill capability" (MX, Pershing II, Trident D-5). The continued American dominance in the technology of accuracy as demonstrated in the MX, the invulnerability and accuracy of the Trident D-5, and the basing mode in Europe of the Pershing II and cruise systems are clearly threatening to Soviet security. To the extent that the Soviet Union deploys first-strike systems (primarily the SS-18), the United States feels threatened. But under attack the Soviet Union, with its heavy reliance on vulnerable ICBMs, could lose many of its weapons as well as command systems. This Soviet vulnerability increases the chance of nuclear war, since the Soviets are more likely than the United States to feel pressured to avoid a "use them or lose them" situation. The United States presses its technological advantage over the Soviet Union at considerable risk to its own national survival.

During "normal" times, the safety mechanisms on these weapons are stringent and have yet to fail in a manner that could lead to an accidental launch or explosion. Nevertheless, as international tensions increase the safety systems will gradually be reduced in preparation for immediate launch. To avoid absorbing a first strike, all systems must be ready to fire within minutes of warning. It is at this stage that the SIOP sets in motion the "automatic phase of the war." As General Snowcroft has said, "that is the time at which the quick-response systems are discharged against predetermined targets, and so on, and the battle plan unfolds more or less automatically."[62] There would be little time to ponder the significance of what was happening. World War III, like World War I, could be caused by automatic military responses that could not be controlled quickly enough to prevent war.

The nuclear weapons of the United States and the Soviet Union have created a doomsday machine that becomes more difficult to control with each passing year. Yet the United States continues to integrate the use or threatened use of nuclear weapons into its foreign policy. Nowhere is this more evident than in the U.S. policy toward Europe.

EUROMISSILES: NUCLEAR WEAPONS AND NATO

Immediately following World War II, a conventional defense of Europe against Soviet attack was not politically or militarily possible. But as Europe recovered from the war, regaining manpower, industrial strength, and technology, initiating a conventional defense for Europe required only a political decision. This decision was not made. At no time since the founding of NATO have the member nations fulfilled the budgetary commitments to the Alliance that would have guaranteed this defense. By the 1980s the NATO nations outdistanced the Warsaw Pact nations in every category of national power except convention forces in being (see Table III).

That a conventional defense was not built is primarily attributable to three causes. First, Europeans did not believe that the Red Army was poised to move west at any moment and were not prepared to make the necessary sacrifices to build up a conventional response to a limited or nonexistent threat. Second, it

TABLE III[63]

COMPARATIVE STRENGTH—NATO AND
WARSAW PACT 1980

	NATO	Warsaw Pact
Population	626 million	380 million
GNP	5,975 billion	2,020 billion
Military spending	$256 billion	$202 billion
Military manpower	5.8 million	4.8 million
Strategic warheads	10,000	7,800
Total nuclear weapons	31,000	20,000
Nuclear warheads in Europe	6,000	4,000 (1984 figure)

was easier and certainly cheaper to rely on the nuclear weapons of the United States to deter any possible attack by the Soviet Union. Third, since 1870, the world has been wary of a militarily strong Germany. Thus, forty years into the Cold War, the Europeans remain dependent on the United States to establish and define European security and to make decisions on European war and peace.

The essential strategy for the defense of Europe remained an initial American conventional "flexible response" to be followed within days, if not hours, by the "first use" of small, battlefield nuclear weapons. This would mean the early first use of tactical nuclear weapons on the battlefield "coupled" to the use of theater, intermediate, and strategic weapons as needed.

With the exception of France, the governments of the NATO nations have acquiesced to these policies; European leaders have been content to place the security and existence of their nations in the hands of the United States. But as the period of absolute American nuclear superiority came to an end in the 1970s, the credibility of the American policies of "flexible response" and "first use" weakened dramatically (see Table IV).

TABLE IV[64]

Weapons	Projected Number	Warheads	Range in Miles	Kilotons	CEP in Feet
SS-20	414	1,242	3,000	150	1,200
Pershing II	108	108	1,100– 1,600	80	100
Cruise	464	464	1,500– 2,200	150	300

* By 1985, the United States had the following forward-based delivery systems capable of reaching Soviet targets: 400 Poseidon warheads assigned to NATO, 161 F-111 bombers, 20 A6 (carrier-based), 48 A7 (carrier-based), and 750 F-16s. The British had 64 SLBMs and 56 Vulcan bombers; the French had 18 IMBMs, 96 SLBMs, and 33 Mirage IV bombers.[65] It was estimated that, excluding Euromissiles, the United States had 2,200 nuclear forward based warheads in Europe capable of attacking Soviet territory.[66]

The 1977 Soviet introduction of the SS-20 missile not only modernized the theater nuclear forces of the Soviet Union but also reaffirmed, in the strongest possible terms, the Soviet policy that all of Europe would be annihilated in the event of a "limited nuclear war" in Europe that threatened Soviet security. The Soviet Union did not share the U.S. belief that a "limited nuclear war" could be fought in Europe without expanding to include the homelands of the superpowers. The SS-20 replaced cumbersome, less-mobile liquid fuel SS-4 and SS-5 missiles already assigned to Europe. The solid fuel and mobile SS-20 meant that the United States could no longer be certain of finding and destroying Soviet nuclear forces in Europe. The American strategy of "limited nuclear war" lost all meaning in the face of the three 150 kiloton warheads on the SS-20. (By 1985 there would be approximately 900 warheads on 300 SS-20s targeted for Europe.)[67] But in spite of its accuracy, the SS-20 was of no use against British, French, or American NATO-assigned submarine forces. Nor could the SS-20 be guaranteed effective against American Euromissiles—the mobile Pershing II and ground launched cruise missiles (GLCMs). Whatever the original reasons for deploying Euromissiles, the end result of their deployment was to further enhance the first-strike capability and threatening posture of the American strategic forces. The introduction of U.S. Euromissiles expanded the boundaries of any European war into the Soviet Union and further served to ensure that any war would be a world war. Both Pershing II and GLCMs in Europe were strategic systems that could attack Soviet nuclear delivery systems and command centers. Deterrence, as well as tactical or theater missions that might be assigned to these Euromissiles, could be just as easily accomplished by other delivery means already in place, leaving the Pershing and GLCMs free for a counterforce, first-strike mission.

The Pentagon insisted that the Pershing II missile could not reach the Kremlin, but only the "western suburbs" of Moscow. This claim was rejected by the Soviets on the premise that the United States would not design a weapon to fall "just short of its obvious target." Soviet leaders could justifiably take the Pershing II "personally" as a weapon designed to ensure their immediate death in the event of war. The 100-foot circle of probable error of the Pershing II meant that all command and control centers in the western part of the Soviet Union were vulnerable to destruction in less than 10 minutes after the outbreak of war. In military language, this weapon could "decapitate" Soviet command centers.[68]

Perhaps the only way to understand how the Soviet Union perceived the Pershing II would be to imagine an American reaction to the Soviet placement of SS-20s in Cuba. In this case, the Soviet Union could protest that the defensive SS-20s were less accurate than the Pershing IIs and were deployed only to prevent an invasion of Cuba. Nevertheless, the presence of the SS-20 less ten minutes from U.S. territory, including Washington, D.C., would logically cause American policy makers to doubt its alleged mission.

In addition to the 108 Pershing II missiles to be sent to Germany, the United States planned on deploying 464 GLCMs throughout the rest of Europe. Deployment of both systems began in 1983, with the following schedule for GLCMs: Britain 160, Germany 96, Belgium 48, the Netherlands 48, and Italy 112.[69] The cruise missiles stationed in Sicily were targeted for the Middle East (not the USSR) and would thereby "couple" American policies in the Middle East to the American strategic policy and the Carter Doctrine of using nuclear weapons first if U.S. interests in the Middle East were threatened.[70]

Ironically, in fact, both the United States and the Soviet Union were following a war policy that dictated annihilating Europe if either side felt that it was losing. The power and mobility of the SS-20 was to make "limited" nuclear war in Europe even more unacceptable to the Europeans. The confusion and increased dangers created by the SS-20 and Euromissiles led many Europeans to search for a different strategy to ensure their security.

The 1979 initiative requesting American Euromissiles (Pershing II and GLCMs) came from Germany in an effort to maintain the credibility of the "coupling" of U.S. strategic forces with the defense of Europe. Thus, the American decision to deploy Pershing IIs and cruise missiles in Europe was allegedly a response to the deployment of the SS-20 as an assurance of an American nuclear response to a successful Soviet attack on Western Europe. In reality, these missiles did not neutralize the presence of the SS-20 in any way, nor were they assigned a mission similar to that of the SS-20. If the goal of the American deployment of Euromissiles (Pershing IIs and GLCMs) was to reassure Europeans in the nuclear age, the United States failed to achieve this goal. Public opinion polls in Germany, France, Britain, Italy, Spain, and the Netherlands showed that less than 20 percent of the population of these nations supported the U.S. deployment of Euromissiles.[71]

The wars of the twentieth century have given the Europeans a catastrophic consciousness not possessed by most Americans. Americans tend to look at the threat of nuclear disaster and believe that it cannot happen to them. Europeans *know* that disasters beyond the imagination are possible. To many Europeans, Euromissiles represent an increased chance of nuclear war, and nuclear war on the crowded continent means disaster. The World Health Organization has estimated that 9 million Europeans would be killed outright with the detonation of 20 megatons in Central Europe. Twenty megatons represents far less than 15 percent of the megatonnage available to the projected number of Soviet SS-20s and less than one-fifth of 1 percent of the total megatonnage available world-wide.[72]

In October 1983 over a million and a half Europeans took to the streets to oppose U.S. Euromissiles. Some European leaders may have wanted Euromissiles, but most Europeans did not. The Europeans did not want the Soviet SS-20 in Europe, but it was the American Euromissiles that they feared most, for they believed that the U.S. missiles targeted on the Soviet Union guaranteed that Europe would immediately be drawn into a U.S.-USSR conflict. Since these missiles could be used for a first strike on Soviet targets, the Soviet Union would obviously make the destruction of these European-based missiles a top priority in its war planning (the Soviet version of the SIOP).

In the United States, efforts were made to convince the American people that these Euromissiles were defensive and intended to match the Soviet SS-20 missiles. American leaders claimed an "INF gap" (intermediate nuclear forces) that was to be closed by Pershings and GLCMs. But as we have seen, the Soviet and American systems were not comparable. Although it was not understood by the American people, it was the official policy of the United States to use nuclear weapons first in response to a nonnuclear attack in Europe. Seventy-seven percent of the American people opposed American "first use" policy; and 81 percent thought that it was the official policy of the United States to use nuclear weapons *only* in response to Soviet use of nuclear weapons.[73] This fundamental contradiction between the public perception of U.S. policy and the avowed policy of the U.S. government has led to enormous confusion in the United States. This confusion demonstrates the success of the government of the United States in creating "myths" in order to justify offensive weapons as defensive.

The contradictions in American policy and the breakdown of a nuclear consensus in Europe led to increased emphasis on building a conventional defense in Europe. Secretary of Defense Weinberger called for military forces to prevent a "world dominated by Soviet hordes."[74] Past American foreign policy leaders, including ex-Secretary of Defense McNamara, began to call for a conventional buildup and a decreased reliance on "first use."[75]

Increasing the conventional forces in Europe might temporarily postpone the use of nuclear weapons, but it would simultaneously lower the threshold of war. The most obvious fact is often ignored in analyzing a possible European war: *Neither side would be willing to lose such a war*. Neither side would allow itself to be ejected from central Europe by military force without resorting to nuclear weapons to prevent such an action. From a European perspective, even a limited conventional war between the United States and the Soviet Union is unacceptable. The goal for Europe must be to prevent *any* war, not to make war "manageable."

The debate over the feasibility of a conventional defense of Europe continues. The Soviet advantage in key categories of conventional power (tanks, artillery, divisions) remains substantial.[76] In the 1970s any conventional defense of Europe could not rely on American reinforcements and this remained true in the mid-1980s for two reasons. First, it takes 10 days to move a single division (approximately 15,000 men) to Europe from the United States if its equipment is already there, or 19 days if the division must be moved with its equipment.[77] Second, even if these divisions could be moved more rapidly, there is no guarantee that they could be safely delivered to the Continent in the event of war. A conventional war in Europe would have to be conducted with the forces in place at the outbreak of hostilities along with European reinforcements. The belief that American reinforcements could play a decisive role in the defense of Europe must be discarded as the myth that it is.

Significantly, there is credible evidence that the United States has never planned on conducting a conventional defense on the Continent. In 1982, the NATO commander, General Bernard Rogers, admitted that conventional warfare by NATO forces in Europe was expected to last a matter of "days" before expanding to nuclear weapons.[78] In 1984, General Rogers admitted that NATO still had less than 30 days of ammunition stockpiled in the event of a conventional war in Europe. At the earliest, stockpiles for 30 days could not be achieved until 1990.[79] Since hundreds of billions of dollars had been spent on the U.S. commitment to NATO, the absence of ammunition stockpiles for more than 30 days is clear evidence that the United States had never planned on fighting a conventional conflict in Western Europe. The assumption had always been made that the conflict would "go nuclear."

By 1983 the United States was spending $133 billion per year, well over 40 percent of the military budget, ostensibly on the defense of Europe.[80] The absence of a conventional capability and of oil and ammunition stockpiles poses an obvious and important question: Where was this money being spent if it was not spent on a conventional defense of Europe? As we saw in Chapter VI, some of the resources claimed to be for use in Europe are actually used to arm and equip American Third World interventionary forces under the guise of a defense of Europe. An example of this type of expenditure is the American effort to dramatically increase its air and sea capability to rapidly deliver troops overseas. The $5.6 billion spent on air and sea lifts in 1984 was expected to increase to $7.4 billion in 1985, a 34 percent increase.[81] The public was told that this expenditure was justified by the need to rapidly reinforce Europe, but military planners knew that this transport capacity was primarily to be used to place large numbers of American troops throughout the world. The American public accepts with relative ease the defense of Europe as a justification for increased spending; spending for interventionary forces for Central America would be more seriously challenged.

DECOUPLING EUROPE: A DIPLOMATIC SOLUTION

There is no doubt that a conventional defense of Europe is possible by the NATO nations, although, historically, neither the United States nor its NATO allies have prepared for such a defense. The most important question on European military policy is rarely asked and even more rarely discussed: How great is the threat of a Soviet invasion of Western Europe? (The answer to questions on conventional defense depends upon empirical evidence on the condition of conventional military capabilities.) The extent of the Soviet threat depends on an assessment of intentions, and, in this, history is our only guide. Although historical evidence on intentions may be less reliable than empirical evidence on capabilities, historical evidence offers valuable insights on the type of behavior we can expect from specific nations.

The Soviet Union would like to remove Western Europe as a potential military threat to its security, providing there is no substantial penalty for obtaining control over this region. Nevertheless, since World War II, the Soviets have shown little inclination to put substantial resources into controlling those areas outside their immediate Eastern European "buffer zone." In three areas of Europe, the Soviet Union permitted its control to be decreased, if not eliminated—Yugoslavia, Austria, and Albania. Even in their primary "sphere of influence," the Soviets have allowed deviation from absolute control. A degree of autonomy for Finland and tolerance for Romanian foreign policy demonstrate this flexibility.

This tolerance of the Soviet Union should not be construed, however, as a change in its fundamental attitude toward Eastern Europe. Like other imperial powers, the Soviet Union has had great difficulty maintaining its client states and has been ruthless in its demand for fundamental allegiance and control— as demonstrated in Hungary, Czechoslovakia, and the German Democratic Republic. There is little likelihood that essential Soviet domination of Poland will be relinquished without a major conflict. Nonetheless, the political stability and military reliability of the satellite states of Eastern Europe remain suspect. At best, in a European war, the satellite armies could not be relied on to conduct offensive operations against Western Europe. They could only be expected to maintain internal order and defend national boundaries. In a worst-case scenario, Soviet supply lines would be disrupted in the satellite nations of Eastern Europe.

During the 1980s, the Soviet Union seemed to have settled on a policy about nuclear war. Ironically, as the leadership of the United States began to speak more of "winning" such a war, the leadership of the Soviet Union was beginning to accept that no victory was possible in such a war. Secretary Brezhnev's 1982 pledge that the Soviet Union not use nuclear weapons first was followed by the 1984 statement by the Soviet Chief of Staff, Marshal Arkomeyev, that publicly reaffirmed official Soviet policy:

> He who fires his missiles first will perish second, but perish just the same. . . . One can turn the adversary into ashes, but cannot thereby emerge victorious. . . . Nuclear might is a means not only of annihilation but also of self-annihilation.[82]

A combination of unrest in the satellite states, attitudes toward nuclear war, confrontation with China, problems in South Asia, and economic weakness at home would indicate that the Soviet Union is not interested in starting a European war. The question then remains: Why does the Soviet Union maintain such a large military force in Europe? In spite of its problems and commitments elsewhere, the Soviet Union cannot afford to ignore Germany. To the USSR, the possible military confrontation in Central Europe would be primarily against an American-supported resurgent Germany.[83] Germany has invaded the Soviet Union twice during this century and under no circumstances will the Soviet Union allow another invasion. In World War II, Hitler's armies started from the Soviet border and moved east; strong Soviet forces in Eastern Europe guarantee that a future war with the West will not begin on its border or be fought on its territory. In the event of a war in Europe, the Soviet Union is determined that this war will be fought in Western Europe and not in the Soviet Union.

Changes in current policies and doctrines in Europe entail risks to the nations involved, but no risk is greater than the present one, which is the absolute destruction of Europe (if not the planet) in the event of accident or miscalculation.

Resolving the lingering problem of Germany is an absolutely essential ingredient in any solution to the dangerous confrontation between the United States and the Soviet Union in Europe. Since German military power has been the most destabilizing force in Europe in the twentieth century, the removal of Germany as a military threat in Europe represents the first step toward a lasting European peace. This can be accomplished by simultaneously disarming, neutralizing, and then unifying the two Germanies. This represents the peace settlement to World War II that should have been imposed in 1945.

At the same time, the establishment of a nuclear-free zone that runs from the Arctic to the Aegean Sea would further disengage Soviet and American military forces in Europe. Nuclear weapons would be removed or banned from Germany, Poland, Czechoslovakia, Hungary, Romania, Bulgaria, Belgium, the Netherlands, Greece, Turkey and Italy. Neutral Austria, Switzerland, and nonaligned Yugoslavia would complete this nuclear-free zone through the center of the Continent. This disengagement would leave nuclear weapons only on the national territories of the nuclear nations—the Soviet Union, Great Britain, and France. Finally, at the Balance Force Reduction Talks in Vienna, the European nations would negotiate the final conventional force levels for Europe, along with the strategic deterrent forces of the European nations with nuclear weapons.

Under such an agreement, all nations would benefit—for Germany, unification; for the Soviet Union, the removal of the German threat; for Europe, a large step away from nuclear war; and for the United States, a dramatically reduced financial and military commitment. The entire world would no longer be threatened by the immediacy of the nuclear war that accompanies current European doctrines and national policies.

THE DEADLY CONNECTION

In Europe nuclear weapons had superseded conventional forces as the primary instrument of American policy. This was not the case in the Third World. In these nations, nuclear weapons became the shield behind which American forces could intervene directly or indirectly world-wide. Thus, the Reagan Administration's escalations of the arms race represented by the hard target "kill capability" of the MX missile, Trident II, cruise technology, and the SDI, which discourage Soviet actions or countermoves, have meant dramatic increases in the ability of the United States to intervene unmolested in the Third World.

The Reagan Administration has not given prominence to the "deadly connection" between nuclear and conventional forces; nor has it totally obscured this connection. At his confirmation hearings as Director of the Arms Control and Disarmament Agency in 1981, Eugene Rostow made it clear that the United States did not believe that mere deterrence was the policy of this country. To have only a "strategic balance" would mean that the United States "would be in no position to use conventional or nuclear forces in defense of our interests in Europe, the Far East, the Middle East or elsewhere." Only an American nuclear advantage and adequate military strength deployed around the world would allow for the maintenance of "a progressive and integrated capitalist world economy which serves the interests of the industrialized and developing nations alike."[84]

Randall Forsberg also articulated the connection between nuclear weapons and interventionary forces:

> The only place the new generation of nuclear weapons actually plays a role, an active role in international politics, is in backing up intervention on our part and deterring intervention on the part of the Soviet Union.[85]

Past political administrations have gone to considerable effort to make American nuclear strategy appear to be separate from American use of nonnuclear military power. A clear admission of this "deadly connection" could lead to opposition by the American people to conventional buildups as well as to nuclear escalations of the arms race. Until this connection is made, it is possible for members of Congress to simultaneously give the appearance of opposing dangerous nuclear weapons while still claiming to be for a "strong national defense" by voting annually for large military budgets.

Perhaps one of the greatest ironies of the nuclear arms race is that no one is exactly certain how effective nuclear weapons are in supporting American policy. Nuclear weapons did not stop Chinese intervention in Korea, prevent American failures in China, Cuba, or Vietnam, or deter Soviet military action in Hungary, Czechoslovakia, or Afghanistan. Nor were nuclear weapons decisive (or even important) in American "successes" in Iran (1956), Guatemala (1954), the Dominican Republic (1965), or Chile (1973). Only the Cuban missile crisis can be called a case of "atomic diplomacy" that "worked"—and in this crisis the world went to the brink of thermonuclear war for reasons that did not justify the risk.

It is impossible to overemphasize the importance of the connection between nuclear and conventional forces. For whether the policy works or not, all eight political administrations since the end of World War II have believed that it does. To understand this official policy is to understand why the Reagan Administration spent over a trillion dollars on the military during its first five years in office, and is escalating the nuclear arms race in spite of the massive overkill capacity already in place.

Secretary of Defense Weinberger stated the administration's military policy in the clearest possible terms when he said: "If we value our freedom, we must be able to defend ourselves in wars of any size and shape and in regions where we have vital national interests."[86] At a later date, Secretary Weinberger called for an increase in U.S. interventionary forces and contended that the United States "must be prepared to dispatch forces promptly to any of a number of regions around the world—possibly simultaneously."[87]

It was thus perfectly consistent with American military policy that the vast increases in spending for strategic weapons would be more than matched by the increased spending to enhance conventional military power world-wide. The Reagan Administration announced its intention to double the rapid deployment force from 200,000 to 400,000.[88] The Department of Defense budget projection for fiscal year 1985 called for an overall increase in the military budget of 13 percent in real dollars while "force projection" expenditures for American interventionary forces were to increase by 34 percent.[89] An examination of this budget proposal revealed that $70 billion was slated for U.S. strategic forces, and $235 billion was requested for general purpose forces.[90] The Reagan Administration was not going to ignore the conventional "sword" while building the nuclear "shield"; these forces were complementary.

American interventionary forces had always been different from those of the Soviet Union. The geopolitical reality of the two superpowers had dictated a frontier-oriented Soviet policy, whereas the United States had been developing large world-wide interventionary forces since the Kennedy Administration. By the 1980s, the United States had established a clear advantage in aircraft carriers, marine amphibious strength, intercontinental airlift capacity, and command capacity. Further, General D. C. Jones of the Joint Chiefs of Staff admitted that the United States was

generally superior to the Soviet Union in those types of combat forces that are most appropriate for rapidly projecting power to areas remote from either homeland.[91]

The rapid deployment force and the 13 American carrier battle groups were the backbone of this interventionary force. In addition, the United States continued to expand its interventionary forces by creating army "light divisions," increasing marine amphibious capability, adding air and sealift units and marine prepositioned ships, and assigning additional manpower.

Although the rapid deployment force was designed to be used world-wide, there was no doubt about the primary mission assigned to it. In addressing a 1983 joint session of Congress, President Reagan served notice that the maintenance of friendly governments in Central America was one of the most vital of America's interests.

> If we cannot defend ourselves there [Central America], we cannot expect to prevail elsewhere. Our credibility would collapse, our alliances would crumble, and the safety of our homeland would be put in jeopardy.[92]

By the mid-1980s it was becoming apparent that the revolutionary forces in Central America could not be placated with fraudulent elections, token land reform, and military support for oligarchical governments. Even the historical willingness of the United States to intervene in this region appeared to be an insufficient threat to guarantee the existence of friendly governments throughout the Caribbean Basin. Iran had proven that no one could predict which country would be the next to be "lost" by the United States. At the beginning of the second Reagan term Central America appeared to be the most likely area of the world where the United States would once again resort to military intervention.

CONCLUSION

When the Reagan Administration came to power in 1980, the United States led the Soviet Union in nuclear delivery systems. President Reagan continued to pursue a policy of arms escalation throughout his first term in order to establish a clear and unquestionable superiority over the Soviet Union. The intertwined doctrines of "first use" and "first strike" had no meaning in an era of nuclear parity, and Ronald Reagan was determined to return credibility to the American-threatened use of nuclear weapons. The "window of vulnerability," the "spending gap," and the SDI represented the now-traditional myth creation used to escalate the arms race and at the same time substantially increase the U.S. capability to intervene militarily in the Third World. By 1985 the Reagan Administration felt that both the nuclear "shield" and the conventional "sword" were in place and all that was needed was the willingness of the American people to support military adventures overseas.

The Vietnam syndrome of resistance to this type of involvement was still present, however. In spite of the best efforts of many Democrats and most members of the Republican Party, the new public consensus needed to support foreign military intervention was not rebuilt. American deaths in Lebanon forced the withdrawal of American troops. "Victory" was achieved in Grenada, but the news blackout on this invasion was a clear indication of a lack of confidence on the part of American military planners. Finally, opposition in Congress prevented an American-funded mercenary war in Nicaragua from obtaining the financial support requested by President Reagan. Nonetheless, by the mid-1980s the Reagan Administration was prepared for the next American war. The national atmosphere of resurgent patriotism and "pride in America" laid the foundation, the interventionary forces were assembled, and the government in Washington was counting on adventurism abroad being matched by docility at home. The only restraint against an interventionary war was the uncertainty about the willingness of the American people to support a war.

Epilogue

By the mid-1980s, the imperial systems of the Soviet Union and the United States had been in conflict for most of the century. The two empires faced each other in a world where nuclear weapons could not maintain the carefully constructed bipolar world each had helped to create. Political nationalism, diverse economic power, and the diffusion of military power were combining to undermine the positions of dominance each nation had carefully constructed after World War II. Imperial client states were increasingly restive, competitive, and independent. Third World nations were demonstrating conclusively that nationalism was the most powerful "ism" of the twentieth century and these nations were no longer willing to submit to the will of an imperial homeland.

Indeed, by midcentury both the United States and the Soviet Union had reached their apex—the high point of their global power. The conclusive signs of decline were in place, if unrecognized. The United States had "lost" China, was stalemated on the Asian mainland (Korea), and faced a nuclear-armed opponent. America had begun a losing struggle to maintain a world-wide status quo. By midcentury, Soviet hegemony over a unified world communist movement was disintegrating. China had chosen its own form of communism, Eastern Europe was challenging Soviet control, and the Soviet Union faced the vastly superior military power of the United States. Like other imperial systems in decline, the United States and the Soviet Union still possessed enough national power to dramatically influence world events. In addition they had sufficient power to essentially destroy the world.

Historically, empires in decline have been the last to recognize that the old imperial world is disappearing and that a new international system is emerging. This remained true in the

235

latter part of the twentieth century. As diplomacy and the economic instruments of foreign policy fail, the United States and the Soviet Union have been forced to rely increasingly on the use or threatened use of military power in each nation's foreign policy. To an even greater extent than the Soviet Union, the United States has continued to try to integrate nuclear weapons into a strategy that would ensure American dominance.

Yet failure has characterized the foreign policy of both systems. Both sides "lost" China and the People's Republic emerged as an international power in its own right. Cuba, Vietnam, Iran, and Nicaragua refused to remain subordinate to the United States. Iraq, Egypt, Somalia, Algeria, and Afghanistan joined the countries of Eastern Europe in resisting Soviet domination. China, Europe, and Japan emerged as major challengers to American or Soviet hegemony. In spite of the continued but declining economic and relative military power of the United States and the Soviet Union, the rest of the world remained restless under Soviet or American domination.

The precise form of the international order that would emerge was not clear. How and under what circumstances would the United States and the Soviet Union recognize this new form and adjust to this changing world? Herein lies the greatest danger of the final years of the twentieth century. With a combined force of 50,000 nuclear weapons, nuclear-armed nations could destroy the world in order to prevent it from changing. By the mid-1980s there was no evidence that either superpower understood what was happening. Nor did either power indicate a willingness to begin to make the adjustments necessary for this transition to occur without resorting to war. In a rapidly changing world that the nuclear powers could not control, is there a point at which nuclear war would seem more desirable (or less threatening) to national leaders than continued change? Or, more aptly put, at what point would the escalation of a regional war seem more desirable than losing such a war?

In the mid-1980s, as relations between the superpowers worsened and the arms race escalated, the world was in turmoil. Wars of national liberation, revolutions, civil wars, and wars between states were so commonplace that the world was in a state of perpetual warfare with more than 40 conflicts taking place at any given time. The slow proliferation of nuclear weapons further complicated these contests. Britain, France, China, India, and Israel had nuclear weapons. The Union of South Africa and Pakistan were developing a nuclear capability. The eventual production of atomic weapons by Black African nations, Arab nations, and the nations of Latin America all threatened to alter the local balance of power, substituting an imperfectly understood balance of terror.

The destruction of empires has always come down to a fundamental question: What will remain of the imperial homeland once the current imperial era has ended? This was as true for the Roman Empire as it was for the British Empire. No empire lasts forever. But in the nuclear age, the critical question has become: Will *anything* remain after the existing imperial system has changed?

Is there a way out of the current impasse? Can the United States back away from the brink of nuclear war?

To begin the process of drawing back the American people must acknowledge the existence of an American Empire. The historical fact of the empires of Greece, Italy, Great Britain, France, Spain, Germany, and Russia has never been challenged in the United States. Yet many Americans are convinced that the United States is the first major power in history that is not · imperial in nature. William Appleman Williams refers to this as the "charming belief that the United States could reap the rewards of empire without paying the costs of empire and without admitting it was an empire."[1] It is exactly the imperial nature of the United States that is being challenged by revolutionary nationalism on a global basis. An awareness of the American Empire and how it operates would enable Americans to understand why the United States is so hated in many parts of the world.

Through an understanding of the imperial goals of American foreign policy and the means used to achieve them, Americans can come to understand how to begin to reverse the arms race. In specific terms, the United States must relinquish its goal of controlling the noncommunist world before it can alter the militarization of its foreign policy. As long as the maintenance of a world-wide status quo is the goal of American foreign policy, military intervention and nuclear threats will remain the ultimate instruments available to achieve this goal. Local domestic oppression and foreign economic intervention are the instruments of first choice to prevent change, but in a revolutionary world the last bulwark of the status quo is military power.

The American commitment to a world without change is based on the assumption that it is reasonable for the United States, with 6 percent of the world's population, to consume over 30 percent of the world's resources. The problem with this disproportionate consumption of the world's resources is that the remainder of the world does not agree with this allocation of wealth and is willing to resist this pattern with any means at its disposal—terrorism, guerrilla warfare, or revolution. The American people should realize that a continuation of this consumption pattern means a continuation of American intervention and war overseas.[2]

If the American people and their leaders can be convinced of the futility and danger of attempting to preserve the current system of global resource and wealth allocation, then, and only then, can such a policy be changed. By redefining the goals of American policy, American leaders can also alter the means of foreign policy to accomplish more modest and limited national objectives. If we relinquish the goal of maintaining an empire, then the costs of empire maintenance (the military budget) can be shifted to meet other needs that reflect a more rational allocation of national wealth. Such a change would not dramatically affect the American standard of living and could lead to an improvement in the quality of life in the United States as national wealth was used to solve social problems.

Both the United States and the Soviet Union follow traditional imperial patterns while denying the existence of an empire. Both sides have hidden an imperial policy behind the idealistic language of each nation's ideology. In the past we have had "the white man's burden," a *mission civilisatrice, Lebensraum,* and "Manifest Destiny" as justifications for imperialism that denied empire. In the 1980s the United States and the Soviet Union cloak their imperial policies in the language of "freedom" and "social equality," "democracy" and "communism."

For Americans, the contradictions between democratic efforts at home and an imperial policy abroad continue to disrupt and fragment their nation. The language of freedom, equality, and self-determination is difficult to rationalize with support for oppression and interventionism abroad.

These rationalizations for imperial policies increasingly face attack and resistance both at home and abroad. But a period of imperial decline need not be a period of total decline. Alan Wolfe has pointed this out.

> The first super-power to acknowledge, implicitly or explicitly, that it no longer is capable of governing its international relations unilaterally will be the first to reap benefits from the transformed world order.[3]

Any attempt at changing an imperial system must be based on Realpolitik rather than utopianism. Long-range interests must be identified and pursued. If in fact imperial systems can be changed, then the United States is one of the more likely historical candidates to accomplish this difficult task. This is true because the American system still allows limited access to power and regularly changes political leadership. The relative openness of the American system means that the United States stands a better chance to adopt fundamental changes in policy than does the Soviet Union, which tolerates only a closed political system.

The openness of the American political system and the superiority of U.S. technology dictate that initiatives for change in the current global system must come from the United States. American leaders need to assess how U.S. policy can be changed in three areas: (1) the Third World, (2) Europe, and

(3) the Soviet Union. In each case leaders must focus on the long-range interests of the United States and realistic possibilities of accomplishing these goals.

In the Third World, the United States must stop intervening to prevent nationalist and revolutionary forces from disrupting existing systems of government. Third World nations must be allowed to find their own form of government, just as the United States went through a revolution and endured a civil war to arrive at its present structure. Continued American interventionism literally increases the number of anti-American regimes in the world. This policy of nonintervention need not be an isolationist policy. As Third World nations stabilize, trade and friendly relations become essential. The goal of the policy is trade, not exploitation. The means is nonintervention, not a rapid deployment force.

In Europe, it is time for both the United States and the Soviet Union to allow Europe to find its own place in the international world. This means a renunciation of "first use" by the United States and a "decoupling" of its nuclear weapons from the defense of Europe. The boundaries of a nuclear-free zone from the Arctic to the Mediterranean could be patrolled by Europeans, with this military strength determined by negotiations. A unified and neutralized Germany would remove a major threat to peace in Europe and establish a nonmilitary buffer zone in the center of the Continent.

In Soviet-American relations, the technological superiority of the United States means that the United States must take the initiative in arms reduction. In a balance of terror, the militarily superior nation must take the first step in order to avoid destabilizing mutual deterrence. American initiatives would be based not on mutual trust, but on shared interests between the United States and the Soviet Union. It seems obvious that it is in the interests of both the United States and the Soviet Union to reduce the possibilities of nuclear war; there are methods of verification that can prevent violations of agreed-upon arms reductions.

The basic goal must not be a "builddown" but a "buildback."

The goal of such a policy would be not only to reduce (or "buildback") nuclear arms so that there was not even the remotest chance of a first strike by either side but also to reduce deliverable nuclear weapons below the megaton level that would induce nuclear winter. The initial steps of this proposal could be accomplished as follows:

(1) An immediate comprehensive nuclear test ban and an agreement to cease testing missiles of any type would stop warhead development and prevent any improvements in missile accuracy or reliability. Since missiles and warheads would be an integral part of any ABM-ASAT system, a freeze on missile development would stop the Strategic Defense Initiative programs on both sides and prevent the militarization of space. A ban on testing warheads and missiles is easily verifiable and would immediately test the good faith of both sides. Simultaneously, the first-strike capability of both sides would be frozen at present levels, including the current lack of *absolute* certainty that a successful first strike could be launched.

(2) Once the first step was accomplished, the next immediate steps would be to freeze the deployment and production of nuclear weapons of any kind, followed by international inspection and supervision.

(3) The final and most important step would be to reduce the number and the accuracy of nuclear warheads to no more than 200 forty-kiloton warheads mounted on missiles that were incapable of delivering a warhead accurately enough to be used for a counterforce attack—that is, a circular probable error of no less than 2,000 feet would be allowed for any operational missile system. The buildback by both sides to a Polaris system would guarantee deterrence but prohibit a successful first strike. The limit of 200 forty-kiloton warheads should prevent nuclear winter even if they were used. This step would require on-site inspection for verification.

(4) Once this position of mutual minimum deterrence was achieved on both sides, then nations could begin negotiations on ridding the planet of nuclear weapons altogether. This would be the most difficult task because of the extensive pro-

liferation of these weapons, the integration of nuclear weapons into national military plans, and the lack of trust among modern nations.

In a nuclear-armed world, the nation-state cannot perform its most fundamental foreign policy function—guaranteeing the security of its population. If more nuclear weapons make every nation-state less secure, then it is clearly in the interests of the national security of all nations to retreat from the nuclear threshold. The policies of the past have produced perpetual warfare and decreased national security. It is time for a change—for an end to U.S. reliance on nuclear weapons and on intervention in the affairs of other countries in order to conduct its foreign policy.

Only by combining a change in the goals of American foreign policy and the means used to implement this policy can the arms race be controlled and then reversed. Until this fundamental truth is recognized by the peace movement in the United States, the arms race will continue. With this understanding, the race to Armageddon can be reversed.

Glossary

This Glossary is intended to help the reader decipher the almost impenetrable jargon that surrounds American military policy and strategy. Where there is disagreement over definitions, I have defined the term as it is used in this book. For more detailed information, see Thomas B. Cochran, William M. Arkin, and Milton M. Hoenig, *Nuclear Weapons Databook* (Cambridge: Ballinger, 1984), and Robert C. Alridge, *The Counterforce Syndrome* (Washington, D.C.: Transnational Institute, 1978).

ABM: Antiballistic Missile. A missile system designed to destroy an enemy's attacking missiles. The current system is called the Strategic Defense Initiative (SDI).

Airborne Alert: An alert system in which a certain number of bombers are kept constantly in the air, ready to retaliate in case of an enemy attack.

ALCM: Air-Launched Cruise Missile. A very accurate cruise missile launched from a bomber.

AMSA: Advance Manned Strategic Aircraft. The name originally given to the American bomber that was to replace the B-52. Currently referred to as the B-1.

ARV: Advanced Re-entry Vehicle. A MIRV system in which the warheads have their own propulsion and guidance systems. The accuracy of this system puts it into the first-strike category.

ASAT: Anti-Satellite warfare. An effort to destroy an opponent's satellites in order to destroy their intelligence gathering and earlier warning capabilities.

BMEWS: Ballistic Missile Early Warning System. This missile warning radar system is designed to give American military planners a little more than a twenty-minute warning of an enemy attack.

Bombers: Soviet Union

TU-4 (named "Bull" by NATO): Early Soviet bomber. Its 2,000 mile range prevented it from reaching the United States.

TU-20 (Bear): This was a turboprop Soviet intercontinental bomber with a range of 7,800 miles. It was operational in 1955–1956 and there are approximately 100 of these aircraft still in operation.

Myasishchev 500 (Bison): Soviet intercontinental bomber. It was operational in 1955, with a range of 7,000 miles; and 43 are still operational.

TU-22M (Backfire): This new Soviet medium-range bomber has a range of 3,400 miles. There is considerable controversy over the refueling capability for this aircraft.

Bombers: United States

B-1 Bomber: Currently entering production, the B-1 is a supersonic intercontinental bomber with a range of 7,500 miles.

B-29: Medium-range U.S. bomber that has to be based overseas in order to reach the Soviet Union.

B-36: Long-range turbojet bomber with a range of approximately 8,000 miles. This bomber became operational in 1951–1952.

B-47: Medium-range bomber with a 3,200 mile range. Forward-based bomber operational in 1952.

B-52G: Heavy bomber with a range of 7,500 miles. This bomber became operational in 1959 and there are currently 150 operational.

B-52H: Heavy bomber with a range of 9,000 miles, deployed in 1961. There are currently approximately 100 of these aircraft operational.

F-111: This medium-range bomber has a range of 3,600 miles and is deployed in Europe. It was first deployed in 1969 and there are currently approximately 100 of these aircraft operational.

C3I: Command, Control, Communications, and Intelligence Systems.

C5A: American supertransport aircraft for moving troops and equipment. It has a range of 5,000 miles and can carry 100 tons of cargo or 500 military personnel.

CEP: Circular Error Probable. A measure of a missile's accuracy and therefore a way to determine its counterforce capability to destroy an enemy nuclear delivery system. CEP is the radius of a circle within which 50 percent of the warheads fired at a given target will land. Thus, a CEP of 300 feet means that half of the missiles fired at a target will land within 300 feet of that target.

Counterforce Doctrine: A first-strike doctrine aimed at the destruction of an enemy's nuclear capability; the goal is to destroy its ability to launch nuclear weapons. After the first strike, the enemy's cities could be held hostage by the remaining nuclear systems and a war could be "won." (See *Second Strike Counterforce*).

Countervalue: The use of strategic nuclear forces to attack population and industrial centers of an opponent.

Coupling: A nuclear strategy aimed at deterring a local battlefield attack by threatening a progressive use of nuclear weapons, from small battlefield tactical weapons to strategic weapons that can destroy an entire nation. Thus, the strategy of "coupling" in Europe means that the United States not only would use nuclear weapons first (see *First Use*) but also would escalate from tactical to theater to strategic weapons in order to "win" a military conflict.

DEFCON: Defense Readiness Condition. The state of alert of American military forces, ranging from DEFCON 5 for normal readiness to DEFCON 1 for maximum readiness, or readiness for nuclear war.

Defense: The act of militarily defending against an enemy attack. Contrasted with deterrence, which is intended to prevent an attack.

Dense Pack: The theory that by placing missile silos close together incoming enemy missiles would destroy each other rather than the densely packed missile silos (see *Fratricide*).

Deterrence: Convincing a potential aggressor, in advance, that it can and will suffer more by aggression than it will gain.

DEW: Distant Early Warning System. An early radar system designed to detect an enemy bomber attack.

DIA: Defense Intelligence Agency. The effort by President Kennedy to consolidate the intelligence services of the Army, Navy, and Air Force in an attempt to reduce confusion within the American intelligence community.

Division (Army): An American division normally has between 14,000 and 20,000 men, whereas a Soviet division normally has between 9,000 and 14,000 men. A U.S. "light" division has 12,000 men.

FDLS: Fast Deployment Logistic Ships, also called Marine Prepositioned Ships. These ships are designed to predeploy the equipment needed by American troops moved to any part of the world for military intervention.

First Strike: A surprise counterforce attack first on another nation in an attempt to disarm its nuclear delivery systems and prevent retaliation.

First Use: The U.S. doctrine that foresees using tactical nuclear weapons first in Europe or the Middle East when the United States feels that U.S. interests demand the use of nuclear weapons.

Flexible Response: An effort on the part of the Kennedy Administration to develop a nonnuclear, conventional military response to perceived aggression. This led to a substantial buildup of American conventional and counterinsurgency forces.

Force de Frappe: The French medium-range bomber force designed to give France an independent minimum deterrent force against the Soviet Union. The Mirage IV bomber can reach either Moscow or Leningrad and this has been more successful as a deterrent than the United States has admitted.

Forward-Based Systems (FBS): United States nuclear delivery systems based in other countries or on aircraft carriers that are capable of delivering nuclear weapons on Soviet territory (e.g., the Pershing IIs or GLCMs in Europe).

Fratricide: The effect of a nuclear explosion on other incoming missiles and their warheads. The unproven belief that the explosion of the first warhead would effectively destroy the other missiles or warheads used in the same attack in the same area. (See *Dense Pack.*)

Galosh: Soviet ABM system deployed around Moscow. Roughly the equivalent of the obsolete American Nike-Zeus ABM system.

GLCM: Ground-Launched Cruise Missile. A small (20 feet long) ground-launched missile with a range of approximately 1,500 miles and a warhead of 10–50 kilotons. Extremely accurate missile with a CEP of 30 meters.

Ground Alert: An alert system in which a certain number of bombers are kept on alert and prepared to be airborne 15 minutes after the command to launch the aircraft has been given.

ICBM: Intercontinental Ballistic Missile. A ballistic missile with a range of over 5,000 miles.

INF: Intermediate Nuclear Force. Refers to those American nuclear forces in Europe that have a range beyond the battlefield and are capable of reaching Eastern Europe or the Soviet Union with a counterforce or countervalue nuclear strike (e.g., Pershing IIs and GLCMs). Also called theater nuclear forces.

IRBM: Intermediate-Range Ballistic Missile with a range of 1,200 to 1,500 miles. The Soviet Union placed 12 to 16 of these missiles in Cuba in 1962. Earlier, in 1959 the United States had placed a number of these missiles in Great Britain, Italy, and Turkey.

Jupiter: United States liquid fuel intermediate-range (1,500 miles) missile once deployed in Italy and Turkey.

Kiloton: A measurement of the power of a nuclear weapon. One kiloton is the equivalent of 1,000 tons of TNT; 20 kilotons is 20,000 tons of TNT and would destroy everything within a radius of 1.25 miles. The Hiroshima bomb was approximately 13 kilotons.

Kneecap: National Emergency Airborne Command Center. The airborne command center for the President of the United States in the event of war.

Looking Glass: The airborne command center that would be used by the Strategic Air Command in the event of war.

LOW: Launch on Warning. The doctrine that missiles and bombers be launched on receipt of a warning that an opponent has launched its missiles.

MAD: Mutually Assured Destruction. A military doctrine of deterrence based on the ability of two opponents to inflict unacceptable damage on each other no matter which side strikes first. Implementation of this doctrine requires only a minimum deterrent system of nuclear weapons.

MAS: Mutually Assured Survival. President Reagan's claim for the ultimate benefit of the Strategic Defense Initiative.

Massive Retaliation: The doctrine formally announced by John Foster Dulles in January 1954. Under this doctrine, the United States would reserve the right to respond to aggression by retaliating at times and places with means of its own choosing. This doctrine was formulated in response to the frustration of the Korean War and was designed to deter any form of aggression, not only a Soviet attack on the United States.

Megaton: A measurement of the explosive power of thermonuclear weapons, with 1 megaton equalling 1,000,000 tons of TNT. One megaton is the equivalent of 1,000,000 tons of TNT and can destroy an area of over 60 square miles.

Minimum Deterrent: A nuclear strike force designed to be only large enough to deter an enemy attack by threatening the destruction of an enemy's population and industrial centers. This is a small force and, in theory, would possess no first-strike counterforce capability.

Minuteman: A hardened, solid fuel U.S. ICBM that serves as one of the principal legs of the U.S. strategic TRIAD. There are more than 1,000 Minuteman missiles, with ranges over 6,500 miles.

MIRV: Multiple Independent Re-entry Vehicle. Multiple warheads launched toward targets by the same missile. A single missile can launch up to 14 warheads independently targeted in an intercontinental range. As the accuracy of these systems increases, they become first-strike systems.

Missiles: Soviet

SS-18: Major Soviet ICBM with MIRVed warheads and a range of 7,000 miles.

SS-20: Intermediate-range Soviet MIRVed three-warhead missile that is operational in Europe and Asia.

MLF: Multilateral Nuclear Force. An American plan that would place a nuclear delivery system under either the joint command of the European NATO allies (with a U.S. veto) or the control of the United States. Discarded after initially proposed by the United States.

MRBM: Medium-Range Ballistic Missile. A short-range (950 miles) ballistic missile. The Soviet Union attempted to place 24 of these missiles in Cuba during the 1962 Cuban missile crisis.

MRV: Multiple Re-entry Vehicle. A precursor to the more sophisticated MIRV systems. The MRV warheads were not independently targeted and therefore not accurate enough for use in a first strike. The MRV warheads were all aimed at the same target and then sprayed over the target area, like a shotgun blast. This is a countervalue and not a counterforce system. U.S. MRVs became operational on Polaris and Poseidon submarines in 1964, several years ahead of the Soviet Union.

MX: Missile Experimental. Designated the "Peacekeeper" by President Reagan. A United States ICBM carrying 10 MIRVed warheads, each warhead with 300 kilotons of explosive power and a CEP of less than 150 meters.

Nike Systems: The Nike Ajax, Hercules, Zeus, and X were all part of the antibomber and antimissile systems developed by the United States. None of these systems is operational in the mid-1980s.

Nuclear Weapons: Usually divided into three categories depending on the target, the range, and the accuracy of the warhead. Tactical with less than 50 miles range, Theater up to 1,000 miles range, and Strategic over 1,000 miles (see below).

Polaris: First-generation solid fuel submarine-launched ballistic missile (SLBM). The Polaris A-1 with a range of 1,380 miles and a payload of 0.7 megatons became operational in 1960. Replaced by the Poseidon and Trident systems.

Poseidon: Navy SLBM carrying a MIRV warhead that became operational in 1970. Each missile had between 10 and 14 warheads and a range of 2,890 miles.

Pre-Emptive War: An attack launched by a nation when it believes that an attack by its enemy is imminent (that is, expected within minutes or hours). In theory, this type of war would prevent the destruction of a nation's nuclear retaliatory forces. To prepare for an immediate attack, a nation might adopt a "launch on warning" system to avoid losing its missile forces.

Presidential Directive #59 (PD #59): Directive issued by President Carter in 1980 indicating that the nuclear strategy of the United States was to be able to fight a "prolonged" nuclear war with the Soviet Union and emerge from such a war with the capability to "recover" after the war was over. Such a strategy had to be based on a first-strike counterforce doctrine.

Preventive War: The launching of a first-strike nuclear attack by a nation when it feels that war is inevitable at some time in the future, although war is not imminent. This sort of attack would be based on a nation's belief that a nuclear war today would be more favorable to its national interests than one in the future when its enemy's strength had increased.

RDF: Rapid Deployment Force, also known as the Central Command. This is a combined force of American military units that could be used to intervene militarily anywhere in the world. This highly mobile force consists of approximately 400,000 men.

Safeguard: The American ABM system approved by Congress in 1969.

SALT: Strategic Arms Limitation Talks.

SDI: A Strategic Defense Initiative. President Reagan's call for an anti-missile defense system based on advanced space technology. Also called "Star Wars."

Second-Strike Counterforce Doctrine: Defined by Secretary of Defense McNamara in a speech at Ann Arbor, Michigan, on June 16, 1962. This doctrine called for a second-strike response by the United States on Soviet military installations (airfield and missile sites). Cities would not be initially attacked, but reserved to "hostage" status for later attacks. The possession of enough nuclear forces to "ride out" a first strike, however, meant that these forces would be powerful enough to threaten a first strike against the Soviet Union.

Sentinel: The ABM system announced by the Department of Defense in 1967. Replaced by Safeguard.

SIOP: Single Integrated Operational Plan. The top-secret U.S. nuclear war plan.

Skybolt: Air-to-surface missile that the United States was going to sell to Great Britain in 1963. Cancelled.

SLBM: Submarine-Launched Ballistic Missile. The U.S. Polaris, Poseidon, and Trident systems are SLBMs.

SRAM: Short-Range Attack Missile. An air-to-surface missile carried by bomber to suppress enemy air defense efforts.

SLCM: Sea-Launched Cruise Missile (Tomahawk).

START: Strategic Arms Limitation Talks. President Reagan's new name for SALT.

Strategic Weapons System: A bomber or missile that is designed to deliver nuclear weapons on an enemy's homeland, attacking either its nuclear delivery systems (counterforce) or its population and industrial base (countervalue).

Tactical Nuclear Weapons: Small nuclear weapons (1–100 kilotons) used on the battlefield to immediately effect the outcome of an individual engagement between smaller combat units. The United States based approximately 6,000 of these weapons in Europe in the mid-1980s.

Theater Nuclear Weapons (sometimes referred to as intermediate nuclear forces (INF): Theater nuclear forces are used in a military geographical area designated as a region within which a war would be fought under a single command. In Europe, American theater weapons are also capable of attacking targets inside the Soviet Union and therefore can be regarded as strategic weapons.

Throw Weight (also Payload): The weight of the missile that remains after the last booster rocket has separated. Normally applies to the various components of the warhead of a missile.

TRIAD: Under U.S. strategic doctrine, U.S. nuclear forces are made up of three fundamental components: (1) bombers with bombs or air-to-surface missiles; (2) submarine-launched missiles (SLBM); and (3) intercontinental ballistic missiles. Forward-based systems are also an integral part of this strategic delivery system, even though these systems are not considered part of the TRIAD.

Trident: A new system of SLBMs, becoming operational in the 1980s. Because of the range and accuracy of the Trident II system, it is considered a first-strike system.

UMT: Universal Military Training. In the mid-1980s the United States relied on a volunteer military force. Demographic studies indicated that by 1992, one of every two qualified males would have to volunteer to meet the manpower needs of a two-million-man military force. Thus, either UMT or more likely a required "national service" seems inevitable by the late 1980s.

Weapons System: Any instrument of combat such as a bomber or missile (with bombs or warheads) together with all related equipment, support facilities, and service required to bring the instrument to its target.

Notes

CHAPTER I

1. This analysis of the period prior to 1953 is very brief. For more detail the reader should consult Gar Alperovitz, *Atomic Diplomacy: Hiroshima to Potsdam* (New York: Vintage Press, 1965); D. F. Fleming, *The Cold War and Its Origins* (New York: Doubleday & Co., 1961), Vol. I; P. M. S. Blackett, *Atomic Weapons and East West Relations* (London: Cambridge University Press, 1956); Dean Acheson, *Present at the Creation* (New York: W. W. Norton & Co., 1969); Ralph E. Lapp, *The New Force: The Story of Atoms and People* (New York: Harper & Bros., 1953); Raymond Garthoff, *Soviet Military Policy: An Historical Analysis* (New York: Frederick Praeger, 1966); Marshall D. Shulman, *Stalin's Foreign Policy Reappraised* (Cambridge, Mass.; Harvard University Press, 1963); and Samuel Huntington, *The Common Defense: Strategic Programs in National Security* (New York: Columbia University Press, 1961).

2. Blackett, *Studies on War* (New York: Hill and Wang, 1962), pp. 214–242; Garthoff, *Soviet Military Policy*, p. 23. See also Appendix B.

3. Lapp, *The New Force*, p. 116.

4. This information was gained by surveying various public sources, primarily *The New York Times*, from 1945 to 1951.

5. Richard C. Hewlett and Oscar E. Anderson, *The New World: 1939–1946: A History of the Atomic Energy Commission* (University Park, Penn.: Penn State University Press, 1962), 1:417.

6. United States Atomic Energy Commission, *In the Matter of J. Robert Oppenheimer*, transcript of Hearing before the Personnel Security Board, April–May 1954, United States Government Printing Office, 1954, p. 33.

7. *The New York Times*, November 27, 1947, quoting Secretary of the Air Force Symington. Even at this early date he was calling for at least 630 heavy bombers near the Soviet Union as part of the "austerity program" imposed on the Air Force. Also, since the United States had several hundred overseas bases at this time, 500 bombers does not sound like a high figure. Huntington, *The Common Defense*, p. 59. Huntington contends that the Strategic Air Command had 18 aircraft wings, or roughly 810 planes (one wing has 45 planes).

8. *The New York Times*, October 2, 1949.

9. *The New York Times*, September 18, 1946, reprint of Secretary Wallace's letter to President Truman of July 23, 1946.

10. *The New York Times,* news article by Hanson Baldwin, "The Defense Hearings," October 27, 1949.

11. Clark R. Mollenhoff, *The Pentagon: Politics, Profits and Plunder* (New York: G. P. Putnam's Sons, 1967), p. 124. At this early stage in the debate, the basic decisions involved in NSC #68 had not been made and the services believed that an increase in one service appropriation meant a decrease in their allocations. (See next chapter.)

12. *The New York Times,* news article by Hanson Baldwin, October 27, 1949.

13. For an excellent study of the Universal Military Training debate, see John W. Swomley, Jr., *The Military Establishment* (Boston: Beacon Press, 1964).

14. *The New York Times,* quoting Secretary of the Air Force Stuart Symington, October 19, 1949.

15. *The New York Times,* news article by Hanson Baldwin, October 26, 1949.

16. *Ibid.,* October 8, 1949. The Navy also had its number of new planes reduced to about 50 per month, as compared to 300 planes a month before Pearl Harbor. The Navy had asked for $1.3 billion for its air arm and the President had cut this request to $687 million. This figure was further reduced to $387 million.

17. *The New York Times,* quoting Admiral W. F. Halsey, October 13, 1949.

18. Shulman, *Stalin's Foreign Policy,* p. 119. This fact seems to have come out by mistake in a television broadcast by Senator Edwin C. Johnson. The official statement that the United States had made the decision to proceed with the development of the H-bomb was not made until January 31, 1950, by President Truman.

19. Lapp, *The New Force,* p. 93.

20. Blackett, *Atomic Weapons and East-West Relations,* pp. 38–48.

21. Dr. Ernest J. Sternglass, Professor of Radiation Physics, University of Pittsburgh, "The Death of All Children," *Esquire,* September, 1969, pp. 1a–1d. Dr. Sternglass' theory that a thermonuclear exchange would genetically destroy all human life has not been definitely proved.

22. Shulman, *Stalin's Foreign Policy,* pp. 28–29.

23. Gabriel A. Almond, *The American People and Foreign Policy* (New York: Frederick Praeger, 1950), p. 104.

24. Huntington, *The Common Defense,* pp. 50–51, quoting Senator Henry Jackson (Dem.-Wash.). Much of the background work on NSC #68 has been done by Huntington, and this author is indebted for this analysis.

25. *Ibid.*

26. *Ibid.,* p. 51, quoting Paul H. Nitze, from "The Need for a National Strategy," address to the Army War College, Carlisle Barracks, Pennsylvania, August 27, 1958. Mr. Nitze was one of the original authors of NSC #68 and was speaking of this paper before the War College.

27. *Ibid.*, p. 51.

28. *Ibid.*, p. 59.

29. James M. Gavin, *War and Peace in the Space Age* (New York: Harper & Brothers, 1958), p. 22.

30. Huntington, *The Common Defense*, p. 54.

31. Walter G. Hermes, *Truce Tent and Fighting Front* (Washington, D.C.: Government Printing Office, 1966), p. 513. It is worth noting that the highest troop commitment in Korea was 300,000 men, whereas by 1968 the United States had over 500,000 men in Vietnam.

32. Seymour Kurtz (ed.) *The New York Times: Encyclopedic Almanac: 1970* (New York: *The New York Times*, 1969), p. 720.

CHAPTER II

1. John W. Spanier, *The Truman-MacArthur Controversy* (Cambridge: Harvard University Press, 1959), p. 259.

2. *The New York Times*, President Eisenhower's State of the Union address (text), February 3, 1953.

3. *Ibid.*

4. *The New York Times*, news article by Hanson Baldwin, October 21, 1953.

5. Samuel Huntington, *The Common Defense: Strategic Programs in National Security* (New York: Columbia University Press, 1961), p. 25. In spite of the awareness of the need for existing military preparedness, the United States continued to plan for industrial mobilization in the event of war.

6. *The New York Times*, January 8, 1954.

7. *The New York Times*, statement by Secretary of State Dulles before the Council on Foreign Relations, January 13, 1954.

8. *The New York Times*, news article by James Reston, January 17, 1954.

9. *U.S. Congressional Record*, 83rd Cong., 2d sess., Vol. 100, pt. 1 (January 6 to February 5, 1954), p. 467; *The New York Times*, speech by Adlai Stevenson to the Southeast Democratic Conference, March 7, 1954.

10. *U.S. Congressional Record*, Vol. 101, pt. 5 (May 5 to May 25, 1955), reprint of speech by Senator Warren Magnuson (Dem.-Wash.), p. 5932. Senator Magnuson's speech also reflects the highly partisan nature of the debate over massive retaliation.

11. John Foster Dulles, "Policy for Security and Peace," *Foreign Affairs*, (April 1954), 32:357.

12. *Ibid.*, pp. 357–358.

13. *Ibid.*, p. 363. When Secretary Dulles referred to a "variety of means and scope for responding to aggression" he must have been referring to alternative nuclear responses, not conventional responses. During this

period there was a steady decline in the combat readiness of the United States Army.

14. *The New York Times*, February 13, 1954. Air Force documents at this time were listing Soviet long-range aircraft at 300–400, but based on Department of Defense official figures this would appear to be an exaggeration by the Air Force. See "How Good Is Russia's Long-Range Turboprop Bear Bomber?", *Air Intelligence Training Bulletin* (published by the United States Air Force, September 1957), 9:39. These Air Force figures would seem to be a precursor to the "bomber gap" that was to develop in 1955.

15. *The New York Times*, February 7, 1951; *ibid.*, March 12, 1951.

16. Ralph E. Lapp, *The New Force* (New York: Harper & Brothers, 1953), pp. 64–67, 133. P. M. S. Blackett, *Atomic Weapons and East-West Relations* (London: Cambridge University Press, 1956), p. 41.

17. *The New York Times*, September 19, 1951. Senator McMahon was chairman of the special Senate committee on atomic energy.

18. Ralph E. Lapp, *The New Force* (London: Cambridge University Press, 1965), quoting Senator Brian McMahon, p. 133.

19. *The New York Times*, February 13, 1949.

20. W. W. Rostow, *The US and the World Arena* (New York: Harper & Brothers, 1967), p. 332.

21. B. H. Liddell Hart, *Deterrence or Defense* (New York: Frederick Praeger, 1960), p. 82.

22. Maxwell D. Taylor (General, United States Army, ret.), *The Uncertain Trumpet* (New York: Harper & Brothers, 1959), pp. 65–66.

23. Dwight D. Eisenhower, *The White House Years: Mandate for Change 1953–1956* (Garden City, New York: Doubleday & Company, 1963), p. 452.

President Eisenhower gave the following figures on manpower and budget reductions.

Manpower	December 1953	October 1954	June 1955
Army	1,500,000	1,400,000	1,000,000
Navy-Marines	1,000,000	920,000	870,000
Air Force	950,000	960,000	970,000

Budget (in billions of dollars)

	Fiscal 1954	Fiscal 1955
Army	12.9	8.8
Navy-Marines	11.2	9.7
Air Force	15.6	16.4

See also, Huntington, *The Common Defense*, p. 75.

24. *Ibid.*, p. 102.

25. When Eisenhower came to office after the Korea build-up in 1952, the United States had 20 Army divisions, 18 regimental combat teams

(roughly the equivalent of 3 divisions), and 3 Marine divisions, *ibid.*, pp. 60–61. When Eisenhower left office, there was a total of 11 combat-ready divisions and of the 11, only 3 were deployed in the United States as a reserve. See Arthur M. Schlesinger, Jr., *A Thousand Days: John F. Kennedy in the White House* (Boston: Houghton Mifflin, 1965), pp. 315–316. Schlesinger goes on to admit that the force for the invasion of Cuba was not readily available following the Bay of Pigs.

26. *The New York Times*, news article by Hanson Baldwin, January 13, 1953.

27. The fact that the United States was not a formal member of CENTO in no way detracts from the fact that it was designed by the United States as a means of achieving its perceived national interests. See John Campbell, *Defense of the Middle East: Problems of American Policy* (New York: Frederick Praeger, 1960), pp. 49–62.

28. *The New York Times*, October 21, 1954.

29. *The New York Times*, quoting Secretary of Defense Charles Wilson, March 30, 1956.

30. Statement by Air Force Chief of Staff, General Hoyt S. Vandenburg, *Aviation Week* (June 11, 1951), 54:11.

31. Huntington, *The Common Defense*, p. 71.

32. Testimony by Secretary of Defense, Neil McElroy, U.S. Congress, Senate, Committee on Appropriations, Department of Defense Appropriations for 1960 (discussing the bomber gap), *Hearings*, 86th Cong., 1st sess. (May 1959), 4:5.

33. Senator Charles Goodell (Rep.-N.Y.), press release quoting General Curtis LeMay, April 3, 1969.

34. Allen Dulles, *The Craft of Intelligence* (New York: Harper & Row, 1963), p. 149.

35. U.S. Congress, House Committee on Appropriations, *Hearings* on Fiscal Year 1960 Defense Budget, 86th Cong., 1st sess., pt. 1 (February 19, 1959), 10:378 testimony by SAC commanding officer, General Thomas Power.

36. *The New York Times*, "Air Manual Hints Soviet Tricked U.S.," April 18, 1960.

37. Raymond Garthoff, *The Soviet Image of Future War* (Washington, D.C.: Public Affairs Press, 1959), pp. 74–75.

38. Marshall D. Shulman, *Stalin's Foreign Policy Reappraised* (Cambridge: Harvard University Press, 1963), quoting Joseph Stalin, p. 185.

39. H. S. Dinerstein, *War and the Soviet Union* (rev. ed.) (New York: Praeger, 1962), pp. 215–217.

CHAPTER III

1. For a closer look at the missile gap, the concerned reader should consult my book, *The Missile Gap: A Study of the Formulation of Military and Public Policy* (Cranbury, New Jersey: Fairleigh Dickinson University

Press, 1970). The author would also like to express his thanks to this publisher for allowing part of this study to be reproduced in this book.

2. Robert Hagan and Bart Bernstein, "Military Value of Missiles in Cuba," *The Bulletin of the Atomic Scientists* (February 1963), 19:11. These figures are confirmed by Senator Stuart Symington (see below, this chapter).

3. Soviet budgetary figures on national defense are notoriously difficult to analyze, if not impossible. However, one of the best efforts at this type of analysis was made by Abraham S. Becker of the Rand Corporation. Becker's analysis showed that the Soviet military budget had been reduced from 1955 to 1959, and then, following a rather drastic increase in 1959, was again reduced in 1960 and possibly 1962. Mr. Becker's figures are given below and are in billions of rubles. The figures represent the "estimate total high" spending in the Soviet Union for defense purposes.

Year	1955	1956	1957	1958	1959	1960	1961	1962
Number of Rubles in Billions	15.00	14.81	14.39	14.63	18.00	17.15	17.0 to 26.1	16.6 to 23.4

See Abraham S. Becker, *Soviet Military Outlays Since 1955* (Santa Monica, Calif.: The Rand Corporation, 1964) (Memorandum RM-3886-PR), p. 91. If Mr. Becker's figures are correct, then these figures offer additional evidence that the Soviet Union was pursuing a policy of "minimum deterrence" during this period.

4. The 25 largest cities in the United States had a combined population of 60.8 million according to the 1960 United States Census.

5. The question legitimately can be asked, Why did the Soviet Union bother with missile development at all? The answer appears to be (1) to avoid a future technological gap in missile development that could not be closed (either with the United States or China); and (2) the increased effectiveness of antibomber surface-to-air missiles raised the possibility that an almost perfect bomber defense *might* be developed by an adversary at some future date.

6. Harry Howe Ransom, *Can American Democracy Survive Cold War?* (Garden City, New York: Doubleday & Company, 1963), p. 209. This report originally appeared in *Aviation Week* (October 21, 1957), pp. 26–27. Also reported in *The New York Times,* November 21 and 24, 1957. In January 1960, Hanson Baldwin identified Soviet missile testing sites as (1) at Kapustin Yar (near Stalingrad/Volgagrad), and (2) near Tyura Tam (near the Aral Sea); see *The New York Times,* January 23, 1960.

7. *The New York Times,* news article on the CIA by Tom Wicker, John W. Finney, Max Frankel, E. W. Kentworthy, and others, April 27, 1966; also reported in Charles J. V. Murphy, "Khrushchev's Paper Bear," *Fortune* (December 1964), 70:225–227.

8. Allen Dulles, quoting Secretary of Defense Gates in 1960, *The Craft of Intelligence* (New York: Harper & Row, 1963), p. 67.

9. *Ibid.*, p. 65.

10. Murphy, "Khrushchev's Paper Bear," pp. 58–59.

11. The possibility remains that President Eisenhower had highly sensitive intelligence sources known to only a few government officials, although the existence of such sources has never been proved. The reports that President Kennedy had intelligence sources (or a source) inside the Kremlin during the 1962 Cuban missile crisis certainly would indicate the possibility that Eisenhower had the same type of source. See the reports on the activities and trial of Oleg V. Penkovsky (former colonel in the Soviet Army) who was accused of passing Russian rocket information to Western intelligence sources. *The New York Times*, May 8, 1963, November 2, 1965, and January 7, 1961; and *The Penkovsky Papers* (New York: Doubleday & Company, 1965). Allegedly, Colonel Penkovsky passed valuable military intelligence information to Western intelligence sources from April 1961 to August 1962. Colonel Penkovsky was arrested on October 22, 1962, tried, and executed as a spy. Edward Crankshaw (who wrote the Foreword to *The Penkovsky Papers*) accepted the authenticity of the "papers" beyond question (p. 4), while the CIA claimed they were a forgery (*The New York Times*, November 2, 1965).

12. Dulles, *The Craft of Intelligence*, p. 164.

13. *Ibid.*

14. Dwight D. Eisenhower, *The White House Years: Waging the Peace* (Garden City, New York: Doubleday & Company, Inc., 1965), p. 221. A writer in *The Boston Globe* claimed that the Gaither Report estimated what the Russians *could* do rather than what they *would* do (capability versus intent). *The Boston Globe*, "Ike Discloses Gaither 'Missile Gap' Report," article by David Wise, September 26, 1965.

15. Eisenhower, *Waging the Peace*, pp. 389–390.

16. Neither side produced large numbers of first-generation missiles.

17. "Next Generation Seen as Missile Race Key," *Aviation Week*, quoting General Bernard Schriever (January 27, 1958), 68:35. Although at one time the United States programmed about 230 first-generation ICBMs (a small number compared to the final production of second-generation missiles), in reality fewer than 200 were produced, counting both the Titan and Atlas systems. In all probability, both the programmed and produced number of first-generation missiles would have been less if the Eisenhower Administration had not been under such heavy pressure to produce more missiles because of the feared missile gap.

18. The Minuteman attained operational status in 1962, while the Polaris was operational in 1960.

19. U.S. Senate, Committee on Armed Services and the Committee on Aeronautical and Space Sciences, Preparedness Investigating Committee, *Joint Hearings on Missiles, Space and Other Major Defense Matters*, 86th

Cong., 1st sess. (January 29 and 30, 1959), p. 46. (Hereafter referred to as the *Joint Hearings, 1959.*)

20. *Ibid.,* pp. 46, 49. During this same testimony, Secretary McElroy indicated that the reduced budget request for missile development in 1960 was due to the fact that the United States had stopped the development of the first-generation Snark and Regulus missiles.

21. *The New York Times,* official Pentagon figures for January 1961, April 1964, and April 15, 1964.

22. American intelligence sources publicly claimed this limited Soviet missile production program in 1960. See U.S. Congress, Senate, Committee on Armed Services and the Committee on Aeronautical and Space Sciences, Preparedness Investigating Subcommittee, *Joint Hearings on Missiles, Space and Other Major Defense Matters,* 86th Cong., 2d sess. (February–March 1960), p. 142. (Hereafter referred to as *Joint Hearings, 1960.*)

23. *Joint Hearings,* 1959, pp. 26–27.

24. *Joint Hearings,* 1960, p. 442. Note: these two sets of estimates made in 1959 were not made public until 1960.

25. U.S. Congress, Senate, Committee on Appropriations, Department of Defense Appropriations for 1960, *Hearings,* 86th Cong., 1st sess. (May 1959), 4:5.

26. *Joint Hearings,* 1960, p. 442. It was impossible to determine which set of figures had upset Senator Symington when presented by Secretary of Defense McElroy, or if Senator Symington had seen both sets and still disagreed.

27. It was possible that Senator Symington's other information came from the "crash" set of figures, but this seems unlikely.

28. As seen above, this statement in books by Schlesinger, Sorensen, Spanier, Huntington, and in the *Joint Hearings,* 1960.

29. The one exception to the 1959 "revision" was found in an article by Joseph Alsop. By the end of 1959, the projected number of Soviet missiles for 1962 was reduced to 400 ICBMs. It is noteworthy that the public estimates that appeared accurate lagged from three to five months behind the changes made in official estimates.

30. See below, this chapter.

31. *The New York Times,* text of President Eisenhower's fiscal 1961 budget message, January 19, 1960.

32. U.S. Congress, Committee on Armed Services, Preparedness Investigating Subcommittee, in conjunction with the Committee on Aeronautical and Space Sciences, *Joint Hearings,* text of General Power's speech before the Economic Club of New York, January 19, 1960, 86th Cong., 2d sess. (February 2, 3, 4, 8, 9, and March 16, 1960), p. 4. This speech had been submitted to the Pentagon and State Department for clearance and was approved. It is worth noting that General Power's "95 percent" destruction was the same figure used in 1970 by Secretary Laird.

33. *Joint Hearings,* 1960, pp. 21, 36. General Power did admit, under intense questioning, that the Soviet Union had only one ICBM base operational at that time. *Ibid.,* pp. 25, 49.

34. *Joint Hearings,* 1960, p. 23.

35. The reader should keep in mind that this advantage had existed since the beginning of the missile gap debate. In 1957, according to the United States Air Force, the United States had 2,500 heavy-combat jet aircraft, 27 overseas bases, and 32 bases in the United States. *The New York Times,* quoting SAC commander, General Thomas Power, September 27, 1957.

36. *The New York Times,* "Washington Finds No Proof Moscow Had Capability to Launch ICBM's," by Hanson W. Baldwin, March 25, 1959; *ibid.,* "McElroy Reports U.S. and Russians Lag on Missiles," news article by Jack Raymond, June 28, 1959; Charles J. V. Murphy, "The Embattled Mr. McElroy," *Fortune* (April 1959), 59:242; "Missiles: Ours and Russia's" (this article reported the alleged strain on the Soviet economy), *Newsweek* (July 13, 1959), 54:52.

37. This downward revision also raised the question of whether United States intelligence estimates were based on Soviet "intent" or "capability."

38. In 1964, one author claimed that after the CIA success with the U-2 photo reconnaissance aircraft, the Air Force bought its own U-2 planes and began to fly "spy" missions over the Soviet Union. (See Murphy, "Khrushchev's Paper Bear," p. 224. Two other authors hinted that the Air Force might have had its own U-2 photographs and stated flatly that the Air Force did use its own photo interpreters to come up with different conclusions than the CIA on Russian missile programs. See David Wise and Thomas B. Ross, *The Invisible Government* (New York: Bantam Books, published by arrangement with Random House, Inc., 1964), p. 226. Neither of these reports could be substantiated by official documents. However, there does not appear to be much doubt that the Air Force did have its own photo interpreters analyzing U-2 photographs.

39. Once this was done, the number of intelligence figures was reduced considerably. (The "crash" estimates had been dropped in early 1960.) However, SAC did not accept the lower figures, so two sets of possible figures were still in existence.

40. This was the stand "high" estimate of Soviet strength.

41. During this period there were reports of "leaks" of intelligence information. See the *Joint Hearings,* 1960, and the reports of the alleged McNamara "background briefing" of February 1961.

42. Schlesinger, *A Thousand Days,* p. 317; McGeorge Bundy, "The President and the Peace," *Foreign Affairs* (April 1964), 42:354.

43. Stewart Alsop, "The Alternative to Total War" (quoting Secretary of Defense McNamara), *Saturday Evening Post* (December 1, 1962), 235:18.

44. Myron Rush and Arnold I. Horelick, *Strategic Power and Soviet Foreign Policy* (Chicago: University of Chicago Press, 1966). This was one of the major themes developed in this book.

45. In the process of explaining the missile gap, Senator Symington attempted to justify his own role in its development and also implied that he was not certain it had really disappeared. U.S. Congress, Senate, Armed Services Committee, *Hearings, Military Procurement Authorization for Fiscal Year 1963*, 87th Cong., 2d sess. (January–February, 1962), 10:49–50; Senator Stuart Symington, "Where the Missile Gap Went," *The Reporter* (February 15, 1962), 26:21–22.

46. U.S. Congress, Senate, Armed Services Committee, *Hearings on Procurement for 1963*, 87th Cong., pp. 49–50.

47. *Ibid.*

48. It was not possible to determine which set of figures or whose estimates Senator Symington based his percentages on, although it is safe to speculate that he used one of the higher sets of intelligence figures available (probably either the "crash" figures or those of the Air Force, if they were different).

49. For those who did not accept the downward revisions, the projected 1,500 Soviet ICBMs by 1962 remained a possible reality.

50. U.S. Congress, House, Appropriations Committee, Department of Defense Appropriations Subcommittee, *Hearings for Fiscal 1963*, testimony by General Frederick H. Smith, Jr., Vice-Chief of Staff, U.S. Air Force, 87th Cong., 2d sess., pt. 2 (February 1962), p. 489.

51. Some of the major aspects of these three factors have been dealt with elsewhere in this study and will not be repeated here.

52. Senator Henry M. Jackson (Dem.-Wash.), "Organizing for National Survival," *Foreign Affairs* (April 1960), 38:446.

53. *Ibid.*, pp. 455–456.

54. Bernard K. Gordon, "The Military Budget: Congressional Phase," *Journal of Politics* (November 1961), 23:692.

55. Also *Air University Quarterly* could be counted on for support of the Air Force position.

56. Also *Military Review* represented the point of view of the Army, while the *U.S. Naval Institute Proceedings* represented the Navy's. See Huntington, "The Military Lobby: Its Impact on Congress, Nation," *Congressional Quarterly Review* (March 24, 1961), 14:466.

57. *Ibid.*, pp. 40–52. A congressional committee investigated the connection between the military and industry in a series of special hearings in 1959. See U.S. Congress, House, Committee on Armed Services, Subcommittee for Special Investigation, *Hearings, Employment of Retired Military and Civilian Personnel by Defense Industries*, 86th Cong., 1st sess., Vol. 8 (July, August, September, 1959). The so-called *Hébert Hearings*.

58. See Fred J. Cook, *The Warfare State* (New York: The Macmillan Company, 1962), pp. 12–15; Victor Perlo, *Militarism and Industry: Arms*

Profiteering in the Missile Age (New York: International Publishers, 1963), pp. 161–170. Mr. Perlo attempted to prove there was (and is) a direct political and financial connection between many of the key personalities in the missile gap controversy and the business community. (Senator Stuart Symington, p. 161; Senator Henry Jackson, p. 161; Robert C. Sprague, co-chairman of the Gaither Report, p. 170.) This book is obviously not about the "military-industrial complex" *per se*. The reader interested in this aspect of the arms race should consult Sidney Lens, *The Military-Industrial Complex* (Philadelphia: Pilgrim Press and The National Catholic Reporter, 1970).

59. For example, see the series of five articles by Joseph Alsop in *The New York Herald Tribune,* starting January 24, 1960. Just prior to this series by Mr. Alsop claiming American strategic inferiority, President Eisenhower had disclosed that the United States Atlas ICBM was operational and that the United States had 2,100 strategic bombers, *The New York Times,* text of President Eisenhower's news conference, January 14, 1960. These 2,100 bombers gave the United States at least a 3–1 advantage over the Soviet Union.

60. For example, see Henry Kissinger, *The Necessity for Choice.* Earlier Kissinger had been one of the major authors of the 1959 Rockefeller Report that accepted the missile gap. In 1964 and 1968 Kissinger was Nelson Rockefeller's major foreign and defense policy adviser. In 1970, he was Nixon's most important defense policy adviser. For the Rockefeller Report see *International Security: The Military Aspect* (Garden City: Doubleday, 1958).

61. *Joint Hearings,* 1960 (Senate), testimony by General Maxwell D. Taylor (U.S. Army, ret.), pp. 190–191; Samuel P. Huntington, *The Common Defense: Strategic Programs in National Politics* (New York: Columbia University Press, 1961), pp. 446–456. Mr. Huntington used the figures: Air Force, 47 percent; Army, 22 percent; and Navy, 29 percent.

62. This was the year of the Soviet ICBM and Sputnik. It was also the year of a recession in the United States.

63. It also appeared that the Alsop brothers, who had done a great deal to create the impression of the missile gap in their writings, escaped any serious damage to their reputations as reporters.

64. *The New York Times,* reprint of the figures submitted by the House Republican Policy Committee on January 25, 1961, and February 9, 1961. In *The New York Times* of April 16, 1965, roughly these same figures were used by the Pentagon as their estimate as of January 1961. See *The New York Times,* April 16, 1964. These figures ignored the various American IRBMs, medium-range bombers, and carrier-based aircraft—all capable of hitting a Soviet target. The Russians had no capability in any of these three categories that could reach the United States. Also, Appendix A indicates that 1961 saw a profusion of estimated missile strengths, yet none of these figures for this year indicates a "missile gap" favoring the Soviet Union, with the possible exception of very early 1961 estimates.

65. *The New York Times,* news article by Jack Raymond, "Kennedy Defense Study Finds No Evidence of 'Missile Gap,'" February 7, 1961; *ibid.,* statement repeated, February 9, 1961; several years later, former President Eisenhower wrote that after his successor assumed office "word conveniently leaked out of the Pentagon that the 'missile gap' had been closed." Eisenhower, *Waging the Peace,* p. 390; also in Schlesinger, *A Thousand Days,* p. 499.

66. *The New York Times,* February 8, 1961.

67. Harold W. Chase and Allen L. Lerman (eds.), *Kennedy and the Press: The News Conferences,* texts of all President Kennedy's news conferences (New York: Thomas Y. Crowell Company, 1965), pp. 19–20.

68. *The New York Times,* "Missile Gap Report Denied by McNamara," February 17, 1961.

69. "Defense: The Missile Gap Flap," *Time* (February 17, 1961), 77:12; "The Ammo Was Political," *Newsweek* (February 20, 1961), 57:24; "The Truth About the Missile Gap," *U.S. News & World Report* (February 27, 1961), 50:41.

70. "The Truth About the Missile Gap," p. 41. See Appendix A, February 27, 1961, for the weapons chart listed.

71. Claude Witze (senior ed.), "Airpower and the News," *Air Force* (March 1961), 44:39.

72. *The New York Times,* text of President Kennedy's news conference, March 2, 1961; *ibid.,* March 9, 1961.

73. From March 8, 1961, to October 11, 1961, President Kennedy held a total of 11 news conferences and the question of the missile gap was not raised in any of them. When a major question of national defense was raised on October 11, 1961, it dealt with the military credibility of the United States to deter aggression during the Berlin crisis rather than directly with the missile gap.

74. *The New York Times,* October 22, 1961.

75. Chase and Lerman, *Kennedy and the Press,* text of news conference by President Kennedy, November 14, 1961.

76. Alsop, "The Alternative to Total War," p. 18.

77. *Developments in Military Technology and Their Impact on United States Strategy and Foreign Policy, Study #8* (prepared at the request of the Committee on Foreign Relations, United States Senate) (Washington, D.C.: Washington Center for Foreign Policy Research, The Johns Hopkins University, 1959), p. 58. Referred to hereafter as *The Johns Hopkins Report,* 1959.

78. For a detailed analysis of this new doctrine see *The New York Times,* text of a major address by Secretary of Defense Robert McNamara at Ann Arbor, Michigan, June 17, 1962; and U.S. Congress, House, Committee on Armed Services, *Hearings on Military Posture,* 88th Cong., 1st sess., Vol. 2 (January 30, 1963).

79. Schlesinger, *A Thousand Days,* p. 245.

80. Numerous writers have expounded this belief and it would seem to be based on sound reasoning. See B. H. Liddell Hart, *Deterrence or Defense* (New York: Frederick A. Praeger, 1958); F. O. Miksche, *The Failure of Atomic Strategy* (New York: Frederick A. Praeger, 1958). Glenn M. Snyder, *Deterrence and Defense: Toward a Theory of National Security* (Princeton, New Jersey: Princeton University Press, 1961).

81. See Horelick and Rush, *Strategic Power and Soviet Foreign Policy.* The authors develop this point as one of the major themes of their book.

82. Donald S. Zagoria, "China's Crisis of Foreign Policy," *The New York Times Magazine,* May 1, 1966.

83. *The New York Times,* March 26, 1962; and *The Communist Bloc and the Western Alliance: The Military Balance 1962–1963* (London: The Institute for Strategic Studies), p. 5.

84. For an example of this kind of "confrontation" thinking see Barry Goldwater, *Why Not Victory?*

CHAPTER IV

1. Arthur M. Schlesinger, Jr., *A Thousand Days: John F. Kennedy in the White House* (Boston: Houghton Mifflin, 1965), p. 500.

2. Robert S. McNamara, *The Essence of Security: Reflections in Office* (New York: Harper and Row, 1968), p. 80.

3. Schlesinger, *A Thousand Days,* p. 318.

4. Clark R. Mollenhoff, *The Pentagon: Politics, Profits and Plunder* (New York: G. P. Putnam's Sons, 1967), p. 242.

5. Stewart Alsop, interview with President John F. Kennedy, *The Saturday Evening Post* (March 31, 1962), 235:14. The reader should also be reminded that President Kennedy learned that the missile gap was a myth within a month of assuming office (see previous chapter).

6. Schlesinger, *A Thousand Days,* p. 318.

7. McNamara, *The Essence of Security.* In his Introduction, Secretary McNamara referred to massive retaliation as "useless."

8. Mollenhoff, *The Pentagon,* pp. 232–235. This was the same committee under Lyndon Johnson that had done more than any other congressional committee to establish the missile gap.

9. *Ibid.,* p. 236. An American division runs approximately 15,000 men, but it can vary from 12,000 to 20,000, as stated previously. A Soviet division runs from 9,000 to 12,000 men. At this time, the Soviet Union was credited with 175 combat divisions (of which 60 percent were considered combat ready) and an army of approximately 2.5 million men. The United States Army had 1,045,000 men.

10. Schlesinger, *A Thousand Days,* pp. 315–316.

11. *Ibid.*

12. McNamara, *The Essence of Security,* p. 82. McNamara claimed that

he had raised the number of "combat assigned divisions" by 66 percent during his term of office.

13. Stewart Alsop, "The Alternative to Total War," in an interview with Secretary of Defense McNamara, *The Saturday Evening Post* (December 1, 1962), 235:19.

14. U.S. Congress, House of Representatives, *Hearings on Military Posture*, 88th Cong., 1st sess., House Doc. No. 4 (January 1963), p. 288. Testimony by Secretary of Defense Robert S. McNamara.

15. *Ibid.*, p. 300. The doctrine of flexible response had definite implications for the role of the United States in NATO (see below in this chapter).

16. McNamara, *The Essence of Security*, p. 97.

17. Alsop, "The Alternative to Total War," p. 16. Official Department of Defense estimates as of 1961 placed the comparative United States-Soviet Union strategic delivery systems in the following manner.

United States	Soviet Union
16 Atlas ICBMs	35 T-3 ICBMs (8,000-mile range)
32 Polaris missiles	None comparable
600 Long-range bombers	200 Long-range bombers

The New York Times, Official Department of Defense figures for 1961, released April 16, 1965. The reader should keep in mind that in 1961 the United States had over 1,200 medium-range bombers that could also reach Soviet territory.

18. U.S. Congress, House of Representatives, *Hearings on Military Posture*, p. 309.

19. Klaus Knorr, "Passive Air Defense for the United States," in *Military Policy and National Security*, William W. Kaufman (ed.) (Princeton: Princeton University Press, 1956), p. 101.

20. David Horowitz, *The Free World Colossus* (New York: Hill & Wang, 1965), p. 367.

21. I. F. Stone, *The New York Review*, series on the military-industrial complex (March 27, 1969), p. 10.

22. Horowitz, *The Free World Colossus*, p. 372.

23. McNamara, *The Essence of Security*, p. 73.

24. *The New York Times*, January 10, 1963; *ibid.*, April 15, 1964.

25. McNamara, *The Essence of Security*, p. 90.

26. J. S. Butz, Jr. (technical ed.), "How Far Is the Red Air Force Ahead?" *Air Force and Space Digest* (September 1961), p. 52.

27. *Jane's All the World's Aircraft, 1963–1964* (New York: McGraw Hill, 1964), pp. 307–309. By 1968 this publication had ceased to mention the Bounder. Some American students of the Soviet Air Force claimed that this bomber was operational as early as 1959; see Ashe Lee, *The Soviet Air Force* (New York: The John Day Company, 1962), p. 138. In 1970,

the Soviet Union still did not have an operational supersonic long-range bomber.

28. *The New York Times,* November 6, 1961. At the same time the Secretary of Defense was attacked for these actions by Senator Henry Jackson (Dem.-Wash.). The reader should keep in mind that Boeing headquarters is located in Seattle, Washington.

29. McNamara, *The Essence of Security,* p. 92.

30. *The New York Times,* April 15, 1964.

31. Noam Chomsky, *American Power and the New Mandarins* (New York: Pantheon, 1969), p. 126.

32. Schlesinger, *A Thousand Days,* pp. 539–548.

33. Seymour Kurtz (ed.), *The New York Times, Encyclopedic Almanac 1970* (New York: *The New York Times,* 1969), pp. 718–719.

34. D. F. Fleming, *The Cold War and Its Origins* (Garden City: Doubleday and Company, 1961), 2:947–948. In spite of Fleming's highly critical analysis of American foreign political and diplomatic policy throughout this large study, he never comes to grips with the fact that the United States maintained strategic nuclear superiority throughout the postwar period. He seems to accept the missile gap as a reality, but it should be remembered that he wrote his study during the height of the missile-gap period.

35. Schlesinger, *A Thousand Days,* p. 345.

36. Some of the best evidence to support this conclusion on the 1961 Berlin crisis can be found in Raymond Garthoff, *Soviet Military Policy* (New York: Praeger, 1966), pp. 115–120; and Myron Rush and Arnold I. Horelick, *Strategic Power and Soviet Foreign Policy* (Chicago: University of Chicago Press, 1966), pp. 108–115.

37. Garthoff, *Soviet Military Policy,* p. 116.

38. Horowitz, *The Free World Colossus,* p. 208, quoting Richard Nixon.

39. Schlesinger, *A Thousand Days,* pp. 252–259.

40. Reported by Fletcher Knebel, "Washington in Crises," *Look,* December 18, 1962.

41. Schlesinger, *A Thousand Days,* p. 315.

42. See Garthoff, *Soviet Military Policy,* p. 120; Schlesinger, *A Thousand Days,* p. 796; and Rush and Horelick, *Strategic Power and Soviet Foreign Policy,* p. 127.

43. *The Communist Bloc and the Western Alliance: The Military Balance, 1962–1963* (London: The Institute for Strategic Studies, 1963), p. 5; *The New York Times,* December 20, 1962; *ibid.,* January 10, 1963.

44. The best examples of this type of thinking can be found in Thomas S. Power (General, United States Air Force, ret.), *Design for Survival* (New York: Coward-McCann, Inc., 1964), p. 21; or Alsop, "The Alternative to Total War," p. 15.

45. There are numerous sources that accept, at least in part, this interpretation. See Allen Dulles, *The Craft of Intelligence* (New York: Harper

& Row, 1963), p. 165; Thomas Wolfe, *Soviet Strategy at the Crossroads* (Cambridge: Harvard University Press, 1964), pp. 23, 33.

46. Garthoff, *Soviet Strategy in the Nuclear Age* (revised) (New York: Praeger, 1962), p. 190. This report indicated that in 1956 the Soviet Union had over 4,000 modern interceptor aircraft for the defense of the Soviet Union.

47. *The New York Times,* October 23, 1962, text of President Kennedy's special address on the Cuban missile crisis.

48. Garthoff, *Soviet Military Policy,* p. 193.

49. Samuel P. Huntington, *The Common Defense: Strategic Programs in National Politics* (New York: Columbia University Press, 1961), p. 120.

50. Garthoff, *Soviet Military Policy,* p. 201.

51. Horelick and Rush, *Strategic Power and Soviet Foreign Policy,* reprint of statement by Premier Khrushchev from *Pravda,* January 17, 1963, p. 177.

52. Jerome Frank, *Sanity and Survival* (New York: Vintage, 1967), quoting a report by the Federation of American Scientists, p. 16.

53. Schlesinger, *A Thousand Days,* pp. 910–912. Among the most prominent early opponents of the Test Ban Treaty were General Thomas D. White (former Air Chief); Admiral Lewis Strauss; Admiral Arthur Radford; General Curtis LeMay; General Thomas Power; Edward Teller (the "father of the H-bomb"); Senator Thomas Dodd (Dem.-Conn.); and Senator Everett Dirksen (Rep.-Ill.).

54. *Ibid.,* p. 910.

55. *Ibid.,* p. 912.

56. *Ibid.,* p. 913.

57. I. F. Stone, "The Test Ban Comedy," *The New York Review* (May 7, 1970), p. 14.

58. *I. F. Stone's Weekly,* September 22, 1969; see also, Stone, "The Test Ban Comedy," p. 21.

59. Alsop, "The Alternative to Total War," p. 17.

60. U.S. Congress, House of Representatives, *Hearings on Military Posture,* p. 430, testimony by Secretary McNamara.

61. *Ibid.,* p. 300.

62. B. H. Liddell Hart, *Deterrent or Defense* (New York: Praeger, 1960), p. 138.

63. Richard J. Barnet and Marcus G. Raskin, *After 20 Years: The Decline of NATO and the Search for a New Policy* (New York: Vintage, 1966), p. 89. This is an excellent study of the development of NATO.

64. McNamara, *The Essence of Security,* p. 43.

65. *The Military Balance, 1968–1969* (London: The Institute for Strategic Studies, 1969), pp. 52–53.

66. McNamara, *The Essence of Security,* pp. 80–81.

67. *Ibid.,* p. 86. The reality of a lack of conventional options and the failure of the Kennedy Administration to develop such an option must have

been realized by Secretary McNamara. Before he left office, he had increased the number of tactical nuclear weapons in Europe by over 100 percent. In 1966, Mr. McNamara claimed that the United States had 7,000 tactical nuclear weapons in Europe (see *The New York Times,* September 24, 1966).

68. *The New York Times,* news article by Henry Tanner, "Rusk Says Pacific Is Flank of NATO," December 16, 1966. Many Europeans rejected the implications of this statement at the time, and the United States government has not mentioned this doctrine since in public.

69. *The New York Times,* Secretary McNamara's Ann Arbor speech, June 17, 1962.

70. Alastair Buchan, "The Future of Western Deterrent Power: A View From the U.K.," *The Bulletin of the Atomic Scientists,* 7:277. In the same issue were articles on the same subject by Raymond Aron (France) and Klaus Knorr (United States).

71. Karl E. Keyer, *The Boston Globe,* November 14, 1968, reprint of a 1968 article in the *New Left Review.* The article covered a report by Richard Neustadt in 1964 on the attitudes of the Labor party toward the MLF.

72. Barnet and Raskin, *After 20 Years,* p. 52.

73. Denis Healey, "What Could Britain Do?" *The New Republic* (December 22, 1962), p. 10.

74. James Warburg, *Germany: Key to Peace* (Cambridge: Harvard University Press, 1953), p. 189; and Marshall Shulman, *Stalin's Foreign Policy Reappraised* (Cambridge: Harvard University Press, 1963), p. 185.

CHAPTER V

1. The Seldon resolution (HR 560) passed the House on September 20, 1965, by a 312–52 roll-call vote. Due to the importance of this shift of attitude on the part of the House of Representatives and its substantial approval by the State Department with minor reservations, part of the resoluton is included here. The resolution stated that "the intervention of international Communism, directly or indirectly, however disguised, in any American state, conflicts with the established policy of the American Republics for the protection of the sovereignty of the peoples of such states and the political independence of their governments. . . ." It expressed the sense of the House that "In any such situation *any one* [emphasis added] or more of the high contracting parties to the Inter-American Treaty of Reciprocal Assistance may . . . take steps to forestall or combat intervention, domination, control, and colonization, in whatever form, by the subversive forces known as international Communism and its agencies in the Western Hemisphere." From *Congressional Quarterly Almanac* (Washington, D.C.: Congressional Quarterly Service, 1965),

21:518. Even a cursory reading of the 1947 Rio Treaty would indicate that both the spirit and letter of this resolution were in direct violation to this treaty.

2. *Public Papers of Lyndon Johnson,* 1966, Vol. II, Public Papers Press of the Presidents (Washington, D.C.: Government Printing Office), p. 1287.

3. *The New York Times,* text of a press conference by Secretary Rusk, October 23, 1967.

4. *The New York Times,* quoting Secretary Rusk, May 25, 1966. It is interesting to note that as of 1966 the United States had not yet made the switch from Russia as "enemy" to China as "enemy"; both were lumped together in spite of their obvious differences toward national "wars of liberation."

5. W. W. Rostow, "The Test: Are We the Tougher?" *The New York Times Magazine* (June 7, 1964), pp. 112–113.

6. Robert McNamara, *The Essence of Security: Reflections in Office* (New York: Harper & Row, 1968), p. 145.

7. *Ibid.*

8. *Ibid.,* pp. 52, 57.

9. *Ibid.,* p. 58.

10. *The New York Times,* November 4, 1969. Some estimates on the total cost of building and maintaining the B-1 over a five-year period have gone as high as $20 billion.

11. *The New York Times,* January 6, 1969. I. F. Stone, *The New York Review,* "The War Machine Under Nixon" (June 2, 1969), p. 10. This writer is indebted to the continuous, excellent analyses of military affairs by I. F. Stone over the years.

12. U.S. Senate, *Hearings,* Department of Defense Appropriations for Fiscal 1969, 90th Cong., 2d sess., Part II, p. 868. At the time of this hearing, the United States Navy was engaged in a major effort to gain additional antisubmarine warfare funds from Congress.

13. *The New York Times,* February 7, 1960.

14. *The Communist Bloc and the Western Alliance: The Military Balance, 1962–1963* (London: The Institute for Strategic Studies, 1963), p. 5; *The New York Times,* December 20, 1962.

15. *The New York Times,* January 10, 1963; *ibid.,* April 15, 1964. Most of these figures represent official Department of Defense figures released in April 1964. It should be noted that by 1964, the B-47 medium-range bomber was being phased out, but that the United States still had fighter-bombers in Europe and on its aircraft carriers that could carry thermonuclear weapons and could reach the Soviet Union.

16. *Ibid.,* July 14, 1966.

17. U.S. Congress, Senate, *Authorization for Military Procurement, Research & Development, Fiscal Year 1969 and Reserve Strength,* 90th Cong., 2d sess., February 2, 1968, testimony by Secretary of Defense McNamara, p. 116.

18. *The Military Balance, 1968–1969,* p. 52.

19. *The New York Times,* May 12, 1969; *The Boston Globe,* news article by George Wilson, January 20, 1969.

20. *The New York Times,* October 29, 1961.

21. *Ibid.,* July 17, 1962.

22. *Ibid.,* November 8, 17, 1963.

23. Marshal V. D. Sokolovsky (ed.), *Military Strategy: Soviet Doctrine and Concepts* (New York: Praeger, 1963), from the Introduction by Raymond Garthoff, p. xix.

24. Raymond Garthoff, *Soviet Military Policy* (New York: Praeger, 1966), p. 57.

25. *Ibid.,* pp. 193–194. It is worth noting here that recently Soviet Marshal I. Krylov challenged this doctrine and stated: "Victory in war, if the imperialists succeed in starting it, will be on the side of world socialism." In the past, statements of this kind by Soviet leaders have reflected insecurity and inferiority, and if this is the case, then the possibility arises that once again the United States had succeeded in frightening the leaders of the Soviet Union. Marshal Krylov's statement appeared in *The New York Times,* September 12, 1969.

26. William Zimmerman, *Soviet Perspectives on International Relations, 1956–1967* (Princeton: Princeton University Press, 1969), pp. 229–230. This quote came from G. Gerasimov, "The First Strike Theory," *International Affairs,* No. 3 (March 1965), pp. 35–39.

27. *Ibid.,* p. 217. This quote came from N. Talenskii, "June 22: Lessons of History," *International Relations,* No. 6 (June 1966), p. 46.

28. Clark Mollenhoff, *The Pentagon: Politics, Profits and Plunder* (New York: G. P. Putnam and Sons, 1967), p. 272.

29. *The New York Times,* March 25, April 18, 1963.

30. *Ibid.,* August 14, 1963.

31. *Ibid.,* news article by Hanson Baldwin, August 15, 1963.

32. Mollenhoff, *The Pentagon,* p. 292.

33. *The New York Times,* Mr. Nixon's "Security Gap" speech, October 25, 1968.

34. *The New York Times,* February 2, 1968.

35. *The Military Balance, 1966–1967,* p. 43.

36. A detailed discussion of the TFX goes far beyond the scope of this study. Suffice it to say that this aircraft has been designated the F-111 and has yet to be successfully tested over a sustained period. It was designed and approved by Secretary McNamara in order to meet the Air Force (and Navy) demand for a new bomber and for tactical air support. By 1969, it has been unable to accomplish either of these missions. The interested reader should see R. J. Art, *TFX Decision: McNamara and the Military* (Boston: Little, Brown, 1969).

37. *I. F. Stone's Weekly* (July 14, 1969), p. 4.

38. Abers, *et al., MIRV* (Cambridge: Union of Concerned Scientists, June, 1969); Ralph E. Lapp, "Can SALT Stop MIRV?" *The New York Times Magazine* (February 1, 1970), p. 40.

39. Lapp, "Can SALT Stop MIRV?" p. 14; *The Boston Globe*, news article by Richard H. Stewart, April 14, 1970; *The Boston Globe*, "Letter to the Editor" from S. A. Forter, director of Polaris and Poseidon Guidance, MIT Draper Laboratory, February 25, 1970. Mr. Forter claimed that the United States already has "an operational MIRV capability." Finally, this planned deployment of MIRV was in *The New York Times*, October 28, 1969.

40. Until August 1970 the United States government was very careful in its press releases and stated only that the Soviet Union has tested a "multiple warhead," but it never said that the Soviet Union has tested an *independently targeted warhead*. This includes the Soviet tests up through the series in April 1970. This same point is also contended by Richard H. Stewart in a news article in *The Boston Globe*, April 14, 1970; and by *I. F. Stone's Weekly* (July 14, 1969), p. 4. Evidently, in August 1970, the Soviet Union conducted its first test of an independently targeted warhead. Secretary of Defense Laird claimed that the Soviet Union tested such a weapon and stated that it would be operational by 1972. Mr. Laird contended that this was "a very realistic projection," *The New York Times*, August 27, 1970. In view of past projections of Soviet behavior by the Department of Defense, I would contend that Laird's prediction is open to some doubt as to its accuracy. Before the Soviet MIRV test, Laird had strongly implied that the Soviet Union had MIRV because they possessed a high-thrust missile (the SS-9) to carry such warheads; but this line of reasoning was patent nonsense. MIRV is mainly a question of technology, not thrust. The earlier Atlas and certainly the Titan could launch MIRV if the MIRV technology had been available to put independently targeted warheads on these missiles.

41. Zimmerman, *Soviet Perspectives on International Relations, 1956–1957* (Princeton: Princeton University Press, 1969), pp. 232–234. The Shelepin quote is taken from *Pravda*, June 3, 1966.

42. *The Military Balance, 1968–1969*, p. 52.

43. Abers, *et al.*, *MIRV*; Secretary of Defense Clark Clifford in his posture statement to Congress before leaving office stated that the Soviet Galosh system (around Moscow) "resembles in certain important respects the Nike-Zeus system which we abandoned years ago because of its limited effectiveness." See *I. F. Stone's Weekly* (February 24, 1969).

44. *The New York Times*, October 28, 1969; Lapp, "Can SALT Stop MIRV?" p. 15.

45. Laird, *A House Divided: America's Strategy Gap* (Chicago: Henry Regnery Company, 1962). Nixon and Laird did not disappoint their supporters. On the first round of escalation of the arms race by the new Administration, the Air Force received MIRV, the B-1, and the C5A transport; the Army got Safeguard; and the Navy got Poseidon.

46. *Ibid.*, p. 41.

47. *The New York Times*, Nixon's "Security Gap" speech, October 25, 1968. In this speech, Mr. Nixon said that the Soviet Union had achieved

superiority over the United States in ICBMs, manned bombers, and nuclear submarines.

48. *Washington Newsletter* (Washington, D.C.: Friends Committee on National Legislation, June 1969), quoting Assistant Secretary of Defense Robert Moot, p. 1.

49. *The New York Times,* February 8, 1970; *ibid.,* May 1, 1970.

50. Abers, *et al., MIRV.*

51. *The New York Times,* February 8, 1970.

52. *The New York Times,* July 19, 1969.

53. *Ibid.,* quoting congressional testimony by Secretary of Defense Laird, January 8, 1970.

54. *Ibid.,* May 12, 1969.

55. *The Boston Globe,* quoting congressional testimony by Secretary Laird, June 18, 1969.

56. *The New York Times,* reprint of Secretary Laird's testimony before the Senate Foreign Relations Committee, February 2, 1969. In the spring of 1970, the Chinese placed an earth satellite in orbit, indicating the reality that eventually they will have a limited ICBM capability.

57. Laird, *America's Strategy Gap,* p. 51.

58. Abers, *et al., MIRV.*

59. Donald C. Winston, "Superhard Silos Seen ABM Replacement," *Aviation Week and Space Technology* (May 13, 1968), 88:32.

60. Abers, *et al., MIRV.* Estimates on the costs of this type of intelligence effort run from $2 to $4 billion a year.

61. *I. F. Stone's Weekly,* report of phone conversation with the Atomic Energy Commission, September 22, 1969.

62. Lapp, "The Fear of First Strike," *The New Republic* (June 28, 1969).

63. U.S. Congress, Senate, *Authorization for Military Procurement,* 90th Cong., 2d sess., Feb. 2, 1968, testimony by Secretary of Defense McNamara, p. 116.

64. *Ibid.,* pp. 126–127.

65. McNamara, *The Essence of Security,* p. 54.

66. U.S. Congress, Senate, *Authorization for Military Procurement,* 90th Cong., 2d sess., Feb. 2, 1968, testimony by Secretary of Defense McNamara, p. 118.

CHAPTER VI

1. Michael Klare, *Beyond the Vietnam Syndrome: Interventionism in the 1980s* (Washington, D.C.: Institute for Policy Studies, 1981). I am deeply indebted to the work done by Michael Klare. This is an excellent book on the impact of the Vietnam War on the United States and its policies.

2. *The Boston Globe,* April 8, 1985, report on a Gallup Poll.

3. Barbara Tuchman, *The March of Folly: From Troy to Vietnam* (New York: Alfred Knopf, 1984), p. 257.

4. For two excellent studies on the Battle of Dienbienphu, the reader should consult Bernard Fall, *Hell in a Very Small Place* (Philadelphia: Lippincott, 1966), and Jules Roy, *The Battle of Dienbienphu* (New York: Harper and Row, 1965). U.S. policy makers could have learned a great deal from either of these books.

5. See Roy, *The Battle of Dienbienphu*, "Operation Vulture," for a discussion on the possible use of nuclear weapons at Dienbienphu.

6. U.S. Department of Defense, Office of Assistant Secretary of Defense (Comptroller), Directorate for Information Operations, March 19, 1974.

7. Secretary of State Dean Rusk was particularly sensitive to this problem because as an Assistant Secretary of State he had earlier predicted that the Chinese would not intervene in Korea. During the late 1960s China was being cast as one of the "enemies" of the United States, and Chinese intervention in Vietnam was feared by U.S. leaders. China had intervened in Korea, annexed Tibet, and conducted a border war with India. It had a historical interest in Indochina. The fear of Chinese intervention was not to end until Nixon's 1972 rapprochement with China.

8. Milton Leitenberg, "The Present Status of the World's Arms Race," citing posture statements by Secretaries of Defense McNamara and Clifford, *Bulletin of the Atomic Scientists* (January 1982), p. 18.

9. Peter Pringle and William Arkin, *SIOP: The Secret U.S. Plan for Nuclear War* (New York: W. W. Norton, 1983), p. 109.

10. Ibid., pp. 120, 124, and 174.

11. Tuchman, *The March of Folly*, p. 337.

12. Richard Nixon, *The Memoirs of Richard Nixon* (New York: Grosset and Dunlap, 1978), p. 606; Herbert Y. Schandler, *The Unmaking of a President: Lyndon Johnson and Vietnam* (Princeton: Princeton University Press, 1977), p. 297.

13. Seymour M. Hersh, *The Price of Power: Kissinger in the Nixon White House* (New York: Summit Books, 1983), p. 118.

14. Nixon, *Memoirs*, p. 606.

15. Tuchman, *The March of Folly*, p. 361; quoting Henry Kissinger.

16. Hersh, *The Price of Power*, pp. 52–53.

17. Ibid., p. 124.

18. Ibid., pp. 361–362.

19. William H. Harris and Judith S. Lavey (eds.), *The New Columbia Encyclopedia* (New York: Columbia University Press, 1975), p. 2891.

20. William Shawcross, *Sideshows: Kissinger, Nixon, and the Destruction of Cambodia* (New York: Simon and Schuster, 1979), p. 272. This is an excellent analysis of the American war in Cambodia.

21. Charles Tyroler II (ed.), *Alerting America: The Papers of the Committee on the Present Danger* (New York: Pergamon-Brassey's, 1984), pp. 240–245, and Hersh, *The Price of Power*, p. 529.

22. Hersh, *The Price of Power*, p. 158.

23. Nixon, *Memoirs*, p. 618.

24. Ibid., p. 415.

25. Ibid., p. 1024.

26. Robert C. Alridge, *The Counterforce Syndrome* (Washington, D.C.: Transnational Institute, 1978), pp. 8–10.

27. Tyroler, *Alerting America,* pp. 50–53.

28. Hersh, *The Price of Power,* p. 639.

29. Alan Wolfe, *The Rise and Fall of the 'Soviet Threat'* (Washington, D.C.: Institute for Policy Studies, 1979), pp. 26–27.

30. Tyroler, *Alerting America,* p. xv. For a complete list of the CPD Board of Directors, see pp. ix–xi.

31. Ibid., p. xv.

32. Hersh, *The Price of Power,* pp. 158–159.

33. Ibid., pp. 3–4, 14 and 65.

34. Ibid., p. 89.

35. Ibid., p. 41.

36. Ibid., p. 4.

37. Ibid., p. 66.

38. Ibid., pp. 82–86.

39. *Newsweek* (March 24, 1980), p. 38; *U.S. News and World Report* (April 7, 1980), p. 37.

40. *The Military Balance: 1977–1978* (London: Institute for Strategic Studies, 1977), pp. 77–79; Alridge, *The Counterforce Syndrome,* pp. 8–10.

41. See Fred M. Kaplan, *Dubious Specter: A Second Look at the Soviet Threat* (Washington, D.C.: Transnational Institute, 1977), for an excellent analysis of American perceptions of the Soviet threat.

42. Alridge, *The Counterforce Syndrome,* pp. 8, 11, and 15. Composite chart.

43. Ibid., pp. 10 and 15. Composite chart.

44. U.S. Military Posture for FY 1978, Chairman, Joint Chiefs of Staff, General George S. Brown (January 20, 1977), p. 14.

45. *World Armaments and Disarmament, Sirri Yearbook 1977* (Cambridge: MIT Press, 1977), p. 24; *The Military Balance,* pp. 77–79.

46. Kaplan, *Dubious Specter,* pp. 30–31.

47. This debate on "first use" and conventional defense forces in Europe did not reach its full intensity until the early 1980s. See McGeorge Bundy, George Kennan, Robert McNamara, and Gerard Smith, "Nuclear Weapons and the Atlantic Alliance," *Foreign Affairs* (Spring 1982); General Bernard Rogers (SACEUR), "The Atlantic Alliance: Prescription for a Difficult Decade," *Foreign Affairs* (Summer 1982).

48. Boston Study Group, *The Price of Defense: A New Strategy for Military Spending* (New York: Times Books, 1979), p. 19.

49. Ibid., p. 199.

50. Boston Study Group, *The Price of Defense,* p. 7.

51. Kaplan, *Dubious Specter,* pp. 30–31. Figures were taken from *The Military Balance* (London: Institute for Statistic Studies, 1976), pp. 73–75, and Jeffrey Record, *US Nuclear Weapons in Europe* (Washington, D.C.: The Brookings Institute, 1974), pp. 23–25.

52. Ibid., pp. 146–151. Composite chart.

53. Ibid., p. 160.

54. Richard Barnet, *The Alliance: America, Europe, and Japan, Makers of the Postwar World* (New York: Simon and Schuster, 1983), p. 322.

55. Ibid., p. 378.

56. Ibid., pp. 368–369.

57. David N. Schwartz, *NATO's Nuclear Dilemmas* (Washington, D.C.: The Brookings Institute, 1983), p. 213.

58. Barnet, *The Alliance*, pp. 344–345; Tyroler, *Alerting America*, p. 66.

59. President Carter did subscribe to the "first use" doctrine and the "tripwire" effect in Europe. Jimmy Carter, *Keeping the Faith: Memoirs of a President* (New York: Bantam Books, 1982), pp. 245–246.

60. Barnet, *The Alliance*, p. 372.

61. Carter, *Keeping the Faith*, pp. 225–229.

62. Barnet, *The Alliance*, p. 376.

63. Klare, *Beyond the Vietnam Syndrome*, pp. 7–9.

64. Ibid., p. 9.

65. Ibid.; for an excellent discussion of the RDF, see Chapter V.

66. *The New York Times*, October 4, 1979.

67. Klare, *Beyond the Vietnam Syndrome*, p. 77, quoting General P. X. Kelley at the Pentagon, June 18, 1980.

68. Carter, *Keeping the Faith*, pp. 245–246.

69. For a superb study of U.S. policies toward Central America and U.S. intervention in this area, see Walter LeFeber, *Inevitable Revolutions: The United States in Central America* (New York: W. W. Norton, 1983), p. 69.

70. Ibid., p. 109.

71. Ibid., pp. 65–66, 81, and 226–242.

72. Carter, *Keeping the Faith*, pp. 471–473.

73. Ibid., p. 472.

74. *The New York Times*, February 1, 1980.

75. Carter, *Keeping the Faith*, p. 483.

76. Klare, *Beyond the Vietnam Syndrome*, p. 81, citing figures from Department of Defense Authorization for FY 81.

77. Quoting Senator Henry Jackson (Dem.-Wash.), "As the Battle for SALT Shapes Up," *U.S. News and World Report* (May 28, 1979), p. 38.

78. Carter, *Keeping the Faith*, pp. 82–83.

79. Ibid., p. 284.

80. Tyroler, *Alerting America*, pp. 150–151. Charts created by Paul Nitze.

81. Pringle and Arkin, *SIOP*, pp. 40 and 186–188.

82. Donald Rumsfeld, U.S. Defense Department, *Annual Report to Congress for FY 1978*, p. 70.

83. Spurgeon M. Keeny and K. H. Wolfgang, "MAD vs. NUTS," *Foreign Affairs* (Winter 1981–1982), pp. 287–289.

84. Pringle and Arkin, *SIOP*, p. 186.

CHAPTER VII

1. Daniel Ford, "U.S. Command and Control," *The New Yorker* (Part II) (April 8, 1985), p. 50. This is an excellent examination by Ford of American C3I systems and problems (Part I, April 1, 1985).

2. Ibid., p. 64.

3. Michael Klare, "The Reagan Doctrine," *Inquiry* (April–May 1984), p. 2.

4. Ford, "U.S. Command and Control," p. 50.

5. Peter Pringle and William Arkin, *SIOP: The Secret U.S. Plan for Nuclear War* (New York: W. W. Norton, 1983), p. 243. See the statements by Deputy Defense Secretary Frank Carlucci and SAC Commanding General Bennie Davis.

6. *The New York Times,* July 14–17, 1980.

7. Robert T. Scott, "Now a Warhead Gap," *Bulletin of the Atomic Scientists* (November 1984), p. 43.

8. William M. Arkin, Thomas B. Cochran, and Milton M. Hoenig, "Resource Paper on the U.S. Nuclear Arsenal," *Bulletin of the Atomic Scientists* (August–September 1984), pp. 3s–5s.

9. *The New York Times,* March 9, 1983.

10. Strobe Talbott, *Deadly Gambits* (New York: Alfred A. Knopf, 1984), pp. 214–215; Charles Tyroler II (ed.), *Alerting America: The Papers of the Committee on the Present Danger* (New York: Pergamon-Brassey's, 1984), p. 86.

11. Randall Forsberg, "A Bilateral Nuclear Weapons Freeze," *Scientific American* (November 1, 1982), pp. 52–61.

12. Arkin, Cochran, and Hoenig, "Resource Paper," pp. 8s–9s.

13. Talbott, *Deadly Gambits,* pp. 219 and 315; Ford, "U.S. Command and Control," p. 85.

14. Ibid.

15. Howard Morland, *U.S. and Soviet First Strike Capabilities* (Washington, D.C.: Coalition for a New Foreign and Military Policy, 1984).

16. Ford, "U.S. Command and Control," p. 63.

17. Thomas B. Cochran, William M. Arkin, and Milton M. Hoenig, *Nuclear Weapons Databook: U.S. Nuclear Forces and Capabilities,* Vol. I (Cambridge: Ballinger, 1984), p. 39.

18. Ford, "U.S. Command and Control," p. 67; Pringle and Arkin, *SIOP,* p. 163.

19. Arkin, Cochran, and Hoenig, "Resource Paper," pp. 8s–9s.

20. See Cochran, Arkin, and Hoenig, *Nuclear Weapons Databook;* Morland, *U.S. and Soviet First Strike Capabilities.*

21. Talbott, *Deadly Gambits,* p. 282.

22. Michael Klare, "Where the Candidates Stand," *The Nation* (October 27, 1984), p. 419.

23. Talbott, *Deadly Gambits,* p. 268.

24. Ibid., p. 273.

25. Ibid., p. 237.

26. Ibid., p. 223.

27. See the article by Fred Kaplan in *The Boston Globe,* March 7, 1985.

28. David Morrison, "ICBM Vulnerability," *Bulletin of the Atomic Scientists* (November 1984), p. 24.

29. "Week in Review," *The New York Times,* March 24, 1985.

30. *The Boston Globe,* March 17, 1985.

31. Department of Defense, *Soviet Military Strength,* 1985.

32. General Bernard Rogers (SACEUR), "The Atlantic Alliance: Prescription for a Difficult Decade," *Foreign Affairs* (Summer 1982), p. 147.

33. Raymond Garthoff, "The Spending Gap," *Bulletin of the Atomic Scientists* (May 1984), p. 5.

34. See the article by Fred Kaplan, *The Boston Globe,* February 26, 1985.

35. Fred M. Kaplan, *Dubious Specter: A Second Look at the Soviet Threat* (Washington, D.C.: Transnational Institute, 1977), p. 14, quoting Les Aspin (Dem.-Wis.).

36. Gordon Adams and Laura Weiss, "Military Spending and the Deficit," *Bulletin of the Atomic Scientists* (April 1985), pp. 26–27.

37. *The New York Times,* March 24, 1983.

38. Ibid.

39. Department of Defense, *Soviet Military Power.*

40. Ibid.; *The Boston Globe,* April 3, 1985.

41. *The New York Times,* February 24, 1985.

42. Daniel Ford in *The New Yorker,* "U.S. Command and Control," Part I, II (April 1, 1985, and April 8, 1985). The author makes this point over and over again.

43. *The New York Times,* February 24, 1985.

44. Hans Bethe, Richard Garwin, Kurt Gottfried, and Henry Kendall, "Space-based Ballistic Missile Defense," *Scientific American* (October 1984), p. 41.

45. Ibid., p. 47.

46. Ashton Carter, *Energy Missile Defense in Space,* U.S. Congress, Office of Technology Assessment, 1985.

47. Raymond Garthoff, "ASAT Arms Control Still Possible," *Bulletin of the Atomic Scientists* (August–September 1984), p. 29.

48. Richard L. Garwin and John Pike, "Space Weapons," *Bulletin of the Atomic Scientists* (May 1984), p. 2s.

49. Associated Press report, *The Boston Globe,* January 16, 1985.

50. Yeugeny P. Velikhow (Vice-President of the Soviet Academy of Science, quoting Yuri Andropov), "Space Weapons: Effects on Strategic Stability," *Bulletin of the Atomic Scientists* (May 1984), p. 13s.

51. Ibid., pp. 12s–14s.

52. Anne Ehrlich, "Nuclear Winter," *Bulletin of the Atomic Scientists* (April 1984).

53. Ibid., p. 3s.

54. Ehrlich, "Nuclear Winter," p. 5s.

55. Bernard Weissbourd, "Are Nuclear Weapons Obsolete?" *Bulletin of the Atomic Scientists* (August–September 1984), pp. 8–9.

56. Ibid., pp. 10s–11s; *The Boston Globe*, March 3, 1985.

57. See the articles by Fred Kaplan, *The Boston Globe*, December 12, 1984, and March 3, 1985.

58. Ford, "U.S. Command and Control," p. 54.

59. Ibid. General Holloway is speaking to Ford, p. 59.

60. Ibid., p. 70.

61. The reference is to the Department of Defense budget; *The Boston Globe*, April 23, 1985.

62. Ford, Part I, p. 90.

63. Composite Chart, Center for Defense Information, Washington, D.C., 1982; and Jeffrey R. Smith, "European Missile Deployment," *Science* (reprint from January 27, February 10, February 17, and March 23, 1984), p. 7.

64. Composite Chart and Smith, see Cochran, Arkin, and Hoenig, *Nuclear Weapons Databook*, and David Schwartz, *NATO's Nuclear Dilemmas* (Washington, D.C.: The Brookings Institute, 1983), p. 203.

65. See the article by Fred Kaplan, *The Boston Globe*, April 10, 1985.

66. William Arkin, "Conventional Buildup: A Deliberate Delusion," *Bulletin* (February 1985), p. 9.

67. See the article by Fred Kaplan, *The Boston Globe*, April 10, 1985.

68. Ford, "U.S. Command and Control," p. 64.

69. Smith, "Missile Deployment," p. 1.

70. Daniel Ellsberg, "Call to Mutiny," in *The Deadly Connection: Nuclear War and U.S. Intervention* (transcripts of a conference held at MIT, December 4 and 5, 1982) (Cambridge: American Friends Service Committee, 1983), p. 26.

71. Smith, "Missile Deployment," pp. 12–14.

72. Weissbourd, "Are Nuclear Weapons Obsolete?" p. 8.

73. Jane M. O. Sharpe, "Reshaping NATO's Nuclear Policy," *Bulletin of the Atomic Scientists* (April 1985), pp. 42–43.

74. *The Boston Globe*, December 6, 1984.

75. McGeorge Bundy, George Kennan, Robert McNamara, and Gerard Smith, "Nuclear Weapons and the Atlantic Alliance," *Foreign Affairs* (Spring 1982).

76. Tyroler, *Alerting America*, p. 229.

77. Boston Study Group, *The Price of Defense: A New Strategy for Military Spending* (New York: New York Times Books, 1979), p. 160.

78. Rogers, "The Atlantic Alliance," pp. 151–152.

79. *The Boston Globe*, December 16, 1984.

80. Richard Barnet, "The Atlantic Alliance," *Bulletin of the Atomic Scientists* (January 1984), p. 8.

81. Michael Klare, "May the Force Protect Us," *The Nation* (February 25, 1984), p. 216.

82. Stephen Shenfield, "Soviet Thinking about the Unthinkable," *Bulletin of the Atomic Scientists* (February 1985), p. 25, quoting Marshal Arkomeyev from *Znamya* 2 (1984), p. 175.

83. Ulrich Albrecht, "European Security and the German Question," *World Policy Journal* (Spring 1984), pp. 575–602. This excellent study by Professor Albrecht of the Free University of Berlin is a detailed discussion of these questions. I am indebted to him for his insights.

84. Eugene Rostow, in *Hearings before the Senate Foreign Relations Committee, U.S. Senate* (Washington, D.C.: Government Printing Office, 1981).

85. Randall Forsberg, "Behind the Facade," in *The Deadly Connection,* p. 14.

86. *The New York Times,* May 6, 1981.

87. Klare, "May the Force Protect Us," *The Nation,* Feb. 25, 1984, p. 216. Quoting Secretary Weinberger, in Department of Defense, *Budget Report* (1985).

88. Michael Klare, "The Conventional Buildup," *Inquiry* (June 1983).

89. Klare, "May the Force Protect Us," p. 215, quoting FY 1985 Department of Defense report.

90. Earl C. Ravenal, "Defense Dollars Buy Foreign Policy," in *Special Report* (San Francisco: Bay Area Institute, 1984), p. 2.

91. Michael Klare, *Beyond the Vietnam Syndrome: Interventionism in the 1980s* (Washington, D.C.: Institute for Policy Studies, 1981), p. 132, quoting Joint Chiefs of Staff report for FY 1982.

92. *The New York Times,* January 18, 1983.

EPILOGUE

1. William Appleman Williams, *Empire as a Way of Life* (New York: Oxford University Press, 1980), p. 170.

2. For a detailed analysis of the problems of world resource allocation, see Richard Barnet, *The Lean Years: Politics in the Age of Scarcity* (New York: Simon and Schuster, 1980).

3. Alan Wolfe, "After Deployment: The Emergence of a New Europe," *World Policy Journal* (Spring 1984), p. 574.

Index

283